AF248884

GOVERNMENT AND GROWTH

The Trade Union Institute for Economic Research, FIEF, is a foundation established in 1985 by Landsorganisationen, the Swedish trade union confederation. FIEF's objective, as defined in its constitution, is to 'deepen the academic economic debate through the promotion of enduring research'.

FIEF Studies in Labour Markets and Economic Policy will be published once a year. The series will provide a forum for out-standing scholars to publish applied, policy-oriented research with generous space available. The length of the papers should be between 40 and 60 pages which allows background surveys of theory, and a review of empirical research. The papers should also contain original contributions either through extensions and/or of empirical analysis.

Normally, two conferences are organized around the papers to be published in the *FIEF Studies*. After the first conference, papers are revised and a final conference is held with FIEF's panel of advisers and specially invited researchers in the field covered by the paper.

FIEF Studies editorial board

Managing Editor:
Villy Bergström Chief Editor, Dala-Demokraten

Editorial Board:
Torben Andersen Professor, University of Aarhus
Michael Hoel Professor, Oslo University
Bertil Holmlund Professor, Uppsala University
Karl-Gustaf Löfgren Professor, University of Umeå
Andrew Oswald Dr, The London School of Economics
Hans T. Söderström Executive Director, Center for Business and Policy Studies, SNS

Government and Growth

edited by

VILLY BERGSTRÖM

CLARENDON PRESS · OXFORD
1997

Oxford University Press, Great Clarendon Street, Oxford OX2 6DP

Oxford New York
Athens Auckland Bangkok Bogota Bombay
Buenos Aires Calcutta Cape Town Dar es Salaam
Delhi Florence Hong Kong Istanbul Karachi
Kuala Lumpur Madras Madrid Melbourne
Mexico City Nairobi Paris Singapore
Taipei Tokyo Toronto Warsaw
and associated companies in
Berlin   Ibadan

Oxford is a trade mark of Oxford University Press

Published in the United States by
Oxford University Press Inc., New York

British Library Cataloguing in Publication Data
Data available

Library of Congress Cataloging in Publication Data

ISBN 0-19-829037-3

1 3 5 7 9 10 8 6 4 2

Typeset by Best-set Typesetter Ltd., Hong Kong
Printed and bound in Great Britain by
Biddles Ltd, Guildford and King's Lynn

Contents

Contents vii

Introduction

VILLY BERGSTRÖM

The neoclassical growth model represented a great step forward from the 'Keynesian' models of Harrod and Domar. By introducing factor prices and substitution of factors of production capital deepening was possible within the model framework and the 'knife edge' instability of the Harrod–Domar scheme was overcome.

In the 1950s and 1960s growth theory was a very active field of research. Interest waned later, probably because most implications of the neoclassical growth model had been revealed. However, interest in growth theory was activated again by the discovery of endogenous growth models. To me it seems astonishing that only a minor technical change in a family of aggregated models—albeit a change with far reaching implications—was needed to trigger the vast empirical and comparative literature on governments, institutions and policy regimes.

These models abandoned the assumption of diminishing returns to capital. By assuming constant returns to the accumulated factor of production, growth became endogenously determined by the parameters of the model. This was in contrast to the neoclassical growth model, where per capita income growth was completely determined by exogenous technological change. But by the assumption of increasing returns to the accumulated factor an instability is reintroduced in growth theory, similar to the instability of the Harrod–Domar model. Returns to capital must be exactly constant.

All these models are highly aggregated. They relate aggregate output to aggregate capital and labour, an aggregated saving rate determines the aggregated level of investment. Schemes like these can be used to analyse certain broad characteristics of the economic growth process, such as conditions for stability, steady state growth, factor substitution and the functional distribution of income. One should not expect to find specific empirical predictions of relevance for the growth history or growth prospects of different existing economies by applying any of these aggregated models.

According to the neoclassical growth framework the equilibrium growth process is determined by (exogenous) technology and population growth. This leaves no scope for economic policy to influence the long-term equilibrium rate of economic growth as opposed to the short-term transitions between so called steady states. ('Short term' in this context can mean decades.) However, the third generation of growth models, initiated by Romer (1986) and Lucas (1988), with growth determined endogenously within the model itself, aroused an interest in institutional arrangements and economic policy as influences on economic growth.

These endogenous growth models have developed in different directions, for instance by assuming external effects of private investment—so called spill overs—so that the national capital stock exhibits increasing returns to capital, while constant returns exist at the firm level. Another development is the recognition of monopoly power and the abandonment of the assumption of price-taking competition among firms.[1]

In the aftermath of this 'new growth theory', a literature has arisen in the 1990s that studies the interrelation of institutions, government policies, distribution and growth. The present book, which is the sixth volume in the series 'FIEF Studies in Labour Markets and Economic Policy', is a contribution to this empirical literature.

This book contains four major papers. The first is written by Alberto Alesina, Harvard University, and Roberto Perotti, Columbia University, entitled 'The Politics of Growth: A Survey'. The second paper is written by Pär Hansson and Magnus Henrekson at FIEF, 'Catching Up, Social Capability, Government Size and Economic Growth'. Kevin B. Grier at the George Mason University writes about 'Governments, Unions and Growth'. Finally, Juhana Vartiainen at FIEF studies four cases of successful growth policies in a paper entitled 'Understanding State-Led Late Industrialization'.

---

[1] For a survey of recent theoretical and empirical results see *The Journal of Economic Perspective* 8: 1 (Winter 1994).

The paper by Alesina and Perotti, 'The Politics of Growth: A Survey', reviews recent literature on the political economy of growth. They discuss topics such as the relationship between income instability and growth, whether democratic institutions and civil liberties influence growth performance, and whether income inequality hampers growth or not. They use data from a variety of sources, such as Summers and Heston (1991) and Barro and Wolf (1989).

Sociological, political and economic factors are used as explanatory variables in regressions to explain economies growth. It is often difficult to imagine an underlying structural model. Still, when one finds robust effects of some variable in different data sets and under different model specifications, which is the case for the effect of political instability on growth as well as for the effect of an unequal income distribution, such results may generate focused hypotheses about politics and growth.

To investigate the effect of democracy on growth and of political and economic freedom, in less than fully democratic societies, on growth different indices are used. Also, variables such as the skewness of the distribution must be measured in a simplified way.

The results reported by Alesina and Perotti on these issues should be compared to the case studies in Juhana Vartiainen's paper in this volume. In his paper the case of two benevolent and economically very successful dictatorships are discussed, namely Taiwan and South Korea. Results reported by Alesina and Perotti from econometric research are supported by Vartiainen's analysis of these two very successful cases of late industrialization under less than fully democratic institutions.

The income distribution effect—equalization seems to stimulate growth—is not easy to interpret. An unequal income distribution may result in tension within society, create political unrest, which is detrimental to investment. In support of this effect, but contrary to the results in the paper by Hansson and Henrekson, there are also robust results indicating that transfer payments have a positive effect on growth. This is puzzling as transfers are disproportionately paid for by high income earners, those who make most of the investments in capital. Redistribution should hurt the agents with the highest propensity to invest.

One interpretation is that transfer payments reduce political instability. Probably this effect will differ between countries on different levels of political and economic development. This illustrates the ambiguity still surrounding this kind of interesting and suggestive growth analysis. This survey is commented on by Torsten Persson of the University of Stockholm.

Hansson and Henrekson's paper is more directly knit to theoretical growth models than the other papers in this volume. The authors study the tendency—predicted by neoclassical growth theory—of per capita income and productivity to converge between countries. Their main interest, however, is the phenomenon of 'catching up', meaning that poor countries can imitate advanced countries, whose technological advancements are dependent on their ability to push forward 'best practice techniques' by research and innovations. By copying production methods and possibly organizational methods in advanced countries, poor countries can grow faster than those countries that have to develop the new technologies (in a broad sense).

But as convergence also follows from pure neoclassical growth theory—under certain similarity assumptions on the available production technologies in different countries—they have to account for differences between countries regarding supplies of capital and labour. The more advanced countries have more capital per labour input. Therefore, marginal productivity of capital should be relatively low there, leading to less capital growth than in poor countries—possibly by foreign direct investment in the relatively poor countries.

Hansson and Henrekson try the catching-up hypothesis in a number of ways by modifying their basic neoclassical growth model. Two different data sets are used, covering different samples of countries. The Summers and Heston (1991) data set covers eighty-one countries—developed and underdeveloped— and OECD's International Sectoral Data Bank (ISOB) covers fourteen countries and fourteen sectors.

When Hansson and Henrekson use Summers and Heston's data set they find clear cut catching up when they take account of capital accumulation and labour input. When they use the ISOB data set to study catching up in two sectors—tradables and nontradables—they find evidence of catching up by analysing total factor productivity, in the nontradables sector. After 1970 they find no evidence of catching up in the tradables sector.

Their results also indicate that the slowdown of productivity growth in the advanced OECD countries since the early 1970s is not a result of a restructuring of these economies from manufacturing to nontradables such as service industries. The nontradables sectors do not show lower capital and labour marginal productivities than these factors do in the tradables sector.

There may be great differences between countries regarding their capability of receiving knowledge and using knowledge about foreign technologies, not so much among industrialized countries as among developing countries. Diffusion of technology to less developed countries may be more or less easy, depending on the levels of education, cultural customs and attitudes towards change, trade orientation and so on. By introducing indicators of 'social capability' such as the level of education of the labour force and the country's exposure to international trade the authors are able to get a stronger catching-up effect than when the capability variables are not considered. The level of education and the openness to international trade are believed to indicate the readiness of an economy to adopt new technologies and production methods in a broad sense.

This analysis is carried through on the Summers and Heston data set with data from the UNDP *Human Development Reports* 1990–2 added. Their result indicates the importance of 'social capability' for the catching-up effect among developing economies.

In the last part of their paper Hansson and Henrekson leave the framework of the pure neoclassical growth model. They turn back to the fourteen OECD countries again and study how government expenditures influence productivity growth in the private sector. This analysis should be seen as an exercise within the framework of endogenous growth models. Government consumption and transfer payments impede productivity growth whereas expenditures for education seem to have a positive effect. In the paper by Kevin Grier in this volume this result on government consumption is reinforced. He uses the growth of the government consumption share of GDP and finds a negative effect on growth.

Nicholas Crafts of the LSE, UK, and Kjell Erik Lommerud of the University of Bergen, Norway, comment on the Hansson–Henrekson paper.

As mentioned above some of the questions treated by Hansson and Henrekson are also analysed by Kevin Grier in his paper 'Governments, Unions and Economic Growth'. He uses a similar neoclassical production function approach but brings in some new explanatory factors for the growth process, such as union density, the existence of corporatist as opposed to economically liberal governments and centralized versus decentralized wage formation. Therefore one should see Grier's paper within the framework of endogenous models. Grier thereby extends the analyses reported on in both the Alesina–Perotti and the Hansson–Henrekson papers. The data set is again that of Summers and Heston.

Grier is critical of how this data set has been used by many growth analysts. By aggregating over time and making cross country comparisons information is wasted. Therefore Grier uses pooled data and computes five-year averages for every country included. Grier is also critical of the way researchers have used arbitrary indices of, for instance, centralization and corporatism. Grier uses dummy variables.

Grier uses 'catching up' in a different way to Hansson and Henrekson. According to Grier there is catching up when countries with relatively low capital intensity—little capital per labour input—grow faster than countries with relatively high capital intensity, because the former countries have higher marginal productivity of capital input. This is what Hansson and Henrekson call convergence, as they use catching up to mean technological transfers from advanced countries to technologically less sophisticated countries and imitation by countries lagging behind the technological leader. This latter phenomenon is not studied by Grier.

There are some very robust results in the Grier paper. One is that growth of government consumption hampers growth. The same is true for the variability of inflation. These results are statistically significant in all reported regressions.

Grier thoroughly discusses the Calmfors–Drifill hump-shaped

relationship between the degree of centralization of wage negotiations and the real wage rate. He tests whether the results on wages carries over to economic growth. It does not. Calmfors in his comment on the Grier paper dwells on this issue, arguing that one should not expect the same result for growth as for wages.

Alesina and Perotti in their paper discuss the relationship between different political variables and economic growth. Grier's paper is complementary to their paper, since he includes some political and institutional variables not considered by Alesina and Perotti. This analysis is closely related to the works by Mancur Olson (1982) *et al.* Variables of this category in Grier's paper are the degree of corporatism and union density. By corporatism is meant the 'participation' in government, mainly by (strong) trade unions and sometimes by employers organisations. Participation means consultation and co-operation in different government functions, such as commissions on different issues and membership of agency boards.

Grier finds no direct effect of union density on economic growth. But when he tests for interaction between union density and corporatism he does find effects. There seems to be a synergy effect. Within the group of corporatist countries increasing union density spurs growth. In non-corporatist countries the reverse seems to be true.

The explanation for this could be that corporatism brings labour into co-operation with governments and therefore labour feels confident that wage restraint is paid off by social transfer payments and macroeconomic policies aiming at full employment. The former may call for higher taxes but according to the Alesina–Perotti paper this may be acceptable to capitalist groups as a means of obtaining social peace and a stable environment for their investments.

Lars Calmfors of Stockholm University is one of the discussants of Grier's paper. Grier's paper is really on the borderline between economics and political science. It is therefore natural that the paper is also discussed by John Stephens who is a political scientist from the University of North Carolina.

Corporatism is one of the concepts used in Grier's empirical analysis. The concept is central to the last paper in this volume,

'Understanding State-Led Late Industrialization' by Juhana Vartiainen from FIEF. His paper differs from the other papers in this volume. Vartiainen neither, even remotely, bases his analysis on a neoclassical growth model or any other growth model connecting factor inputs to general output, nor uses econometric or other quantitative methods of analysis. He does analyse a two-sector theoretical model to show that under certain conditions decentralized market solutions of the problems of resource allocation are inferior to state planning and corporatism (co-operation) with or without government involvement. The basic idea is the existence of externalities related to investment, which tend to lead to a corporatist structure of society.

Vartiainen's analysis relates to the great debate in political science on corporatism and in economics on economic systems. He points to the fact that small industrialized economies have to concentrate their resources on a few sectors to reap economies of scale. One example is the pulp and paper industries in the Scandinavian countries. This economic concentration of resources results in few branches of industry and large corporations within small countries. This creates not only economic power but also political. Because of this fact countervailing powers develop and societies tend to be organized around large economic power centres such as federations of industries, employers' organizations, and trade unions.

In such surroundings corporatism tends to thrive in the form of co-operation between government, unions and employers' organizations. Is this good or bad? Neoclassical economics has no place for such political co-operation. Believers in neoclassical economics usually, in their role as citizens, condemn corporatist organizations and societies. Vartiainen shows that corporatism, or looser co-operation between economic agents and governments, can be welfare enhancing. Although his model is static Vartiainen's analysis brings to mind the dynamic model used by Kelvin Lancaster (1973).

Vartiainen looks at four cases of late, that is post-World War II, successful industrialization of formerly dominantly agricultural societies. The countries Vartiainen discusses are South Korea, Taiwan, Finland and Austria.

Vartiainen finds certain common traits in these four countries, such as an efficient and uncorrupted bureaucracy, a relatively small home market in an economy open to foreign trade, a threatened foreign political situation between great military powers. According to Vartiainen this exposed situation created a corporatist, co-operative society, where the state succeeded in co-ordinating national efforts to the best of society. Because the state recognized property rights and a liberal market-oriented economy, planning (in a loose sense) was never looked upon as an outpouring of ideological socialism, and could work smoothly within a capitalist environment. Vartiainen's findings on the benevolent non-democratic societies of Taiwan and South Korea support the hypothesis in the Alesina–Perotti paper that economic liberties within dictatorships can be conducive to economic growth. Jonas Agell of the University of Uppsala and Villy Bergström of FIEF comment on Vartiainen's paper.

References

Barro, R. J. and Wolf, H. C. (1989), 'Data Appendix for Economic Growth in a Cross Section of Countries', unpublished, National Bureau of Economic Research.

Lancaster, K. (1973), 'The Dynamic Inefficiency of Capitalism', *Journal of Political Economy* 81.

Lucas, R. E., Jr. (1988), 'On the Mechanics of Economic Development', *Journal of Monetary Economics* 22(1): 3–42.

Olson, M. (1982), *The Rise and Decline of Nations* (New Haven: Yale University Press).

Romer, P. M. (1986), 'Increasing Returns and Long-Run Growth', *Journal of Political Economy* 94(5): 1002–37.

Summers, R. and Heston, A. (1991), 'The Penn World Table (Mark 5): An Expanded Set of International Comparisons, 1950–1988', *Quarterly Journal of Economics* 106(2): 327–68.

PART I

The Politics of Growth: A Survey

ALBERTO ALESINA AND ROBERTO PEROTTI

1

Introduction

The literature on the political economy of growth is immense: both political scientists and economists have written extensively on this topic. In this paper we do not even attempt to provide a comprehensive survey of the literature; our more modest purpose is to evaluate what we have learnt from the recent outburst of research on the political economy of growth that has occurred in the last few years. This recent literature has developed at the intersection of the new 'endogenous growth theory' and the new 'macro-political economy'.

What is new about these two areas of research? In the growth literature the novelty is in the attempt to view economic growth as an endogenous variable influenced by several factors beyond technological progress and population growth. The macro-political economy literature introduces endogenous determination of policy choices in otherwise standard macroeconomic models.[1] Economists typically view policy choices as exogenous or as chosen by a benevolent social planner. The novelty in the macro-political economy approach is the emphasis on the political process and on interpersonal conflicts as determinants of policy choices.

This paper reviews the recent literature which has grown at the intersection of these two very active areas of research. Specifically, we analyse what we have learned and what puzzles (and there are many!) are left unsolved in the area of the socio-political determinants of growth.

We thank Douglas Hibbs, Torsten Persson and other conference participants for very useful comments. This chapter builds upon a paper that circulated under the title: *The Political Economy of Growth: A Critical Survey of the Recent Literature and Some New Results*, and was published in the *World Bank Economic Review 1994*. We are very grateful for the comments received from Shanta Devarajan, William Easterly and Lant Pritchett. We also acknowledge financial support from the National Science Foundation.

[1] For recent surveys see Persson and Tabellini (1990), Alesina, Roubini and Cohen (1997), and Alesina and Perotti (1995).

Several recent papers have investigated various links between income distribution and growth; political instability and growth; political rights, democracy and growth; savings, investment and political instability. The goal of this paper is to clarify how all these contributions to the literature fit together, by taking a systematic view of the interactions between the variables described above.

We begin in Chapter 2 with a discussion of the relationship between political instability and growth. The two key issues here are how to define and measure political instability and how to account for the fact that neither of the two variables is exogenous to the other. Chapter 3 reviews the basic insight of several recent papers that have argued that income inequality is harmful for growth through its effects on taxation and therefore the return to capital accumulation. In Chapter 4 we propose a way of integrating the literature reviewed in the preceding sections. This section draws on a recent paper of ours, Alesina and Perotti (1996). Chapter 5 begins to explore the intermediate links between income distribution and growth by focusing on fiscal policy. Finally, Chapter 6 concludes.

2

Political Instability, Quality of Governments and Growth

Researchers studying the relationship between political instability and growth have to tackle two major issues. First, how to define political instability. Second, does political stability foster growth or vice versa, or both?

Political instability can be measured in two different ways. The first uses some index of socio-political unrest. The second approach focuses on the frequency of government changes, namely on executive instability.

The first approach, which we label the 'socio-political instability' (SPI) approach, focuses on variables such as riots, political demonstrations against the government, assassinations etc.[2] Some researchers, for example, and among many others, Barro (1991), and Easterly and Rebelo (1993), consider the 'raw' data of these variables (for instance, political assassinations) as their measures of political instability. Other researchers, instead, construct an aggregate index that summarizes in one dimension this multitude of variables. The statistical method often used is the method of 'principal components', which permits a summary of the information contained in a set of original variables in a smaller number of components, typically one or two.[3]

The variables typically used to construct these indices of political instability are of three types: indicators of mass political violence (for example, assassinations or riots), indicators of nonviolent forms of political protest (peaceful demonstrations, strikes), and forms of illegal and violent transfer of power (*coups d'etat*, revolutions).

The results on the relation between these measures of political instability and growth vary. For instance, Hibbs (1973) finds

---

[2] The most widely used sources for these variables are Jodice and Taylor (1988) and Banks (various issues).

[3] The 'classic' reference for this approach is Hibbs (1973); more recently, the same technique has been used by Venieris and Gupta (1986) and Gupta (1990).

no effect of the former on the latter, Benhabib and Spiegel (1992) find weak effects of political instability on investment, while Barro (1991) and Easterly and Rebelo (1993) find stronger effects on growth. All these papers consider cross-sectional studies involving large samples of countries. The differences in the results can be explained by the different definitions of political instability, that is, by which variables are included in the index, and by different specifications of the growth equation. We discuss this point further in Chapter 4.

The second approach to modelling political instability focuses on government changes, that is, on executive turnover. This 'executive instability' (EI) approach begins by estimating the propensity of government collapses by means of probit regressions. The independent variables in these regressions are political variables (protests, riots, executive reshuffling etc.), economic variables (past growth, inflation etc.) and institutional variables (whether the country is a democracy or not, the electoral system etc.). A high estimate of the probability of government change is viewed as an indicator of executive instability. Thus, one can estimate the probability of a government collapse, and then use this estimate as one of the independent variables in a regression where growth is the dependent variable.

Which of the two concepts of political instability is preferable is not obvious on a priori grounds. One argument holds that political instability is harmful for growth because it creates policy uncertainty: a high propensity to change governments implies more policy variability, since new governments may implement new policies. According to this view, the crucial variable that captures political instability is government turnover. Phenomena of mass political violence are relevant only insofar as they help to predict the occurrence of government changes. Thus, according to this argument the definition of political instability focusing on government turnover is preferable. On the other hand, one may argue that mass violence and social unrest can create economic disruption even when they are not associated with frequent executive changes. This is more likely to be the case at high levels of mass violence.

Regardless of the approach taken to measuring instability, the researcher has to deal with the important problem of the direction of causality. Political instability can disrupt economic growth, and on the other hand low growth may generate political instability.

Londregan and Poole (1990) suggest a clever way of dealing with this problem. They estimate a two-equation model. One equation is a probit regression where the dependent variable captures the occurrence of *coups d'état*. The dependent variable in the second equation is per capita income growth. They find that poverty and, to some extent, low growth increase the likelihood of coups. Furthermore, *coups d'état* are 'persistent': past coups increase the likelihood of more coups. Thus, if a country has a history of coups, it is likely to experience more coups in the future. On the contrary, and somewhat surprisingly, they find that the propensity to have a coup does not reduce growth. In a later paper, the same authors (Londregan and Poole, 1992) confirm these results using a different sample and estimation techniques.

Alesina, Ozler, Roubini and Swagel (1996) adopt Londregan and Poole's technique but use different specifications. First, they control for many more economic determinants of growth. Second, they focus not only on coups but on a broader definition of government changes, which includes both coups and constitutional changes of the executive. While they confirm Londregan and Poole's results on the effects of poverty on coups, they find that a high propensity to executive instability reduces growth. This result is quite robust and holds in several different specifications of the system.

These authors also address an important problem for models of executive instability. They distinguish three different types of government changes: *coups d'état*, that is, unconstitutional executive turnovers; 'major' government changes, that is, coups plus those constitutional changes of government that imply a significant modification in the ideological orientation of the government; and 'regular' government changes, which include all of the above plus any other change of government, even without a 'significant' change of leadership. They find that, according to intuition, the largest effects on growth are generated by a large propensity to major government changes and coups, rather than by 'regular' changes. They also find that low growth tends to increase the propensity to observe government changes. Therefore, the joint endogeneity issue has to be taken seriously. On the one hand, political stability reduces growth, on the other hand low growth increases political instability.[4]

An additional insight which both Londregan and Poole (1990) and Alesina *et al.* (1996) emphasize is that the variable that influences growth is not the actual occurrence of a government collapse but the expectation of it, which is estimated exogenously and can assume any value between 0 and 1. This implies that a country with a politic-economic environment which leads to a persistently high expectation of a collapse is considered unstable even though the actual frequency of collapses may be not as high as expected. Needless to say, however, countries with frequent government changes are also countries with a persistently high probability of changes.

The picture that emerges from this line of research is the following. Poor countries tend to have frequent radical government changes and are socio-politically unstable. Since political instability reduces the incentives to save and invest and therefore reduces growth, poor countries may fall into a 'trap'. They are unstable because they do not manage to become rich; they find it hard to become rich because they are politically unstable.

A somewhat different view on this topic has been put forward by Huntington (1968), who concentrates on the causal link from growth to socio-political instability. He argues that it is not always true that 'all good things go together'. When poor countries experience a period of take-off and rapid growth, social unrest may actually increase: new demands are generated, the process of urbanization accelerates, the entire society is in turmoil. This is not in general true for those rich countries that, for some reason, experience a period of high growth: rich countries, unlike poor ones, have already the institutions in place to cope with social and economic transformations. Therefore, according to Huntington, the relationship between instability and growth is nonlinear, and its sign depends on the level of development: positive for poor economies, negative for richer economies.

Some summary statistics on the data typically used in this area of research are quite suggestive. These statistics are reported in

---

[4] Block-Bomberg (1992) presents results consistent with this view.

TABLE 2.1. *Definition of variables and data sources*

GDP	GDP in thousands of 1980 dollars, from the Summers–Heston data set
GR	Rate of growth of GDP 1960–85 or 1970–85
EDUC	Primary school enrolment rate in year 1960 or 1970
MID	Share of the third quintile of the population in or around year 1960 or 1970
MIDCLASS	Share of the third and fourth quintiles of the population in or around 1960 or 1970
TOPBOT	Ratio of the share of the fifth quintile to the share of the first and second quintiles, in or around 1960 or 1970
URB	Urban population as percentage of total in year 1960 or 1970. *Source*: World Bank Tables
AGE	Percentage of population over age 65 in year 1960 or 1970. *Source*: World Bank Tables
GTRAN	Nominal government transfer payments as ratio to nominal GDP (average from 1970 to 1985)
INV	Ratio of real domestic investment (private plus public) to real GDP (average from 1970 to 1985 or from 1960 to 1985)
PRIVINV	Ratio of real private domestic investment to real GDP (average from 1970 to 1985)
PPPIDE	Deviation of the PPP value for the investment deflator from the sample mean, 1960
GCHANGE	Dummy variable taking the value of 1 for every change of the executive, both constitutional and unconstitutional. *Source*: Jodice-Taylor (1982), corrected by Alesina *et al.* (1991)
MJCHANGE	Dummy variable taking the value of 1 for every unconstitutional change of the executive *and* every constitutional change of government with a change in the party (or group) leading the executive. *Source*: Alesina *et al.* (1991)
COUPS	Dummy variable taking the value of 1 for every unconstitutional change of the executive. *Source*: Jodice-Taylor (1982)
EXADJUST	Dummy variable taking the value of 1 for every adjustment in the composition of the executive, without a change of leadership. *Source*: Jodice-Taylor (1982)

Note: This table describes the data used in the regressions. All the data are from the Barro–Wolf [1989] data set, except for the income distribution data (which are from a variety of sources detailed in Table A.1 in the Appendix) or unless otherwise indicated.

TABLE 2.2. *Sample means of the data, 1960–82*

	All	Latin	Africa	Asia	Indust.	Other
GCHANGE	0.28	0.29	0.21	0.30	0.39	0.37
	(0.45)	(0.45)	(0.41)	(0.46)	(0.49)	(0.48)
MJCHANGE	0.11	0.16	0.11	0.07	0.12	0.16
	(0.32)	(0.36)	(0.31)	(0.25)	(0.32)	(0.37)
COUP	0.048	0.078	0.057	0.040	0.00	0.058
	(0.21)	(0.27)	(0.23)	(0.20)	(0.00)	(0.23)
EXADJ	0.49	0.49	0.42	0.54	0.53	0.57
	(0.50)	(0.50)	(0.49)	(0.50)	(0.50)	(0.50)
DEM	2.24	2.18	2.83	2.33	1.07	2.23
	(0.93)	(0.92)	(0.50)	(0.89)	(0.37)	(0.91)
GR	0.024	0.022	0.015	0.033	0.029	0.041
	(0.069)	(0.065)	(0.084)	(0.068)	(0.035)	(0.060)
EDUC	0.827	0.963	0.625	0.826	1.020	0.995
	(0.30)	(0.18)	(0.33)	(0.25)	(0.17)	(0.22)
GDP60	2626	2170	881	3379	6021	1879
	(4202)	(1003)	(499)	(8521)	(1801)	(163)
Countries	113	24	41	21	21	6
Obs. (60–82)	2592	552	943	476	483	136
Obs. (70–82)	3259	759	1051	572	693	184

Note: This table is from Alesina *et al*. 1996. For some variables, units of measurement may be different from those utilized in this paper. Region breakdowns uses the IMF coding system. Hence, the 'other' category refers to non-industrialized European countries.

Table 2.2. Table 2.1 defines all the variables used not only in Table 2.2 but also in the rest of this paper.[5] Table 2.2 shows that Latin America is the region which has had the highest frequency of major government changes and *coups d'état*.[6] It is also the region with the second lowest rate of growth, after Africa. Africa

[5] Table 2.2 is adapted from Alesina *et al*. (1996).

[6] 'Major government changes' are coded by Alesina *et al*. (1996) as changes which include all the coups plus any regular government change which implies a significant turnover of leadership. See Alesina *et al*. (1996) for more details.

also has a very low frequency of constitutional changes of government and a high frequency of coups and the lowest income per capita. The variable *DEM* varies from close to 1 (fully democratic systems) in the industrial countries, to almost 3 (dictatorships) in Africa (see Table 2.1). A monotonic relationship between this variable and growth does not jump out of Table 2.2. Africa is the least democratic region and has the lowest growth rate. However, Asia is less democratic than Latin America but has grown more rapidly.

These simple observations point to the following hypothesis: what influences growth is not so much the type of regime (dictatorship or democracy) but regime instability, that is, the propensity to coups and major changes of government. In Chapter 3 we provide a more systematic discussion of the relationship between growth and political freedom.

A related topic is the one of the 'quality' of governance, namely the level of corruption, the degree to which the rule of law and property rights are respected and the quality of the bureaucracy. These variables are obviously very difficult to measure, even more difficult than the concept of political stability. Several authors, including Mauro (1995), Knack and Keefer (1995) and Clague, Keefer, Knack and Olson (1996), have used various subjective measures of these variables to evaluate their influence on economic growth. Generally these papers find that a low level of corruption, respect of the rule of law and of property rights and an efficient bureaucracy are growth enhancing. However, these indicators of 'good governance' are highly correlated with each other and with measures of political stability and civil liberties. In other words, 'good things go together'. As a result it is often difficult to disentangle the separate effects of all these different variables.[7] Borner, Brunetti and Weder (1995) use a self-constructed survey to evaluate the extent of credibility of contract enforcement, rule of law and political stability. They find that these indicators are associated with growth in the expected direction.

---

[7] Some of this high correlation may be induced by the way in which these variables are measured. In fact these variables on the quality of government are obtained by the subjective evaluation of correspondents in different countries of private consulting groups. An observer is likely to assign bad marks on any dimension to the country for which he or she is responsible rather than trying to disentangle in a more refined (and difficult) way the difference between various aspects of good governance.

3

Democracy, Freedom and Growth

The concept of 'political freedom' can be viewed in two ways, which are related but not identical. The first defines 'democracy' and 'political freedom' based upon the existence of free competitive (that is, more than one party) elections. This definition was used in Table 2.2 above. The second focuses on the amount of civil and economic rights that are available to the population: the existence of competitive elections is obviously one major civil right, but others include freedom of the press, freedom of movement, etc.

The two definitions are not identical. All dictatorships are not democratic according to the first criterion, that is they do not allow free competitive elections. On the other hand several dictatorships may grant a certain amount of civil and especially economic rights to their citizens.

One line of argument emphasizes the possibility of a negative relationship. With political freedom various pressure groups have a 'voice' in the political arena. Their conflicting demands for redistributive policies either imply legislative deadlocks or are resolved by increasing the size of the government. Furthermore, democratic governments (particularly coalition governments) may be slow at responding to shocks with appropriate policies. For example, Alesina and Drazen (1991) propose a model that explains delays in the adoption of efficient policies as a result of a 'veto game' among conflicting groups. Finally, incumbent politicians are expected to engage in suboptimal and short-sighted policies to be re-elected.[8]

Each of these arguments, however, can be questioned. First, even dictators need to please various constituencies to avoid being overthrown (Ames, 1987). Redistributive struggles between various socio-economic groups can certainly occur in

[8] On pressure groups and lobbying see Krueger (1974), Bhagwati (1982) and Mueller (1979). On fiscal deadlocks see Alesina (1988) and Alesina and Drazen (1991).

various forms even without democratic institutions. In fact, lacking a constitutional way of changing a leader, political change often requires violence and disruption of market activities. Thus, *a priori*, there seems to be no obvious relationship between democracy and growth.

As a matter of fact, Alesina *et al.* (1996) find no relationship between democracy defined in this way and growth. This inconclusive result is consistent with much of the earlier literature (reviewed by Roubini, 1990). Basically, the point is that several dictators have followed growth-enhancing economic policies (again, think of South-East Asia) while many others have severely damaged their economies (think of several countries of Africa). Indeed, after examining the evidence, Helliwell (1994) concludes that 'it is still not possible to identify any systematic net effects of democracy on subsequent economic growth'.

A difficult problem of this line of research is that democratic institutions are very highly correlated with per capita income which, in turn, is highly correlated with education.[9] Thus, when a democracy variable is found significant in a regression where the dependent variable is growth, one has to worry about whether what is really being captured is the effect of per capita income or education. Disentangling the individual effects of these three highly correlated variables (GDP, education and democracy) is not a simple matter (see Helliwell, 1994 and Barro, 1996, for some progress on this point).

The second definition of democracy does not focus on elections, but on the level of political and, to some extent, economic freedom. The most widely used index of civil liberties is the Gastill index that ranks countries in seven groups. As an indicator of economic rights one might use measures of restrictions on capital mobility, trade restrictions or other measures of economic regulations.

As before, one can think of arguments which are consistent with either a positive or a negative correlation between civil

---

[9] Table 2.2 illustrates this correlation. Recently there has been a welcomed push towards democratization in many parts of the world. However, in the sixties, seventies and early eighties (the sample typically covered in growth studies) there were very few democracies outside the OECD group of countries.

liberties and growth. One may argue that economic liberty fosters entrepreneurship, market activities and growth. On the other hand, more economic liberty may translate into more conflicts over distribution. On balance, there are probably reasons to believe that it is civil liberties that are conducive to growth, rather than the presence of competitive elections *per se*. In fact, results by Barro (1991) and Ozler and Rodrik (1992) suggest that civil liberties are conducive to growth and capital accumulation. As to economic freedom, it is more straightforward to argue that less regulation and fewer obstacles to individual market activities should spur growth.

The problem with these concepts of economic liberty is that the results obtained by using them are virtually undistinguishable from statements like 'economic inefficiencies are bad for growth'. It is not completely clear whether these results on economic freedom are implying something other than the fact that economic inefficiencies are not conducive to growth.[10]

What one can conclude from the research effort summarized in this section is that the hypothesis that democratic institutions reduce growth prospects is not supported by the available evidence. Certain dictatorships, which score very low in terms of political rights because they do not allow free competitive elections, have grown very fast and have created the necessary environment for market activities to prosper. Other dictatorships have performed very poorly. On the contrary, regardless of the existence of free competitive elections, the evidence suggests that other civil liberties are growth enhancing.

The related question is whether growth influences the likelihood of democratization, and more generally what are the economic determinants of democracy. The most recent studies on this point are by Barro (1996a,b), who argues that (not surprisingly) high levels of income per capita increase the propensity to become a democracy. Other factors which favour democratization include a low gap between male and female education and a low level of urbanization and reliance on natural resources. While the levels of income reflect past growth

---

[10] Roubini and Sals-i-Martin (1991) find that a measure of openness is positively related to growth. In some sense, openness, like the black market premium, can be thought of as a proxy for economic liberty.

performance, and thus historical patterns of growth influence the likelihood of democratization, the evidence does not revel any particular influence of current growth on the likelihood of democratization.

4

Income Distribution and Growth

A third strand of literature focuses on the relation between income distribution and growth. Needless to say, this is not a new topic in economics. What characterizes the new contributions is their close connection with the new theories of endogenous growth, and a focus on previously neglected links *from* income distribution *to* growth, rather than from growth to income distribution.

In particular, the recent literature has focused on three links.[11] The first approach stresses the role of imperfect capital markets. With perfect capital markets, anybody could borrow for his education against his expected future earnings. However, various departures from perfect market conditions, including imperfect information about individual abilities and imperfect enforcement of loans, severely restrict the option of borrowing for education. Thus, most people (particularly the less well off) must rely on their own resources to invest in education. Thus, the initial distribution of these resources determines how many agents can invest, and therefore what is the resulting rate of growth of the economy. Important contributions to this line of research are Galor and Zeira (1993), Banerjee and Newman (1991) and Aghion and Bolton (1996). For instance Galor and Zeira show that the effects of wealth distribution on growth depend on the level of wealth per capita. If a country is relatively poor, then wealth inequality may be growth enhancing, because in this case at least someone will have enough resources to acquire education, generating positive externalities that will benefit other agents later on. By contrast, if wealth is equally distributed no group might be above the necessary threshold to invest in education. As aggregate wealth grows, less inequality becomes more beneficial because even the middle class can start investing in education, provided wealth is not too concentrated in few hands.

---

[11] For an excellent recent survey see Benabou (1996).

In the second approach, the more unequal is the distribution of resources, the larger the incentives for agents in the lower tail of the distribution to engage in rent-seeking activities, and crime, which hinders investment and therefore growth. Recent formalizations of these arguments are Benhabib and Rustichini (1991) and Fay (1993). A third approach focuses on the size of the market. Murphy, Shleifer and Vishny (1989) argue that income inequality has negative effects on growth by reducing aggregate demand. Ades and Glaeser (1994) provide some evidence consistent with this approach. Finally Benabou (1996b,c) investigates the connections between income inequality, segregation, school achievements and growth.

A fourth approach, on which we mostly focus here, emphasizes a *political* channel linking income distribution and growth. One crucial idea that is common to several papers in this area is that the level of government expenditure and taxation is the result of a voting process in which income is the main determinant of a voter's preferences; in particular, poor voters will favour a high level of taxation.[12] This is because they either pay a lower share of taxes, or disproportionately benefit from government spending. In an unequal society, with many poor agents relative to the average, the majority of voters will then vote for high taxation, which again will discourage investment and therefore growth. Alesina and Rodrik (1994) (henceforth A&R), Bertola (1993) (B) and Persson and Tabellini (1994) (P&T) are three contributions in this area.[13]

These papers share a common structure. Each of them consists of an *economic mechanism* and a *political mechanism*.[14] The

---

[12] This line of research generalizes to a dynamic context static models of voting on the tax rate by Romer (1975), Roberts (1977) and Meltzer and Richard (1981).

[13] Perotti (1993a) and Saint-Paul and Verdier (1991) are two other recent contributions that study the politico-economic determinants of growth. In both papers the agents vote over the level of government expenditure and growth is driven by accumulation of human capital, but the two mechanisms are different. In the former, individuals vote over the level of purely redistributive transfers: this determines the post-tax income of the agents of the economy and therefore who can privately invest in education. In turn, this determines the rate of accumulation of human capital. In the latter, agents vote over public expenditure on education: therefore, income distribution affects the accumulation of human capital through this channel.

[14] For a more complete detailed survey of these models, see Perotti (1992) and Benabou (1996a).

 Alesina and Perotti

former describes the effects of fiscal policy on growth. The latter describes how income distribution determines fiscal policy (taxes and government expenditure) through the voting process. The papers differ in the type of government expenditure they consider: public services (A&R), redistribution from capital to labour (B), purely redistributive transfers (P&T). The common element is that, whenever the share of government expenditure on GDP rises, the accompanying increase in taxation reduces the after tax marginal product of capital that can be appropriated by private investors: this reduces the rate of accumulation of capital and therefore growth. The distribution of initial resources comes into play because it determines the distribution of preferences over fiscal policy.

In A&R the key distributional variable is the relative share of labour and capital endowments, which is monotonically related to the distribution of income. Public services needed for production are financed only by a tax on private capital. Because government services are productive a 'small' tax benefits everyone, including those agents who have only capital income. A certain level of taxation maximizes growth, and this is the tax rate preferred by the 'capitalists'. Beyond this point an increase in the tax rate decreases the rate of investment and therefore the rate of growth of an economy.

Now consider the political mechanism: the higher the proportion of capital income in an individual's total income (or, equivalently, the higher the individual's total income), the higher the price that individual has to pay for the benefits of public services. Pure capitalists prefer the tax rate that maximizes growth; generally, the higher the proportion of labour in the total endowment of an individual, the higher the desired tax rate and the desired size of government services. This observation implies that the higher is the proportion of labour in the endowment, the lower is the desired growth rate for the economy. It is worth emphasizing that this result is in no way due to myopia or 'excessive' discounting: in this model everybody has the same discount rate and is rationally forward looking. An increase in the tax rate beyond the growth-maximizing level has two effects: a growth effect and a redistributive effect. The first one is second order for tax rates close to the level that maximizes growth. In fact, the relationship between growth and the tax rate is an inverted

U and is 'flat' (or, more precisely, the first derivative is zero) at the level of the tax rate that maximizes growth. The second effect arises because an increase in taxes and public services redistributes resources from capital to labour. Thus, while a capitalist would never choose to tax beyond the growth-maximizing level, a 'worker' would weigh these two effects on growth and redistribution.

The 'median voter theorem' implies that the equilibrium tax rate is the one preferred by the median agent in the distribution of resources; namely, the agent with the minimum relative endowment of labour and capital.[15]

By combining the economic and the political mechanisms one obtains that, the higher the proportion of capital income to total income of the median voter, the lower the tax rate that prevails through the voting process and the higher the resulting rate of investment and growth. The result can also be restated in terms of income distribution: the poorer is the median voter relative to the voter with average income, the higher is the equilibrium tax rate and the lower is the growth rate. Therefore, this model implies an inverse relation between growth and income or wealth inequality.

Since reliable data on wealth distribution are not available for a sufficiently large sample of countries, A&R focus on income distribution and land distribution as a proxy for wealth distribution. Note that the distribution of wealth is more skewed than the distribution of labour income: this implies that, if in country A the median income is lower than in country B, the same is true for their median wealth/labour ratios. Thus, one can use data on the distribution of income to proxy for the data on wealth/labour ratios. The testable implication of this model is therefore that there should be a positive relation between income inequality and the rate of growth of the economy.

Bertola (1991) also focuses on the functional distribution of income, but the economic mechanism is different: revenues from taxation are used for redistribution, not for public services. Capital income is taxed and the proceeds are directly redistributed to agents who derive their income from labour. The effect of a higher level of taxation is then similar to the A&R model:

---

[15] Note that in this model, 'labour' has to be interpreted as unskilled labour, and 'capital' has to be interpreted as inclusive of physical and human capital.

it decreases the after-tax marginal product of capital that an investor can appropriate, and therefore it decreases investment and growth. The difference is that in A&R the government serves two purposes, a productive one and a redistributive one, while in B the government is only redistributive. The political mechanism is also similar to that of A&R: the higher the proportion of capital income to labour income, the more an agent has to lose from a proportional tax rate on capital that is redistributed to an individual in proportion to his labour income. Thus, the tax rate that prevails through the voting process is again a negative function of the wealth/labour ratio of the median voter. Combining the two mechanisms, one obtains the same reduced-form prediction as in A&R: the higher the wealth/labour ratio of the median voter, the higher the rate of growth of the economy. By applying the same reasoning used above, this can be translated into a testable prediction, that is, that there should be a positive association between the income of the median voter and the rate of growth of the economy.

P&T also analyse the effects of redistributive policies, but they focus on redistribution from rich agents to poor agents rather than from capital to labour; therefore, the relevant concept is now that of the personal distribution of income. In the economic mechanism, agents work and invest in human capital. Taxes are proportional to income, and the revenues are redistributed lump sum to all agents. Again, higher taxes discourage investment in human capital and therefore reduce growth. As to the political mechanism, since taxes are redistributed lump sum, poor voters pay a relatively small amount in taxes, but receive the same benefits as rich voters; thus, the tax rate favoured by an individual is inversely related to his income. When preferences are aggregated through the voting process, the implication is that the poorer the median voter relative to the average, the higher the tax rate and again the lower the rate of investment and growth.

In summary, the common testable prediction of all these models is that there should be a negative relationship between growth or investment and inequality. Although one might not want to take the median voter result too literally, the main message is fairly clear: societies with more unequal income distributions have a higher level of government expenditure and taxation resulting from the political process, will invest less and therefore will grow more slowly. A literal interpretation of the theory suggests that the inverse relation between income distribution and growth should hold only in democracies, where voting is a relevant part of the political process. Because of this, we discuss below results obtained on a sample of democracies. However, one may not want to interpret the 'median voter theorem' too literally and may want to apply these theories to non-democratic countries as well. Dictators can ignore the desires of a majority only up to a point: the fear of insurrections may keep even a dictator from deviating too much from the median citizen's preferences, although the link between the median voter's preferences and the policy implemented is less direct in a dictatorship than in a democracy.

Table 4.1 displays several regressions where the dependent variable is the average growth in per capita GDP from 1960 to 1985. The regressions in the first four columns use the sample of democracies: we present estimates of the reduced form using three different data sets on income distribution variables (from Perotti, 1996 (P), Alesina and Rodrik, 1994 (A&R) and Persson and Tabellini, 1994 (P&T) respectively) with the corresponding samples of democracies, based on slightly different definitions. The last column includes all the sixty-four countries for which data are available. The list of countries in the sample from Perotti (1996), which we will use for the next estimates, is reported in Appendix I.1.[16] Our income distribution variables are measured in or around 1960, therefore at the beginning of the sample period on which growth is computed. This is appropriate because in all these models the initial distribution of income is taken as predetermined.

Table 4.1 displays a few examples of various growth regressions in which a measure of income inequality is used as an independent variable. The table highlights a positive relationship

---

[16] For the precise definition of 'democracy' used to select the twenty-nine countries see Perotti (1996). In any case, the results presented in Table 4.1 are robust to 'sensitivity tests' on this definition; the results do not change when 'dubious' cases are kept in or left out from the group of democracies. On this point see Alesina and Rodrik (1992) and Perotti (1996).

TABLE 4.1. *Reduced form growth regressions, 1960–85*

	(1) P	(2) A&R	(3) P&T	(4) P	(5) P
Constant	−0.24	−4.93	−5.07	−1.70	1.69
	(−0.13)	(−1.96)	(−3.51)	(−0.66)	(1.19)
GDP	−0.43	−0.62	−0.61	−0.43	−0.63
	(−2.82)	(−3.20)	(−3.84)	(0.26)	(−3.75)
PRIM	0.02	0.06	0.05	0.03	0.04
	(1.08)	(3.04)	(3.98)	(3.73)	(3.74)
MID	0.20	0.26	0.30	0.14	−0.04
	(1.81)	(2.06)	(3.06)	(1.20)	(−0.48)
PPPIDE				−1.64	−0.08
				(−1.38)	(−0.12)
URB				0.01	0.01
				(0.54)	(0.70)
LAAMER				−0.85	−2.38
				(−0.95)	(−3.96)
AFRICA				3.59	−1.31
				(2.38)	(−1.71)
ASIA				−0.03	−0.46
				(−0.23)	(−0.72)
NOBS	29	24	29	29	64
$\bar{R}^2$	0.17	0.30	0.49	0.46	0.40
SEE	1.22	1.21	1.22	0.98	1.34

Note: OLS. Dependent variable: $\Delta GDP6085$. In column (2) the Alesina–Rodrik data and sample of democracies have been used. In column (3) the Persson–Tabellini data and sample of democracies have been used. *t*-statistics in parentheses. Botswana is the only African country in the sample of democracies.

between the income share of the third quintile of the population and growth in democracies, as predicted by the theory.

These regressions are suggestive of an intriguing regularity linking income inequality and growth. One has to be aware, however, of some issues of robustness. As for many regressors in what are by now 'standard' cross section growth regressions, whether or not the income distribution variable remains statistically significant depends on the specification of the regression, namely on what other variables are used in the right hand side.[17] Sensitivity analysis performed by Clarke (1993), Persson and Tabellini (1994) and Alesina and Rodrik (1992, 1994) suggests that these results are quite robust.

A caveat has, however, to be mentioned, namely the high correlation between the income distribution variable and the Latin American dummy variable. In fact, income distribution is more unequal and growth lower in Latin America relative to other regions. Therefore, in some (but not all) specifications the income distribution variable becomes insignificant when the Latin American dummy variable is introduced. In other specifications the opposite occurs: the distribution variable remains significant. Column 4 of Table 4.1 presents an example of one regression in which the presence of a regional dummy for Latin America reduces the significance of the coefficient on *MID*.

Column 5 shows a specification in which the inverse relationship between inequality and growth does not hold when the non-democracies are added in the sample. Whether or not this comparison between democracies and non-democracies is a robust result is an open question. Persson and Tabellini (1994) argue that it is, in the sense that the relation between growth and inequality holds only for democracies. Alesina and Rodrik (1994), using a different set of data, argue that this result is not robust: democracies and non-democracies are indistinguishable. Clarke (1993) using yet another data set and different specifications presents results consistent with Alesina and Rodrik (1994): like the latter authors, Clarke does not find a significant difference in the sample of democracies and non-democracies. Perotti (1996) explains how to reconcile these results in terms of different specifications of the regressions and argues that the evidence is inconclusive on this point and although one cannot exclude a different effect

---

[17] Levine and Renelt (1992) have shown that very few right-hand side variables in cross section growth regressions retain their statistical significance regardless of which other variables are used in the same regression.

between democracies and dictatorships, this effect is not very robust.

These somewhat inconclusive results on dictatorships versus democracies can be interpreted in two ways. One is that, as argued above, dictators may face similar redistributive pressure to democratically elected governments. The other is that other channels, in addition to the political one, may link income inequality and growth.

Several criticisms have been raised against these models. First, they assume a very stylized voting process, where all proposals are chosen by pairwise comparison in a referendum-type competition. In defence of these models one can argue that the empirical analysis concerns the long-run relations between income distribution, growth, investment and fiscal policy, not their year-to-year relations. Therefore, even though year-by-year fiscal decisions may be taken based upon many considerations which have nothing to do with the median voter's preferences and wealth, in the long-run it is not implausible to assume that the political equilibrium will reflect to some extent the position of such 'focal points' as the 'median voter' and the 'middle class'. It is not even obvious that voting is the only way the middle class can express its voice. Even a dictator cannot depart too much from the policies desired by a majority, for fear of uprising or political violence. This argument also responds to a second criticism of these models, namely that they are applicable only to a restricted sample of democracies. On the other hand it is quite possible that the political influence of the upper middle class, even in a democracy, extends beyond their one-person–one-vote influence, for instance through campaign contributions. In this case the median voter model would not be appropriate even for long-run predictions.

A third objection is that the predictions of these models can be quite sensitive to the type of taxation and government expenditure considered. For example, in Bertola's model when taxes are used to redistribute income from owners of capital to labour (as we have assumed up to now) it is intuitive that the rate of investment and growth will decrease. However, if taxes are used to subsidize investment, a high level of taxation promotes investment and growth by decreasing the price of capital relative to consumption and therefore by inducing agents to postpone consumption. In both cases, rich agents oppose high taxation: in the first case for obvious reasons, in the second because a high level of subsidization of investment reduces the price of the capital these agents already own. Thus, in a society where the median voter has a relatively low income the resulting high level of taxation will hamper growth if taxes are used to redistribute income from capital to labour, while it will promote growth if taxes are used to subsidize investment. One can shed more light on this issue by disaggregating the relation between income distribution and growth into its two components: the effects of income distribution on a *specific* type of government expenditure (the *political mechanism*) and the effects of that government expenditure variable on growth and investment (the *economic mechanism*).

We will attempt to explore this point in Chapter 6. First, however, we investigate another link between income distribution and growth, one that passes through socio-political instability.

5

Income Distribution, Political Instability and Growth

The idea we test in this chapter, which is based on Alesina and Perotti (1996), is at the same time simple and plausible: when income distribution is very unequal, the resulting tensions within a society induce a high level of political instability. This instability discourages investment and therefore generates a low rate of growth of the economy.

As pointed out in Chapter 2 two definitions of political instability can be adopted: socio-political instability (SPI) and executive instability, that is, the frequency of government collapses (EI). In Alesina and Perotti (1996) we adopt the first definition, and use two related indices of SPI. The first one is our own construction of an index based on a principal component analysis applied to a relatively small number of key variables. The second index is taken from Gupta (1990), which applies the same method to a larger set of political variables. The results obtained with the two models are fairly similar, indicating robustness to the choice of an index. Since in Alesina and Perotti (1996) we emphasize the first index, here we report the results obtained using the Gupta index, which is constructed as follows:

$$
\begin{aligned}
SPI = {} & 1.14 + 0.0007 PROTEST + 0.0049 RIOT \\
& + 0.0086 STRIKE + 0.0000043 DEATH + 0.13 ASSASS \\
& + 0.0008 ATTACK + 0.0033 EXECUTION \\
& + 1.38 SCOUP + 0.264 UCOUP + 0.92 DEM,
\end{aligned} \tag{1}
$$

where $PROTEST$ is the number of political demonstrations against a government; $RIOT$ is the number of riots; $STRIKE$ is the number of political strikes; $DEATH$ is the number of people killed in conjunction with any domestic political violence; $ASSASS$ is the number of politically motivated assassinations; $ATTACK$ is the number of politically motivated attacks on individuals; $EXECUTION$ is the number of politically motivated executions; $SCOUP$ is the number of successful coups; $UCOUP$

is the number of unsuccessful coups, and *DEM* is a dummy variable that identifies democracies, taking a value of 0 for democracies, 0.5 for semi-democracies and 1 for dictatorships. A democracy is defined in the first way discussed in Chapter 3: a country is a democracy if its leaders are elected in free competitive elections. The democracy variable corrects for the fact that a given level of unrest is an indicator of more serious socio-political instability in a dictatorship than in a democracy, since in the former demonstrations and political activities in general are severely limited.[18]

A simple bivariate system captures the basic mechanisms we are investigating:

$$INV = \alpha_0 + \alpha_1 SPI + \alpha_2 PPPIDE + \alpha_3 EDUC + \varepsilon_1 \qquad (2)$$

$$SPI = \beta_0 + \beta_1 MIDCLASS + \beta_2 GDP + \beta_3 INV + \beta_4 URB$$
$$+ \beta_5 AFRICA + \beta_6 LAAMER + \beta_7 ASIA + \varepsilon_2 \qquad (3)$$

In the first equation we estimate the effects of socio-political instability (*SPI*) on investment, after controlling for some obvious economic variables, common in the literature. The variable *EDUC* (enrolment ratio in primary school in 1960) captures complementarities in production between human and physical capital. *PPPIDE* is the deviation of the PPP value of the investment deflator from the sample mean in 1960. It thus captures distortions that make investing in physical capital more costly. We expect a higher level of socio-political instability to discourage investment, i.e. $\alpha_1 < 0$.

The second equation specifies what can be regarded as plausible determinants of socio-political instability. The variable *GDP* measures the level of economic development. *URB* captures the degree of urbanization of a country. The regional dummies are meant to capture region-specific cultural factors. We are particularly interested in the two remaining variables. *INV* is a proxy for the growth performance of an economy: it is plausible to assume that socio-political instability should be a decreasing function of the rate of growth of the economy. Furthermore, it is quite plausible that the effect of political instability and uncertainty about property rights should be

---

[18] See Alesina and Perotti (1993b) for more discussion on the properties of this index and for additional results obtained using other *SPI* indices.

particularly harmful to investment activities, particularly long-run investment in plants and equipment. As to *MIDCLASS*, the income distribution variable, the hypothesis is that socio-political instability is a positive function of the degree of inequality in the distribution of resources across individuals.

The variable *MIDCLASS* has a very high negative correlation (−0.93) with *TOP*, the share of income of the richest quintile of the population. Thus, in our sample an increase in *MIDCLASS* corresponds almost one-to-one to a decrease in the share of income of the richest quintile. It follows that a higher value of *MIDCLASS* implies both a wealthier middle class *and* more equality in the distribution of income.

TABLE 5.1. *Summary statistics (sample 1960–85)*

	NOBS	Mean	Std. Err.	Min	Max
INV	72	19.34	7.32	6.82	36.91
SPI	70	1.68	1.26	0.00	3.21
GDP	72	2.05	1.88	0.021	7.38
EDUC	72	79.14	30.77	5.00	144.00
MIDCLASS	72	33.08	5.73	20.10	41.90
TOPBOT	72	4.31	2.40	1.32	13.85
URB	65	39.33	23.19	4.00	82.00
PPPIDE	72	−0.004	0.25	−0.49	0.86

Note: For definitions of variables and units of measurement, see Table 2.1. For sources, see Appendix I.2.

TABLE 5.2. *Correlation matrix (sample 1960–85)*

	INV	SPI	GDP	EDUC	MIDCLASS	TOPBOT	URB	PPPIDE
INV	—	−0.64	0.52	0.64	0.29	−0.08	0.51	−0.30
SPI	−0.64	—	−0.73	−0.69	−0.45	0.30	−0.60	0.05
GDP	0.52	−0.73	—	0.69	0.41	−0.24	0.77	0.08
EDUC	0.64	−0.69	0.69	—	0.23	−0.06	0.74	−0.03
MIDCLASS	0.29	−0.45	0.41	0.23	—	−0.61	0.35	−0.11
TOPBOT	−0.08	0.30	−0.24	−0.06	−0.61	—	0.24	−0.09
URB	0.51	−0.60	0.77	0.74	0.35	−0.24	—	0.04
PPPIDE	−0.30	0.05	0.08	−0.05	−0.11	−0.09	0.04	—

Note: For definitions of variables and units of measurement, see Table 2.1. For sources, see Appendix I.2.

TABLE 5.3. *Investment and SPI equations, 1960–85 and 1970–85*

	INV (1a)	SPI (1b)	PRIVINV (2a)	SPI (2b)
Constant	28.00 (3.50)	29.35 (6.23)	28.64 (3.71)	24.84 (3.24)
EDUC	0.07 (1.98)	−0.11 (−2.80)	0.06 (1.71)	−0.09 (−1.41)
SPI	−0.78 (−2.63)		−0.98 (−3.39)	
PPPIDE	−10.36 (−4.26)		−10.70 (−3.79)	
GDP		0.73 (−1.50)		−1.25 (−1.99)
INV		0.17 (0.89)		
PRIVINV				0.29 (0.86)
MIDCLASS		−0.23 (−2.05)		−0.07 (−0.33)
URB		0.06 (1.51)		0.06 (0.97)
AFRICA		0.95 (0.44)		−3.17 (−0.85)
LAAMER		1.92 (1.09)		1.56 (0.63)
ASIA		1.82 (1.00)		0.38 (0.14)
SEE	4.78	4.13	5.21	5.83

Note: *2SLS*. *t*-statistics in parentheses. Estimates using *3SLS* are very similar. First two columns: 1960–85. Last two columns: 1970–85. Number of observations: 64 (1960–85) and 53 (1970–85).

Before presenting the results of the regressions, we present in Table 5.1 and Table 5.2 the sample statistics and the correlations between the variables used in our system. Our sample consists of sixty-four countries. Both tables refer to the period 1960–85. The two key correlations for our purposes are those between *SPI* and *INV*, and between the income distribution variable (*MIDCLASS*) and *SPI*. The first correlation is –0.60, while *MIDCLASS* has a correlation of –0.50 with *SPI*. All of these signs are consistent with our hypothesis. *SPI* is highly negatively correlated with both the level of income and the level of education. However, the latter two variables are highly correlated with each other: this explains why we did not include both variables in our *SPI* equation. The same argument applies to the investment equation, where we included only *PRIM* and not *GDP*. For more discussion of these correlations and of various identification issues, see Alesina and Perotti (1996).

Table 5.3 presents the estimates of our system for the periods 1960–85 (first two columns) and 1970–85 (last two columns). Note that, for the 1970–85 period, the income distribution variables are measured as close as possible to 1970. The two coefficients of interest have the expected sign and are statistically significant, except for the coefficient of *MIDCLASS* in the 1970–85 sample. In the investment equation, socio-political instability depresses investment, while in the second equation inequality generates socio-political instability. All the other coefficients have the expected sign and are generally statistically significant. For instance, education has a negative effect on *SPI* while urbanization has a (weak) positive effect.

The negative effect of socio-political instability on investment is indeed a very robust result: it holds for the 1970–85 subperiod as well, when the dependent variable is private investment rather than total domestic investment, and for several different specifications of the two equations. Alesina and Perotti (1996) discuss the robustness of these results in much more detail.

6

Income Distribution, Fiscal Policy and Growth

In the models of income distribution and growth surveyed in Chapter 4, fiscal policy plays a crucial role in both the political mechanism and the economic mechanism. In the former, government expenditure and the tax rate depend on the distribution of income through the voting process. In the latter, government expenditure and the associated tax rate affect the incentives to invest and therefore the rate of growth. We estimate these two mechanisms in this section: thus, we go beyond the results presented before by decomposing the reduced form regression into its two main components.

The difficulty in pursuing this analysis is that the policy instruments used to achieve redistribution may vary across countries and time periods. In some cases redistribution may be achieved by a very progressive labour income taxation, in other cases by a certain composition of government spending, in others still by trade policy. It may be hopelessly restrictive to focus on one specific policy tool to test these models of income distribution and growth. Nevertheless, it is instructive to make an attempt at going into the 'transmission mechanism' from income distribution to growth, while keeping in mind that all the results we present will have to be evaluated with the above important caveats.

We concentrate on the case of purely redistributive government transfers for at least two reasons. First, transfers are the main component of virtually all government budgets in the countries in our sample of democracies. Second, when public investment or investment subsidies are involved one should be careful about what type of taxation finances them. For instance, in the Alesina and Rodrik model results are likely to be reversed if public expenditure on infrastructure is financed by proportional taxes on labour income. On the other hand, they would continue to hold with sufficiently progressive taxation on total income. In addition to this theoretical complication, the existing breakdown in the tax data does not easily allow a satisfactory use of tax data in these regressions.

The idea that redistributional transfers reduce the incentives to invest seems fairly robust. By their very nature, transfers are associated with a redistribution of income from the high income agents to low income agents, and are financed by distortionary taxes. As we discussed in Chapter 4, high income agents also tend to own a disproportionate share of the capital stock and to make most of the investment in physical capital. Therefore, redistribution tends to hurt the agents with the highest propensity to invest.

We use data on a sample of twenty-nine democracies[19] to estimate the following model:

$$INV = \alpha_0 + \alpha_1 GTRAN + \alpha_2 PPPIDE + \alpha_3 EDUC$$
$$+ \alpha_4 AFRICA + \varepsilon_1 \tag{4}$$

$$GTRAN = \beta_0 + \beta_1 MID + \beta_2 GDP + \beta_3 AGE + \beta_5 AFRICA$$
$$+ \beta_6 LAAMER + \beta_7 ASIA + \varepsilon_2 \tag{5}$$

The equation for investment is similar to the one estimated in the previous section, except that now we want to estimate the effects of government transfers ($GTRAN$) on investment. According to the theories of income distribution and growth discussed in Chapter 4, $\alpha_1 < 0$. The second equation estimates the main determinants of government transfers. The income level, GDP, controls for Wagner's law, which states that the share of government expenditure in GDP increases with GDP itself. The proportion of individuals over age 65, AGE, appears as a regressor because a large component of government transfers is social security benefits, which obviously depend on demographic factors. As usual, the regional dummies capture region-specific cultural and political factors that affect the share of transfers in GDP.[20] Finally, and most importantly for our purposes, MID is the share of the third quintile of the population in GDP. Since the median voter lies in the middle of the third quintile, this variable is the right measure if one wants to test the political

---

[19] We focus on the sample of democracies for the reasons emphasized above.

[20] Note that the African dummy is really a dummy variable for Botswana, which is the only African country in the sample. In terms of the estimate of the other coefficients, including the African dummy variable is therefore equivalent to excluding Botswana from the sample.

mechanism of the models of income distribution and growth. The hypothesis is that the richer the median voter, the lower the tax rate and therefore the share of transfers in GDP. Thus, we expect $\beta_1 < 0$.

The results are presented in Table 6.1. One can see immediately that both the coefficient of government transfers in the investment equation and the coefficient of the third quintile in

TABLE 6.1. *Investment and government transfers equations, 1960–85 and 1970–85*

	INV	GTRAN	INV	GTRAN	PRIVINV	GTRAN	PRIVINV	GTRAN
	(1a)	(1b)	(2a)	(2b)	(3a)	(3b)	(4a)	(4b)
Constant	13.06	−3.07	13.58	−1.47	11.98	−12.55	11.76	2.74
	(1.85)	(−0.26)	(1.80)	(−0.13)	(1.63)	(0.98)	(1.61)	(0.27)
EDUC	0.03		0.04		0.04		0.04	
	(0.31)		(0.42)		(0.47)		(0.55)	
GTRAN	0.53		0.50		0.33		0.31	
	(2.26)		(2.10)		(2.15)		(1.99)	
PPPIDE	−7.20		−7.48		−4.82		−4.98	
	(−1.52)		(−1.59)		(−1.22)		(−1.26)	
AFRICA	11.07	−10.99	11.20	−11.22	13.70	−12.29	13.60	−8.79
	(1.75)	(−1.78)	(1.79)	(−1.54)	(2.58)	(−1.63)	(2.57)	(−1.16)
GDP		−0.14		−0.13		−0.44		−0.29
		(−0.21)		(−0.21)		(−0.76)		(−0.53)
INV		0.45		0.42				
		(1.13)		(0.92)				
PRIVINV					0.58		0.56	
					(1.28)		(0.18)	
MID		0.07				0.64		
		(0.13)				(0.89)		
TOPBOT				0.02				−1.31
				(0.03)				(−1.25)
AGE		0.97		0.99		0.97		0.82
		(1.86)		(1.90)		(2.05)		(1.70)
LAAMER		−3.58		−4.08		−2.55		−3.16
		(−0.68)		(−0.61)		(−0.85)		(1.06)
ASIA		−2.24		−2.39		−3.00		−3.79
		(−0.59)		(−0.61)		(−0.85)		(−1.06)
SEE	5.49	5.54	5.43	5.50	4.88	5.46	4.85	5.33

Note: *2SLS*. *t*-statistics in parentheses. Estimates using *3SLS* are very similar. First four columns: 1960–85. Last four columns: 1970–85. Number of observations: 29. Botswana is the only African country in the sample.

the government transfers equation, that is, the coefficients that define the economic and the political mechanisms respectively, have the wrong signs. Transfers have a positive effect on investment and they increase with the share of the third quintile. The other variables of the system have essentially the expected signs. In particular, *AGE* is an important determinant of transfers, and a higher price of investment goods (*PPPIDE*) deters investment. These results suggest that the reduced form results of the preceding section are not well explained by a specific focus on the transfer variable.

As we did for the system of Chapter 5, we subjected our estimates to several checks. First, we used *MIDCLASS* and *TOPBOT* as income distribution variables instead of *MID*. In so doing, we test a looser implication of these models, according to which societies with unequal income distribution express more demands for redistribution and therefore experience lower growth. However, in most cases *MIDCLASS* has a positive sign and *TOPBOT* a negative sign in the *GTRAN* equation, although they are never statistically significant. Thus, even when using these measures the seemingly robust finding is that more inequality is associated with *less* transfers, not more.[21]

These rather counterintuitive results suggest what we regard as an important direction for future research. The basic idea of the models by Alesina and Rodrik, Persson and Tabellini, and Bertola is that more inequality raises demand for fiscal redistribution. It would appear that just looking at the ratio of transfers on GDP is not enough to capture the general idea of redistributive policies: the latter may take more complex and hard to pinpoint forms. For instance, the composition of public expenditure in different programmes, the degree of progressivity of the tax system and the relative share of income versus property taxes are only a few of the many channels that fiscal redistributions can take.

Easterly and Rebelo (1992) address some of these issues. Some of their results are more consistent with the models by Alesina and Rodrik, Persson and Tabellini and Bertola than our

---

[21] As a matter of fact, we are not alone in finding that government transfers have a positive effect on growth. Sala-i-Martin (1992) finds the same correlation in a large sample of countries including both developed economies and LDCs.

evidence on transfers. For instance, they find that in a large sample of countries for the period 1970–88, income inequality prior to 1970 was associated with higher income taxes and more publicly provided education. These findings suggest that public education might be the channel through which income inequalities are mitigated. In the Alesina and Rodrik model, in fact, redistribution can occur via two channels: direct transfers from the rich to the poor and an increase in the size of government, which raises labour productivity and therefore the real wage. Perhaps one can interpret the results by Easterly and Rebelo as an indication that this second channel is, in fact, operative.

Engen and Skinner (1992) present another piece of evidence that is consistent with the sign of the effect of fiscal policy in the Alesina and Rodrik model. They find that, after correcting for serious problems of endogencity of fiscal policy, in a sample of 107 countries for the period 1970–85, a balanced-budget increase in government spending and taxation reduces growth.

Perotti (1996) presents the most comprehensive tests of various channels linking income distribution and growth. He finds very robust evidence of the link from income inequality to political instability to investment and growth. In this regard his results are consistent with our discussion in the previous chapter. He also finds that the level of inequality is linked to the fertility/education choice. Inequality is inversely related to investment in human capital and directly related to the fertility rate. Thus, the negative effect of inequality on growth could also pass through this channel. As for the fiscal policy channel, Perotti (1996) presents a much richer set of empirical results well beyond those in the present chapter, and based on his evidence he cannot support this channel. However, the difficulties in testing this channel discussed above suggest that further work on this point using more disaggregated data and more types of fiscal policy may be quite useful.

7
Conclusions

We conclude by summarizing the main results and puzzles of this literature and by indicating which are, in our view, the next steps in this area of research. Several results appear fairly robust. First, political instability is harmful for growth, and to some extent low growth fosters political instability. This result is not overly sensitive to different measures of political instability. Second, income inequality is harmful for economic growth, but the exact channels linking these two variables are less clear. One possible channel is political instability and mass violence. We presented evidence consistent with the hypothesis that income inequality creates social discontent which in turn fuels unrest, violence and political instability. The latter has negative effects on growth. Evidence on the other political channel, fiscal redistribution, is for the moment less clear. Part of the problem is the variety of different policy instruments that can be used to achieve the desired redistribution.

Third, there is no evidence suggesting that democratic institutions are not conducive to growth. A variable 'democracy' which identifies those countries with relatively free competitive elections is not correlated with growth. A variable that captures the extent of 'civil liberties' may, in fact, be positively associated with growth; namely, more individual liberties enhance growth.

Several issues are still open. First, the role of political instability deserves a closer look, along several dimensions. Thus far, we have considered two definitions of instability, socio-political and executive instability. At least another concept seems to be potentially relevant, one that has to do with 'legislative instability'. In fact, variables like the number of parties in a coalition and dummies for coalition governments and for majority governments are economically and statistically significant in explaining inflation and the share of transfers in GDP. This suggests that legislative instability could play an important role in affecting the policy outcomes and therefore the growth performance of an economy. Another interesting question is whether different concepts of instability have different explanatory power and different impacts on policy outcomes depending on the level of income of a country and/or its democratic status.

The relationship between political instability and the government budget is also worth considering. One may argue that social unrest may require an increase in the amount of transfers, to 'buy' social peace. For instance, Grossman (1994) and Sala-i-Martin (1992) argue that since government transfers are used by policy-makers to appease citizens in periods of discontent and unrest, transfers can *reduce* political instability. By reducing political instability, transfers could positively affect investment. The interactions of these three variables—investment, political instability and transfers—deserve to be investigated empirically.

A second important direction for research is to make use of the time-series dimension of the data more extensively. For instance, in trying to understand the positive effects of government transfers on investment, it would be interesting to investigate whether the positive cross-section association between investment and transfers is dominated by short-lived periods of high growth, in particular government expenditure. Then, as government expenditure remains high, growth declines in consequence of the distortionary effects of taxation. Similarly, it would be useful to explore in time-series data if the relation between the different concepts of political instability and government expenditure depends on the level of instability, and what is the timing of this relation. This analysis might go some way in trying to explain the first puzzle pointed out in Chapter 6: the positive association between government transfers and investment.

APPENDIX I.1

List of Countries and Democracies

Tanzania; Malawi; Sierra Leone; Niger; Burma; Togo; Bangladesh; Kenya; Botswana (D); Egypt; Chad; India (D); Morocco; Nigeria; Pakistan; Congo; Benin; Zimbabwe; Madagascar; Sudan; Thailand; Korea; Zambia; Ivory Coast; Honduras; Senegal; Gabon; Tunisia; Taiwan; Philippines; Bolivia; Dominican Republic (D); Sri Lanka (D); El Salvador; Malaysia (D); Ecuador; Turkey (D); Panama; Brazil; Colombia (D); Jamaica (D); Greece (D); Costa Rica (D); Peru; Hong Kong; Iran; Mexico; Japan (D); Spain (D); Iraq; Ireland (D); South Africa (D); Israel (D); Chile; Argentina; Italy (D); Uruguay; Austria (D); Finland (D); France (D); Netherlands (D); UK (D); Norway (D); Sweden (D); Australia (D); Germany (D); Venezuela (D); Denmark (D); New Zealand (D); Canada (D); Switzerland (D); US (D).

Note: A '(D)' indicates that the country is in the sample of democratic countries.

APPENDIX I.2

Sources of Income Distribution Data

Flora, P., Kraus, F. and Pfenning, W. (1987), *State, Economy and Society in Western Europe*, vol. 2 (Chicago, IL.: St James Press).

Ginneken, W. van and Jong-Goo Bak (eds.) (1984), *Generating Internationally Comparable Income Distribution Estimates* (Geneva: ILO).

Jain, S. (1975), *Size Distribution of Income: A Compilation of Data* (Washington, DC: World Bank).

Kuznets, S. (1963), 'Quantitative Aspects of the Economic Growth of Nations VIII: Distribution of Income by Size', *Economic Development and Cultural Change* 2: 1–80.

Lecaillon, Jacques *et al.* (1984), *Income Distribution and Economic Development* (Geneva. ILO).

Paukert, F. (1973), 'Income Distribution at Different Levels of Development: A Survey of Evidence', *International Labor Review* 108: 97–125.

Pryor, F. L. (1989), 'Income Distribution and Economic Development in Madagascar: Some Historical Perspectives', World Bank Discussion Paper no. 37 (Washington, DC: World Bank).

United Nations (1981), *A Survey of National Sources of Income Distribution Statistics* (New York: UN Department of International Economic and Social Affairs).

World Bank (1979), *World Development Report 1979* (Washington, DC: World Bank).

——(1986), *World Development Report 1986* (Washington, DC: World Bank).

8

Comment

TORSTEN PERSSON

It is a great pleasure to read and comment on this paper. What it does is to survey recent theoretical and empirical research on political factors in the growth process. The authors are indeed two of the main contributors to this emerging field, which runs across the conventional boundaries between macroeconomics, development economics and political science. In addition, the paper sheds some new light on two specific hypotheses regarding an empirical relation that has been emphasized in recent research: countries with a more unequal distribution of income turn out to have lower growth rates. I shall organize my comments into four parts, each part corresponding to a question: (1) What are the stylized facts regarding political factors and growth? (the material treated in Chapters 2–4); (2) Does the measured negative effect from income inequality to economic growth run via political instability? (Chapter 5); (3) Or does it run via redistributive fiscal policies? (Chapter 6); (4) Where should we go in future research on politics and growth?

8.1 What do we know?

Instability and growth

On purely theoretical grounds we may plausibly argue that there ought to be a two-way negative relation between political instability and economic growth. On the one hand major political instability may lead to economic policies—or expectations of policies—that seriously hamper the incentives for private accumulation of physical capital, human capital, or productive knowledge. On the other hand, bad growth performance is likely to produce discontent with incumbent leaders and thus generate political turnover, by legal or illegal means. As Alesina and Perotti stress in Chapter 2, the resulting simultaneity problem should be taken seriously in any attempt to confront any one of the two hypotheses with data. Recent empirical work, notably by Alesina *et al.* (1991) and by Londregan and Poole (1992), does just that by jointly estimating growth and political instability regressions in data sets that exploit both the cross-country and time-series variation in large international data sets. This work also rightly focuses on the *likelihood* of government turnover as the appropriate measure of political instability. Indeed, this empirical work finds a significant and robust negative link from economic performance increases political instability, and—at least Alesina *et al.*—a significant and robust negative link from instability to growth. I will come back to what to make of the latter relation later.

Inequality and growth

A large literature in development economics and economic history has focused on the link from growth, or more precisely the level of development, to the distribution of income, ever since Kuznets's seminal contributions in the mid-1950s. Whether any systematic relation—a Kuznets curve—can be detected in the data is unclear, at best. More recently, researchers have begun analysing the prospective links in the opposite direction, from income distribution to growth. In particular, some work has tried to marry together insights from the theory of 'endogenous growth' and from the theory of 'endogenous policy' in formulating a simple politico-economic hypothesis. Inequality is bad for growth, because it breeds political demands for redistribution, because a democratic majoritarian system will aggregate these demands into redistributive policies, and because such policies will hurt the incentives to accumulate those factors that foster long-term growth. Empirical research in Alesina and Rodrik (1994) and Persson and Tabellini (1994), investigating the validity of this hypothesis, has indeed found a significant and sizable negative reduced-form relation from measures of inequality on to growth. This relation seems to be robust to reverse causation and to a number of statistical pitfalls. Furthermore, it holds for different data sets and for inequality in the distribution of personal income, as well as in the distribution of land.

Democracy and growth

As the authors stress, it is hard to disentangle any systematic relation between different measures of political democracy and economic growth, in either direction. The only stylized fact that clearly stands out is a positive association between the level of income and the incidence of democratic institutions—such institutions are definitely a 'luxury good' in country income. There is also an 'interaction effect'; at least in the Persson–Tabellini data set, the negative effect of inequality on growth is present only in the set of democracies.

8.2 Does inequality hurt growth through instability?

In Chapter 5 of Part I Alesina and Perotti consider the hypothesis that the reduced-form relation between inequality and growth runs through socio-political instability, the argument being that more inequality in the distribution of income *ceteris paribus* fosters more instability. To investigate this possibility, they estimate versions of a two-equation system on a cross-country data set, where a measure of instability is regressed on measures of inequality and a standard set of other variables, whereas growth—here actually investment—is regressed on instability and a set of other variables. The empirical results seem to support the hypothesis, in that inequality comes in significantly positive in the instability equation, and instability comes in significantly negative in the investment equation.

The hypothesis that inequality affects investment *solely* through the channel of generating instability warrants the authors' identifying assumption that inequality does not enter the investment regression. But that assumption is not warranted if inequality also affects investment via some other channel. Thus one wonders what happens when inequality is entered in the investment regression alongside with instability: if the authors' hypothesis is correct, inequality should simply drop out.

On a more theoretical note, I think there are several reasons as to why we may expect the link between income inequality and political instability to be pretty fuzzy. First, we would expect a prime cause of instability to be socio-political *conflict* and a prime cause of conflict, in turn, to be *polarization*. Now, it is possible for more income inequality—as it is typically measured—to be associated with *less* income polarization. In Fig. 8.1, I have plotted two hypothetical income distributions to illustrate this point. In the upper one, the median income level is below the mean, indicating income inequality according to a common measure, whereas the mean and median coincide in the lower distribution. Yet, the bimodality of the lower distribution makes income more clearly polarized than in the upper distribution. For more on the distinction between distribution and polarization, see the recent paper by Esteban and Ray (1994).

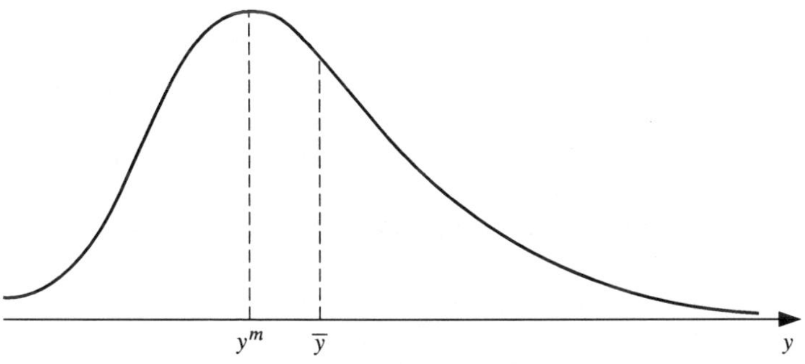

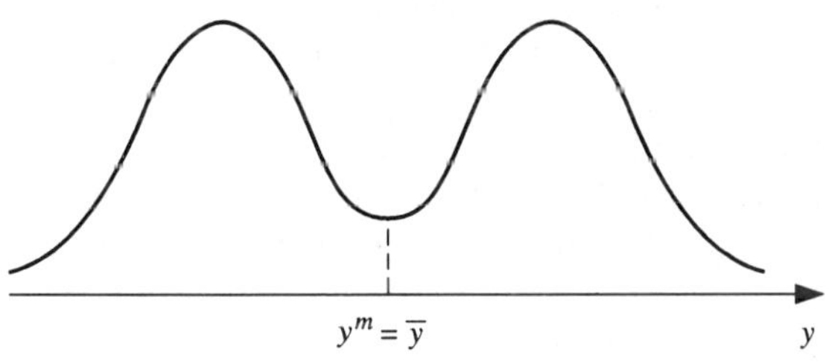

Fig. 8.1.

Second, even if income inequality would correctly measure political polarization, the same amount of polarization could generate different amounts of conflict. For one, different political institutions may aggregate conflicting interests in very different ways: a majoritarian electoral system may promote more conflict than a proportional one, for example. We know from Grilli, Masciandaro and Tabellini (1991), for example, that such broad features of the electoral system systematically seem to affect fiscal policy. For another, how much conflict a given degree of income polarization will generate largely depends on how permanent the income differences are expected to be. In an economy with high social mobility we would expect the conflict to be much smaller than in an economy where people can expect to see themselves, or their heirs, in the same relative position for ever.

Third, the same conflict over income may generate different degrees of socio-political conflict in different countries. Generally speaking, we would expect conflict over income alone to generate more polarization and conflict, the more it is correlated with differences in other social or cultural attributes, such as language, race or religion.

In further studies of the link from income distribution to instability, one may thus want to take these three additional considerations into account. Empirically, they would all give rise to interaction effects.

8.3 Does inequality hurt growth through redistributive policies?

In Chapter 6, Alesina and Perotti focus instead on the theoretical 'redistribution hypothesis' underlying the recent empirical studies of inequality and growth, namely that inequality hurts growth via more distributive policies that distort investment incentives, broadly defined. They estimate a two equation system—where inequality affects government transfers and transfers affect investment—on a cross-country data set, comprising a set of democracies. The results are disconcerting: both the relations seem to run in the direction opposite to the one suggested by the redistribution hypothesis, even though the estimated coefficients are not statistically significant.

Now, the authors mention some important caveats about testing the redistribution hypothesis in this way, including problems of finding comparable data, and the possible pitfalls of concentrating on one policy variable out of many possible channels of redistribution. They also mention some more favourable results in recent work by Easterly and Rebelo (1993) on marginal income tax rates. Here one may also mention some other work. Looking at smaller samples composed of the OECD countries—for which more reliable and comparable data do exist—Kristov *et al.* (1992) find a positive association between inequality and redistributive transfers, whereas Nordström (1993) finds a negative link from transfers to growth.

Encouraged by these findings, Persson and Tabellini (1994) look at basically the same two-way relations as those Alesina and Perotti estimate in Chapter 6, but in a smaller OECD-country data set. Their results are weakly supportive of the redistribution hypothesis, in that the relevant coefficients have the right signs, but only reach marginal significance at best. All in all, the question whether the reduced-form relation between inequality and growth emanates from a redistributive mechanism, remains open. It clearly merits further study.

8.4 Where do we go from here?

The work on politics and growth to date suggests an exciting agenda for future research. In their concluding chapter, Alesina and Perotti suggest some topics for further work. At the end of sections 8.2 and 8.3 above, I have also mentioned some open issues, both theoretical and empirical. Let me suggest a few more topics. One is the precise mechanism whereby political instability would hamper growth. In Chapter 2, Alesina and Perotti mention the possibility that instability generates policy *volatility* and hence policy uncertainty. But *a priori* it is not clear that this will lead to lower investment. Indeed Hopenheyn and Nicolini (1993) demonstrate in a theoretical model that the opposite may well be the case: more volatility in the policies that set the incentives for private investment can increase average investment. Another possible mechanism is that instability combined with polarization generates policy *myopia* and hence produces policies that try to strike short-run benefits to the incumbent government, at the expense of long-run growth, a mechanism which is similar to the one at play in Persson and Svensson (1989), and in Tabellini and Alesina (1990).

Whatever the theory of instability, it would be worthwhile to confront sharper hypotheses regarding the intervening mechanism with the data. A more structural empirical approach is thus warranted, much in the same way as the tests of the redistributive mechanism between inequality and growth discussed above. Let me conclude by mentioning an example of such an approach. Svensson (1994) formulates a model where political instability makes incumbent policymakers myopic. As a result, they become reluctant to build up a legal infrastructure protecting individual property rights, something which hurts private investment. This composite hypothesis is confronted with cross-country data from developing countries. The preliminary results support both parts of the hypothesis: instability is bad for property rights and property rights are good for investment.

References

Ades, A. and Glaeser, E. (1994), 'Evidence on Growth, Increasing Returns and the Extent of the Market', NBER working paper no. 4714.

Aghion, P. and Bolton, P. (1996), 'A Trickle-Down Theory of Growth and Development with Debt-Overhang', *Review of Economic Studies*, forthcoming.

——and Drazen, A. (1991), 'Why are Stabilizations Delayed?', *American Economic Review* 81: 1170–88.

——and Perotti, R. (1994), 'The Political Economy of Growth: A Survey with Some New Results', *World Bank Economic Review* 8: 351–72.

————(1995), 'The Political Economy of Budget Deficits', *IMF Staff Papers* 42: 1–31.

————(1996), 'Income Distribution, Political Instability, and Investment', *European Economic Review* 40: 1202–29.

——and Rodrik, D. (1992), 'Income Distribution and Economics Growth: A Simple Theory and Some Empirical Evidence', in A. Cukierman, Z. Hercovitz and L. Leiderman, *The Political Economy of Business Cycles and Growth* (Cambridge, MA: MIT Press).

——and Rodrik, D. (1994), 'Distributive Politics and Economic Growth', *Quarterly Journal of Economics* 109: 465–90.

——Ozler, S., Roubini, N. and Swagel, P. (1996), 'Political Instability and Economic Growth', *Journal of Economic Growth* 1: 189–212.

Alesime, A., Roubimi, N. and Cohen, D. (1997), *Political Cycles and the Macro Economy* (Cambridge, MA: MIT Press), forthcoming.

Ames, B. (1987), *Political Survival: Politicians and Public Policy in Latin America* (Berkeley, CA: Berkeley University Press).

Banerjee, A. und Newman, A. (1991), 'Risk Bearing and the Theory of Income Distribution', *Review of Economic Studies* 58: 211–35.

Banks, A. (various issues), *Political Handbook of the World*.

Barro, R. J. (1990), 'Government Spending in a Simple Model of Endogenous Growth', *Journal of Political Economy* 98: S103–25.

——(1991), 'Economic Growth in a Cross-Section of Countries', *Quarterly Journal of Economics* 106: 407–44.

——(1996a), 'Democracy and Growth', *Journal of Economic Growth* 1: 1–31.

Barro, R. J. (1996b), 'The Determinants of Democracy', unpublished manuscript.

Benabou, R. (1996a), 'Inequality and Growth', *NBER Macroeconomic Annual 1996*, forthcoming.

——(1996b), 'Heterogeneity, Stratification and Growth: Macroeconomic Implications of Community Structure and Public School Finance', *American Economic Review* 86: 584–609.

——(1996c), 'Unequal Societies', NBER working paper no. 5583.

Benhabib, J. and Rustichini, A. (1991), 'Social Conflict, Growth and Income Distribution', mimeo.

——and Spiegel, M. (1992), 'The Role of Human Capital and Political Instability in Economic Development', Economic Research Report (New York: C. V. Starr Center for Applied Economics, New York University).

Bertola, G. (1993), 'Factor Shares and Savings in Endogenous Growth', *American Economic Review* 83: 1184–98.

Bhagwati, J. (1982), 'Directly Unproductive Profit-Seeking (DUP) Activities', *Journal of Political Economy* 90: 250–75.

Block-Bomberg, S. (1992), 'Growth, Political Instability and the Defense Burden', unpublished manuscript.

Borner, S., Brunetti, A. and Weder, B. (1995), *Political Credibility and Economic Development* (London: Macmillan).

Clarke, G. (1993), 'More Evidence on Income Distribution and Growth', unpublished manuscript.

Clague, C., Keefer, P., Knack, S. and Olson, M. (1996), 'Property and Contract Rights in Autocracies and Democracies', *Journal of Economic Growth* 1: 243–76.

Easterly, W. and Rebelo, S. (1993), 'Fiscal Policy and Growth', *Journal of Monetary Economics* 32: 417–58.

Engen, E. and Skinner, J. (1992), 'Fiscal Policy and Economic Growth', NBER working paper 4223.

Esteban, J.-M. and Ray, D. (1994), 'On the Measurement of Polarization', *Econometrica* 62: 819–51.

Galor, O. and Zeira, J. (1993), 'Income Distribution and Macroeconomics', *Review of Economic Studies*, January.

Grilli, V., Masciandaro, D. and Tabellini, G. (1991), 'Institutions and Policies', *Economic Policy*.

Grossman, H. (1994), 'Productive Appropriation and Land Reform', *American Economic Review*, forthcoming.

Gupta, D. K. (1990), *The Economics of Political Violence* (New York: Praeger).

Helliwell, J. (1994), 'Empirical Linkages between Democracy and Economic Growth', *British Journal of Political Science* 24: 225–48.

Hibbs, D. (1973), *Mass Political Violence: A Cross-Sectional Analysis* (New York: Wiley).

Hopenheyn, H. and Nicolini, J.-P. (1993), 'Investment and Policy Instability', mimeo, Pompeu Fabra University.

Huntington, S. (1968), *Political Order in Changing Societies* (New Haven: Yale University Press).

Kaldor, N. (1956), 'Alternative Theories of Distribution', *Review of Economic Studies* 23: 83–100.

Knack, S. and Keefer, P. (1995), 'Institutions and Economic Performance: Cross-Country Tests Using Alternative Institutional Measures', *Economics and Politics* 7: 207–27.

Kristov, L., Lindert, P. and McClelland, R. (1992), 'Pressure Groups and Redistribution', *Journal of Public Economics* 48: 135–64.

Krueger, A. (1974), 'The Political Economy of the Rent-Seeking Society', *American Economic Review* 64: 291–303.

Londregan, J. and Poole, K. (1992), 'The Seizure of Executive Power and Economic Growth: Some Additional Evidence', in A. Cukierman, Z. Hercovitz and L. Leiderman, *The Political Economy of Business Cycles and Growth* (Cambridge, MA: MIT Press).

Mauro, P. (1995), 'Corruption and Growth', *Quarterly Journal of Economics* 110: 681–712.

Meltzer, A. H. and Richard, S. F. (1981), 'A Rational Theory of the Size of Government', *Journal of Political Economy* 89: 914–27.

Mueller, D. (1979), *Public Choice* (Cambridge: Cambridge University Press).

Murphy, J., Shleifer, A. and Vishny, R. (1995), 'Income Distribution, Market Size and Industrialization', *Quarterly Journal of Economics* 104: 537–64.

Nordström, H. (1993), *Studies for Trade Policy and Economic Growth*, Monograph no. 22, Institute for International Studies.

Ozler, S. and Rodrik, D. (1992), 'External Shocks, Politics and Private Investment: Some Theory and Empirical Evidence', *Journal of Development Economics*, forthcoming.

——and Tabellini, G. (1991), 'External Debt and Political Instability', mimeo.

Perotti, R. (1992), 'Income Distribution, Politics and Growth', *American Economic Review*, Papers and Proceedings, May, pp. 343–7.

——(1993), 'Political Equilibrium, Income Distribution, and Growth', *Review of Economic Studies*, September.

——(1996), 'Growth, Income Distribution and Democracy: What the Data Say', *Journal of Economic Growth* 1: 149–88.

Persson, T. and Svensson, L. E. O. (1989), 'Why a Stubborn Conservative Would Run a Deficit: Policy with Time-Inconsistent Preferences', *Quarterly Journal of Economics* 104: 325–46.

Persson, T. and Tabellini, G. (1990), *Macroeconomic Policy, Credibility and Politics* (Amsterdam: Harwood Academic Publishers).

——— (1994), 'Is Inequality Harmful for Growth? Theory and Evidence', *American Economic Review* 84: 600–21.

Roberts, K. W. S. (1977), 'Voting Over Income Tax Schedules', *Journal of Public Economics* 8: 329–40.

Romer, T. (1975), 'Individual Welfare, Majority Voting, and the Properties of a Linear Income Tax', *Journal of Public Economics* 14: 163–85.

Roubini, N. (1990), 'The Interaction Between Macroeconomic Performance, Political Structure and Institutions: The Political Economy of Poverty, Growth and Development', unpublished manuscript.

Sala-i-Martin, X. (1992), 'Transfers', unpublished manuscript.

Svensson, J. (1994), 'Political Instability, Insecure Property Rights, and Investment: Theory and Evidence', mimeo, Institute for International Economic Studies; forthcoming in *European Economic Review*.

Tabellini, G. and Alesina, A. (1990), 'Voting on the Budget Deficit', *American Economic Review* 80: 37–49.

Venieris, Y. and Gupta, D. (1983), 'Socio-Political and Economic Dimensions of Development: A Cross-Sectional Model', *Economic Development and Cultural Change* 31: 727–56.

——— (1986), 'Income Distribution and Socio-Political Instability as Determinants of Savings: A Cross-Sectional Model', *Journal of Political Economy* 96: 873–83.

—— and Sperling, S. (1989), 'Saving and Socio-Political Instability in Developed and Less-Developed Nations', unpublished manuscript.

PART II

Catching up, Social Capability, Government Size and Economic Growth

PÄR HANSSON AND MAGNUS HENREKSON

9

Introduction

There is a long tradition of expecting long-term convergence of per capita incomes in different countries. This forecast can be based on two different theories, both of which predict that incomes and productivity ought to grow faster in relatively poorer countries. According to the first theory, it is much easier for relatively poorer countries to imitate and adopt modern technology from more highly developed countries than it is for the technologically most advanced countries, through innovations, to improve their technology further. This theory is generally called the catching-up hypothesis. The same prediction follows from the neoclassical growth model introduced by Solow (1956) and further refined by Cass (1965) and Koopmans (1965). In this case, the rate of return on investment is assumed to decline with increasing capital intensity (capital stock per employed). Since the capital intensity is higher in richer countries, the return on investment, according to the theory, is higher in relatively poorer countries. The capital stock, and thereby production and labour productivity, tend therefore to grow faster there, producing a trend towards income convergence over time.

Although the predictions of the two theories are identical, the theoretical points of departure are very different. In neoclassical growth theory it is assumed that all countries have access to the same technology, whereas the catching-up hypothesis assumes that countries are at different technological levels and that diffusion of technology from leaders to followers is the main driving force towards convergence. The work presented in this paper follows the latter tradition.

The main purpose of this study is to make a thorough empirical appraisal of the catching-up hypothesis. The catching-up view is also contrasted to neoclassical and endogenous growth theory,

Magnus Henrekson gratefully acknowledges financial support from Jan Wallanders och Tom Hedelius' stiftelse för Samhällsvetenskaplig forskning.

and the effect of government spending on productivity growth is studied.[1]

The paper is organized as follows. Chapter 10 is a presentation of the catching-up hypothesis. We emphasise that the catching-up hypothesis assumes that countries are at different technological levels and that diffusion of technology from leaders to followers is the main driving force towards convergence in income and productivity.

In Chapter 11 we briefly review how income and productivity convergence is dealt with in neoclassical and endogenous growth theory. Notably, we emphasize that neoclassical growth theory assumes that all countries have access to the same technology. Chapter 12 contains tests of the simple catching-up hypothesis both at the aggregated level (for an extended sample of countries) and at the industry level (in fourteen OECD countries).

A necessary condition for the catching-up factor to be operative is that a follower country has a sufficient degree of 'social capability', that is, it must be sufficiently sophisticated in order to be able to assimilate the more advanced technology. In Chapter 13 we suggest and test a model which incorporates the effect of differences between countries in terms of their social capability to adopt technology from abroad.

Among rich countries there exist only slight differences in trade orientation, human capital, the security of property rights, the degree of political stability and other factors often cited as important determinants of social capability and economic growth. On the other hand, the size of the public sector varies greatly across countries, a fact which may potentially be an important determinant of the variation in productivity growth across industrialized countries. This hypothesis is explored in Chapter 14, in an extension of the disaggregated model developed in Chapter 12.

In Chapter 15, we briefly discuss the limitations of our study. Chapter 16 concludes.

---

[1] Many of the results and discussions in this paper are based on Hansson and Henrekson (1994a–c).

10

The Catching-up Effect

The notion of a catching-up effect can be traced back (at least) to Gerschenkron (1952), who maintained that, where a country's growth prospects are concerned, an advantage may lie in 'relative backwardness'. The catching-up hypothesis states that when the productivity level is substantially higher in one or more countries as compared with a number of other countries, it is possible for the countries in the latter group to start a catching-up process by adopting more advanced production technology from the more developed countries. More advanced technology should be seen in a broad sense. The growth potential of laggard countries is not large solely because of the possibility of replacing obsolete capital with best-practice equipment. In addition, there is a chance to adopt advanced management practices, better marketing strategies etc. As a result, we ought to expect technologically less developed countries to experience faster growth than the technologically leading countries.

In the literature on the catching-up hypothesis, this possibility is not regarded as necessarily realizable. A further necessary condition for the catching-up factor to be operative is a sufficient degree of 'social capability', that is, the poorer country must be sufficiently sophisticated in order to be able to assimilate the more advanced technology. Accordingly, the catching-up effect may be expected to be strongest in technologically backward but socially advanced countries. West Germany and Japan after World War II may be regarded as good examples in point. Labour productivity was reduced to less than half in each country between 1938 and 1950 because large parts of the capital stock had been destroyed by war. On the other hand, the general level of knowledge was high and the countries were well organized. The prospects for fast growth with the help of technology borrowed from other countries were therefore unusually favourable.

A major problem with the concept of social capability is its imprecision. As Abramovitz (1986, p. 388) puts it: 'no one knows just what it means or how to measure it'. Despite these problems he proceeds to enumerate a number of factors that are important determinants of a country's social capability: the level of education, the organization of firms, openness to foreign competition, the ease by which new firms can be established, the power of vested interests in opposing change, the functioning of the labour market and the degree of competitiveness in domestic product markets. Stern (1991) has identified a number of other factors that are potentially important, notably managerial competence and the quality of infrastructure including features of the social infrastructure such as honesty, benevolence of the bureaucracy, and how clearly property rights are defined.

In summing up, it may be worth stressing once more that technologically backward countries have a *potential* for closing the productivity gap vis-à-vis the technological leader. However, the pace at which this catching-up potential is *realized* is governed by a country's degree of social capability. The full story is of course subject to a host of further refinements and qualifications, which will not be pursued here.

A major purpose of the present paper is to operationalize and test the importance of social capability for the realization of catching up. This will be done in Chapter 13 below.

11

The Neoclassical and Endogenous Growth View of Income and Productivity Convergence

In the 1950s, Robert M. Solow developed a model that has come to be a standard instrument in the study of economic growth. In this model, the rate of economic growth depends on the speed with which the input of the factors of production—capital and labour—increases. Ongoing growth may be a result of an increase in input of either or both the factors of production.

In Solow's model, increased saving and capital accumulation leads to a rise in the steady state of production and thereby to only a temporary increase in the rate of growth. Initially, the capital stock per capita rises, and thereby also production per capita. But since capital is assumed to show decreasing returns, the increase in production will decline until the higher saving is matched exactly by the input of capital required to keep the capital stock per capita constant. Production per capita does not increase in the steady state. To the extent that growth occurs, it is determined by technical progress that is not explicable within the framework of the theory.

Let us discuss the dynamics in Solow's model more in depth. We assume that the savings ratio, s, and the rate at which capital depreciates, δ, are constant. In addition, we ignore population growth, which means that the capital intensity, k, is affected only by changes in the capital stock. As a result of a decreasing marginal rate of return on capital, a decrease occurs in the rate at which the capital stock increases. The decreasing rate of growth of the capital stock leads in turn to a proportionally decreasing rate of growth of production per capita. The capital stock does not increase in the steady state, that is, investment, I, is equal to capital depreciation, δK, and capital stock per capita, k^*, is constant.

Formally, this can be shown, for instance, by assuming that the production function is of the Cobb–Douglas type with constant returns to scale. The rate of growth of production per capita is

$$\frac{\dot{y}}{y} = \alpha \frac{\dot{k}}{k}, \tag{11.1}$$

where $0 < \alpha < 1$. The rate of growth of the capital stock is given by

$$\frac{\dot{K}}{K} = \frac{\dot{k}}{k} = \frac{I}{K} - \delta = sAL^{1-\alpha}K^{\alpha-1} - \delta = sAk^{\alpha-1} - \delta, \tag{11.2}$$

where A is the level of technology and L is population (labour force). Since $\alpha - 1 < 0$, the larger the capital stock, the slower its rate of growth in proceeding towards zero growth in the steady state.

In Fig. 11.1 a state is described where two countries have the same savings ratio, technology level, labour force and rate of capital depreciation. Both countries are at a lower income level than in the steady state and will therefore experience a period of economic growth. Country P is poor and country R is rich, which means that the capital intensity, production and productivity are higher in the rich country than in the poor one, $k_R > k_P$. Since the return to capital is decreasing, the marginal productivity of capital is higher in the poor country. This means that

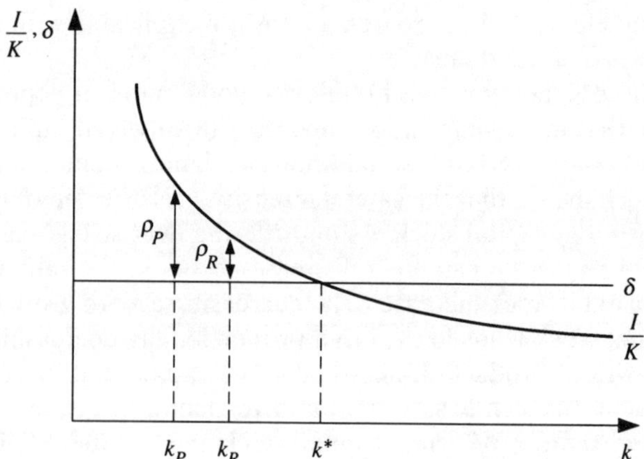

FIG. 11.1. *Growth and Convergence in the Neoclassical Model*

the capital stock grows faster in the poor country and that capital intensity and production per capita grow faster there. ρ_i is the rate of growth of capital in country i, $i = R, P$, and the rate of growth of production is proportionally related to ρ_i; $(\dot{y}/y)_i = \alpha\rho_i$, since $\rho_i = (\dot{k}/k)_i$. Fig. 11.1 shows that a poor country grows at a faster rate than a rich country, if the initial capital intensity is the only feature that distinguishes them.

If the countries also differ from each other in some other respect, for example, if the poor country has a lower savings ratio, the rich and the poor countries will not move towards the same steady state. In Fig. 11.2 the capital intensity in the poor country is less than that in the rich country in the steady state, $k_P^* < k_R^*$. In this example, growth in the rich country is faster than in the poor country, $\rho_P < \rho_R$. In contrast to absolute convergence, each country is converging with a decreasing rate of growth in capital intensity and production per capita towards its own steady state, which means that the steady-state production per capita, y_i^*, varies between countries. This has generally been described as *conditional* convergence.

Growth also appears in the model if the technological knowledge increases, that is, if the production function is shifted such that greater production is obtained for given amounts of capital and labour. Growth is then the combined effect of capital

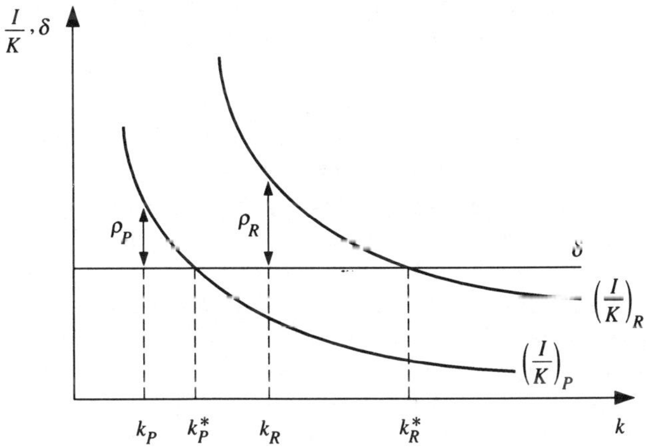

FIG. 11.2. *Conditional Convergence in the Neoclassical Model*

accumulation and technical progress, and growth in production per capita becomes:

$$\left(\frac{\dot{y}}{y}\right)_i = \alpha\left(\frac{\dot{k}}{k}\right)_i + \lambda_i = \alpha\left(s_i A_i k_i^{\alpha-1} - \delta\right) + \lambda_i \qquad i = P, R. \qquad (11.3)$$

λ_i is determined by the pace at which new technology is developed and spread. The catching-up effect can thus be smoothly reconciled with the neoclassical model. If it is easier to imitate existing technology than to shift the technological frontier, the rate of technical progress is lower in the leading country, which gives rise to convergence. From equation (11.3) it appears that per capita incomes will converge if the poor country has a lower capital intensity (applies by definition), higher savings ratio, higher technological level or more rapid technical progress.

The standard neoclassical growth model assumes a closed economy. With free, international movements of capital, rapid growth can be attained in a country even when the savings ratio is low. The opening up of an economy speeds up the predicted rate of convergence to the steady state. In practice, however, if capital consists of both physical and human capital, even in an open economy, the accumulation of human capital must be financed primarily by domestic savings. Human capital provides little collateral for lenders, and accordingly, cannot be financed by borrowing. In addition, the adjustment costs of human capital accumulation are much higher than for the accumulation of physical capital. Buildings and machinery can be assembled quickly, while the education of people is a long process. Finally, the migration propensity of skilled labour is still rather low. All in all, this indicates that the convergence rates in an open economy model with human capital do not differ significantly from the rates of the standard neoclassical model.

If, unlike in the neoclassical model, the marginal productivity of capital is constant irrespective of the size of the capital stock, then there will be no convergence. Constant returns to scale to a factor of production that can be accumulated is a characteristic of the endogenous growth models developed in recent years.[2] Such a production factor can be physical capital, human capital or a combination of these. The models are generally character-

---

[2] Lucas (1988) and Romer (1986) are seminal articles in this area.

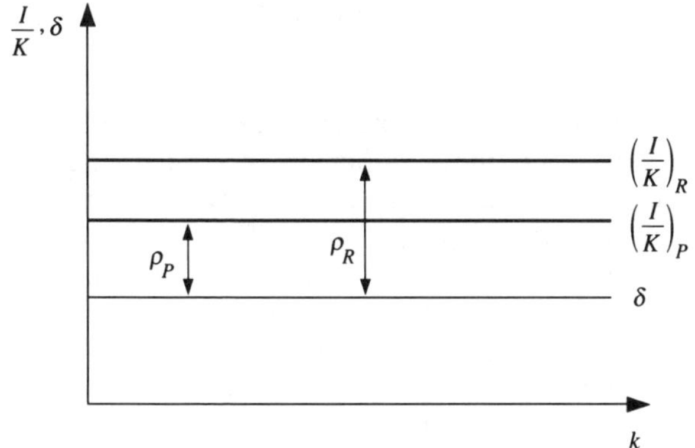

FIG. 11.3. *Growth in Endogenous Growth Models*

ized as endogenous since growth, which in Solow's model consists of exogenous technical change, is determined within the model.

In the endogenous models, the rate of growth of the capital stock is independent of the capital intensity, which is shown in Fig. 11.3. If investment exceeds capital depreciation, growth of the economy will be positive and constant. Variations in the rate of growth between countries may, for example, depend on differences in the savings ratio and the technological level.[3]

Technological progress provides the engine of growth in most growth models. One could argue that technology is a good with particular properties (Romer, 1994). First, it is nonrival, which means that it is possible for every firm to make use of it at the same time. Second, technology is partially excludable or excludable for at least some period of time. Because of that a firm can control access to an innovation and therefore, at least temporarily, obtain a monopoly position. This implies that technology cannot be considered as a pure public good, which is both nonrival and nonexcludable.

In the neoclassical model, on the other hand, technology is a pure public good. Improvements in technology are not the result

---

[3] An example of a production function where capital has constant returns to scale is $Y = AK$ (see, e.g., King and Rebelo, 1990). The rate of growth of the capital stock is constant, $\dot{K}/K = \dot{k}/k = I/K - \delta = sA - \delta$, and is determined by the savings ratio, the technological level and the rate of capital depreciation.

of intentional investments of resources by profit-seeking firms or entrepreneurs, but hits the economy like 'manna from heaven'. Obviously, this is an unsatisfactory feature of the neo-classical model, since the commercial exploitation of scientific ideas almost always requires resources. The endogenous model described above may capture the fact that technological change comes from investments people make. This is the case if we assume that research is an ordinary input in the production. On the other hand, the technology in this model is nonrival.

Models incorporating both that technological advance comes from things people do and that owners of innovations earn monopoly profits are the neo-Schumpeterian models.[4] In these models the driving force behind the innovative process is temporary monopoly power. Firms invest resources to develop new products or processes and expect to reap profits from their research efforts. The monopoly position they attain if they succeed makes it possible to sell their products at prices in excess of production costs and recover their research outlays.

In brief, the models of endogenous innovation consist of a competitive consumer goods industry which uses different intermediate inputs in the production of a single, homogeneous product. Prospective innovators invest in R&D to invent new intermediates or to improve the quality of existing intermediates. A patent system gives the innovator the exclusive right to produce the new product and earn monopoly profits. The economy grows because access to more intermediates or improved quality of existing intermediates raise the productivity in the consumer goods industry. Long-term growth is determined by the costs and benefits of industrial research. These models of endogenous innovation have, among other things, been used to analyse the effects on growth of international trade, capital accumulation and technological diffusion between countries.

The theoretical developments and the compilation, by Summers and Heston (1991), of an easily accessible set of comparative national accounts data have revived the interest in growth theory and inspired a great deal of empirical

---

[4] e.g., Grossman and Helpman (1991) and Aghion and Howitt (1992).

research.[5] These empirical studies loom large throughout this volume.

Barro and Sala-i-Martin (1992) start out from the neoclassical model and obtain support for absolute convergence when they study growth in the states of the USA. Unlike countries which may differ from one another as regards the saving ratio and in other respects that are important for steady state, y_i^*, the USA states may be assumed to converge to the same steady state. Factors that can influence y_i^* are government policy with regard to taxation, maintenance of property rights, provision of infrastructure services, the human capital of the countries at the beginning of the period etc. The rate of convergence is defined by the proportion of the gap between the per capita income of a USA state, y_i, and its steady state position, y_i^*, that is eliminated in one year. In their study, Barro and Sala-i-Martin estimate this rate to be on the order of 2 per cent. This means that 50 per cent of the initial gap vanishes in thirty-five years and 90 per cent in 115 years. In a comparison of growth between ninety-eight countries during the period 1960–85, Barro (1991b) obtains the same rate of convergence when account is taken of factors that influence y_i^*, for example, the human capital level of the countries at the beginning of the period.

Mankiw, Romer and Weil (1992) study the same period. They also proceed from a neoclassical model, where they include a proxy for accumulation of human capital. They obtain support for convergence; the income level at the beginning of the period is negatively correlated with growth. In other words, the neoclassical growth model, where convergence is conditional, is compatible with the variations in growth between countries during the period 1960–85. In addition, the empirical studies above indicate that human capital plays an important role in a country's growth. The latter is a line of reasoning we will develop further in Chapter 13.

One objection to the discussed empirical studies is that they are based on the assumption that equivalent technologies are

<hr>

[5] Helpman (1992) and Verspagen (1992) are good surveys of the new growth models, and a collection of articles in the winter 1994 issue of the *Journal of Economic Perspectives* evaluate the insights gained from the recent research on economic growth.

available in all countries. For instance, Mankiw *et al.* (1992) postulate that all countries have experienced the same rate of technological progress, which seems unjustifiable. Helliwell (1992) has shown that over the last twenty-five years the levels and rates of growth of total factor productivity differ significantly among nineteen OECD countries. In our empirical studies, in Chapters 12–14, we acknowledge differences in technology levels and rates of growth in technology; for example, by allowing for catching up on either the sectoral or the country level.

12

The Simple Catching-up Effect:
Some Empirical Tests

12.1 Catching up at the aggregated level

Strong empirical support for the catching-up hypothesis was provided, for example, by Baumol (1986) and Abramovitz (1986) when they tested it on sixteen developed countries for which Maddison (1982) had compiled productivity data dating back to 1870. Productivity is defined as GDP per hour worked. In Table 12.1, the trends of GDP per hour worked are compared in Maddison's sixteen countries during the period 1870–1970. The countries are ranked according to the rate of increase in productivity. As we see, there is a very strong negative correlation between a country's productivity level in 1870 and the rate of growth during the next 100-year period.

This finding does not provide as strong support for the catching-up factor as one might believe at first sight. First, the average productivity level does not approach that of the USA (the USA is defined as the technologically leading country) over the entire period. On the whole, an approach to the USA occurs only during the 1950s and 1960s. Rather than catching-up there is *convergence*, a decrease in the variance in productivity levels between the countries. These two concepts should be kept distinct: convergence means a reduction in the variance of productivity among a group of countries, while catching up implies a diminished gap between a leader and the followers. In addition, substantial shifts occur in the rank order between countries where productivity is concerned, which does not follow from the theory. For example, Sweden's position improved from fourteenth to third between 1870 and 1970.

Second, the selection of countries compared in Table 12.1 was naturally restricted by the access to data. The fact that data for these particular countries covering such a long period is available is no coincidence. Interest on the part of economic

TABLE 12.1. *Growth Rate of GDP per Hour in Sixteen Countries 1870–1970 (in 1970 USD)*

	Rank		GDP per hour		
	1870	1970	1870	1970	1970/1870
Sweden	14	3	0.31	5.33	17.2
Japan	16	16	0.17	2.79	16.4
Finland	15	12	0.29	4.16	14.3
Norway	13	7	0.40	4.78	12.0
France	12	6	0.42	4.92	11.7
Germany	10	9	0.43	4.62	10.7
USA	5	1	0.70	6.96	9.9
Canada	6	2	0.64	5.96	9.3
Italy	8	13	0.44	4.10	9.3
Austria	10	15	0.43	3.99	9.3
Denmark	8	14	0.44	4.00	9.1
Switzerland	7	10	0.55	4.31	7.8
Netherlands	3	4	0.74	5.19	7.0
Belgium	3	8	0.74	4.71	6.4
UK	2	11	0.80	4.27	5.3
Australia	1	5	1.30	5.02	3.9

Source: Maddison (1982).

historians in producing comparable data on a number of countries has largely been governed by the questions which they wished to answer. To try to understand why particularly those countries that are rich today have become rich is a question of this kind. Perhaps, towards the end of the nineteenth century, there were several other countries which had equally good prospects for industrialization, but which for different reasons did not succeed? As a rule, no corresponding compilation of data on growth is available for these countries, despite the fact that it now appears an equally interesting question why these countries never succeeded in embarking on a similar process of development as the most developed countries today.

De Long (1988) notes this in his criticism of Baumol's study. He maintains that since Maddison's sixteen countries are an *ex post* selection of countries that have become rich, convergence is almost certain to be found in the statistical analysis. Instead, he states that the statistical analysis must be carried out on a selection of countries which were considered in 1870 to have good growth prospects. By studying countries to which foreign direct investment was channelled during this period, he identifies another seven countries which were considered by investors at that time to have good development potential—namely, Chile, Portugal, Spain, Argentina, Ireland, New Zealand and East Germany. In a corresponding statistical analysis of the *ex ante* selection of countries, the catching-up effect disappears.[6]

A third factor which counterindicates the relevance of the catching-up effect is that when the selection of countries is extended to market economies outside the group of OECD countries, the negative relationship between original income level and rate of growth disappears. This is shown in Figure 12.1, where we compare GDP per capita in 118 countries relative to the level in the USA in 1960 and the rate of growth in GDP per capita during the period 1960–85. According to the catching-up hypothesis, the 118 countries ought to lie relatively well assembled along a negatively sloping curve starting from the north-western corner of the figure, but, as we see, some poor countries have shown rapid growth (Botswana, Taiwan), and others slow growth (Chad, Mozambique). Some rich countries have shown slow growth (Uruguay, New Zealand), while others have shown rapid growth (Canada, Norway).[7]

A fourth criticism of earlier attempts to test the catching-up hypothesis is that if the reason for convergence of income and productivity is technological diffusion, convergence of total factor productivity (TFP)[8] ought to be observed rather than convergence of GDP per capita or labour productivity. Otherwise, it is fully possible that what appears to be a technological catching-up effect is due only to the fact that the rate of investment differs from country to country, that is, that capital intensity increases at different rates.

[6] Streissler (1979) arrives at the same conclusion for the postwar period in a comparison of an *ex post* and *ex ante* selection of industrial countries.

[7] In fact, the correlation between the rate of growth in GDP per capita and initial level of GDP per capita relative to the USA is positive; $r = 0.14$.

[8] This measure is generally defined as the change in production volume that cannot be attributed to increased inputs of the two production factors labour and capital.

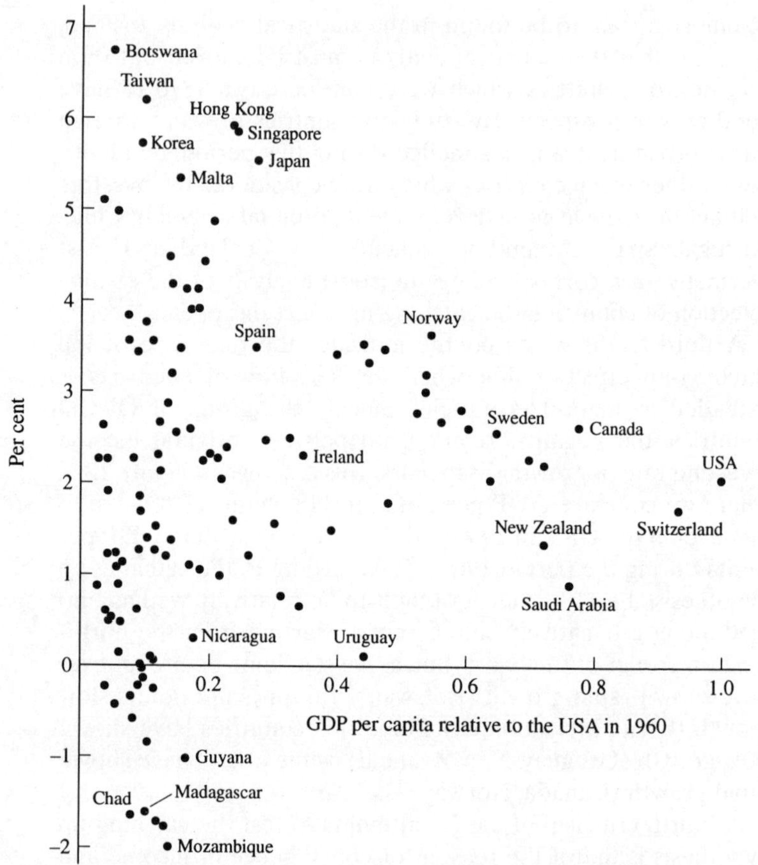

FIG. 12.1. *Growth Rate of GDP per capita, Compared with GDP per capita in the USA in 1960, for 118 Countries, 1960–1985*
Source: Summers and Heston (1991).

In order to examine the catching-up process at the most aggregate level econometrically we start out from a production function. Total production in each country is assumed to be determined as:[9]

[9] As a consequence of data constraints we have to choose a restrictive functional form; a quasi Cobb–Douglas production function with Hicks-neutral technical change.

$$Y_{kt} = A_{kt}\mathrm{f}(K_{kt})L_{kt}^{\mu}, \tag{12.1}$$

where Y_{kt} is GDP in a country k at time t, K_{kt} is the capital stock and L_{kt} total employment. A_{kt} denotes the technological level (the level of total factor productivity, TFP).

As we emphasized above, the catching-up hypothesis predicts convergence in TFP, not in GDP per capita. However, lack of data on capital stocks forces us to use GDP per worker, y, as a proxy for TFP. Therefore the simplest test of catching up, that is whether there is a negative correlation between initial TFP and subsequent growth in TFP across countries, cannot be carried out. Instead of TFP we have to use y. For this reason it is more convenient to formulate the model in terms of GDP per employed throughout:

$$y_{kt} = \left[\frac{Y}{L}\right]_{kt} = A_{kt}\mathrm{f}(K_{kt})L_{kt}^{\mu-1}. \tag{12.2}$$

Differentiation with respect to time and some rewriting gives us an expression for the relative rate of growth of output per employed:

$$\left[\frac{\dot{y}}{y}\right]_k = \left[\frac{\dot{A}}{A}\right]_k + \left(AL^{\mu}\mathrm{f}_K\right)_k\left[\frac{\dot{K}}{Y}\right]_k + (\mu-1)\left[\frac{\dot{L}}{L}\right]_k. \tag{12.3}$$

In the simple catching-up model the relative growth in TFP in country k, $(\dot{A}/A)_k$, is determined by the technological gap between country k and the technologically leading country in the world. Following the empirical practice of many others we measure the technological gap as $\log(\tau_k/\tau_l)$,[10] where τ_k is the technological level in country k and τ_l is the technological level in the leading country. Inserting that expression into (12.3) and assuming constant marginal productivity of capital across countries,[11] we obtain the following regression equation:[12]

---

[10] e.g. Dowrick and Nguyen (1989), Dowrick (1989) and Dowrick and Gemmell (1991).

[11] This may be seen as a somewhat heroic assumption. However, Dowrick and Gemmell (1991) have tested whether the marginal productivity of capital differs between different stages of economic development, and they cannot reject the hypothesis of constant marginal productivity across countries.

[12] This means that $\gamma_1 = (AL^{\mu}\mathrm{f}_K)_k$ and $\gamma_2 = \mu - 1$.

TABLE 12.2. *Descriptive Statistics*

Variable	Mean	Std Dev.	Min	Max	Obs
$\dot{Y}/Y$	0.041	0.017	0.007	0.099	81
$\dot{L}/L$	0.020	0.009	0.001	0.037	81
I/Y	0.185	0.084	0.018	0.372	81
$\tau_k/\tau_{US\ 1960}$	0.260	0.219	0.030	0.809[a]	81
$\tau_k/\tau_{US\ 1985}$	0.329	0.265	0.026	0.854[a]	81

[a] By definition the maximum is 1.000. We therefore report the second highest value instead.

$$\left[\frac{\dot{y}}{y}\right]_k = \alpha + \gamma_1 \left[\frac{\dot{K}}{Y}\right]_k + \gamma_2 \left[\frac{\dot{L}}{L}\right]_k + \beta \log\left[\frac{\tau_k}{\tau_l}\right] + \varepsilon_k. \qquad (12.4)$$

The data source for all variables is Summers and Heston (1991). As the dependent variable we use GDP per worker, y, unlike most other studies which use GDP per capita. Assuming a constant marginal productivity of gross capital investment across countries, $\dot{K}/Y$ can be proxied by gross investment as a share of GDP, I/Y.[13]

The growth rates used in the regressions for a country k are calculated as averages over a period $t = 0$ and $t = T$ as

$$\frac{\dot{X}}{X} = \frac{\left(\log X_T - \log X_0\right)}{T}, \qquad (12.5)$$

where X denotes Y and L. I/Y is the arithmetic mean during the studied period. τ_k/τ_l is proxied by initial y_k/y_l. The USA is taken to be the leading country in all regressions (subscript US). Due to data limitations only eighty-one countries can be included in the regressions. A complete list of these countries is given in Appendix II.1.

In Table 12.2 some descriptive statistics of the variables used are shown. It is noteworthy that there are large variations between countries in all variables. The technological gap between the USA and the followers has decreased between 1960 and 1985, whereas the dispersion among countries in techno-

---

[13] This has also been done by, among others, Dowrick and Gemmell (1991) and Dowrick (1992).

TABLE 12.3. *The Effect on the Rate of Growth in Labour Productivity of Catching Up and Growth in Factors of Production 1960–85*

Variable	Parameter	(i)	(ii)
$\log\left[\dfrac{\tau_k}{\tau_{US}}\right]$	β	0.001 [0.35]	−0.006 [−2.51]
$\dfrac{I}{Y}$	γ_1		0.128 [3.80]
$\dfrac{\dot{L}}{L}$	γ_2		−0.056 [−0.31]
Constant	α	0.022 [7.77]	−0.012 [−1.08]
$\bar{R}^2$		0.011	0.280
n		81	81

Note: Brackets [ ] give White's (1980) heteroscedasticity consistent t-statistics.

logical levels has increased. In other words, there is evidence of catching up, but not of convergence.

We begin our empirical analysis by the simplest possible test of the catching up hypothesis. This is reported in specification (i) in Table 12.3. The catching-up parameter is insignificant. Thus, the simple catching-up hypothesis is not supported.[14] The result is not entirely unexpected. As is clear from equation (12.3), catching up affects the relative growth in TFP. Therefore, the possible effect on labour productivity of capital accumulation and labour growth should be controlled for, which we do in specification (ii). Here we obtain a highly significant catching-up effect. The point estimate for the catching-up parameter indicates that the labour productivity growth is approximately 0.4 percentage points higher in a country at half the productivity level of the USA ($-0.006\log 0.5$) and 1.4 percentage points higher in a country at one tenth of the US level ($-0.006\log 0.1$).

[14] This result is similar to that of other researchers, such as Baumol (1986), Barro (1991b) and Dowrick (1992), although they test for convergence in GDP per capita rather than in labour productivity.

Hence, a catching-up effect seems to have been operative at the most aggregate level during the period 1960–85.

12.2 Catching up at the disaggregated level

As previously noted by Dollar and Wolff (1988) it may be inappropriate to test for the existence of catching up at the most aggregate level. A regression analysis restricted to the GDP level may spuriously attribute income convergence to catching up. For instance, Dowrick and Nguyen (1987) and Dowrick (1989) have suggested that a lower marginal productivity in the production of services and a faster-growing service sector in richer countries would account at least for part of the observed convergence. Preference shifts towards activities of self-expression and enhancement of 'quality of life' in richer economies have also been put forward as explanations (Gruen, 1986). The main reason, however, for using starting levels of sector productivity rather than aggregate productivity or GDP per capita in testing technological catching up is that there may be systematic differences between sectors in technological catching up.[15] In order to discern whether technological catching up is important, it is advantageous to make a study of disaggregated data, measuring catching-up potential within industries across countries, rather than just across countries at the most aggregate level.

Earlier studies have always used catching-up variables that define the USA as the technological leader. Even if it is uncontroversial to claim that the USA was the technological leader in virtually all industries at the end of World War II, this has gradually changed. Now technological leadership is likely to be spread among different countries. To account for this possibility it is necessary to use disaggregated data.

There is a very strong tendency towards catching up among the OECD countries during the post-war period. The first quarter of a century following World War II was exceptionally

[15] Dowrick and Gemmell (1991) found that the productivity levels in agriculture tended to diverge across countries in 1960–85, whereas there was convergence in the nonagricultural sector. Moreover, a specification test showed that their sectoral model was superior to models using aggregate measures.

TABLE 12.4. *Sector Classification and Countries*

Sector 1: Tradables	*Sector 2: Nontradables*
Food, beverages, tobacco	Electricity, gas, water
Textiles	Construction
Wood, wood products	Transport, storage, communication
Paper, printing, publishing	Finance, insurance, real estate
Other manufactured products	Wholesale, retail trade,
Nonmetallic mineral products	restaurants, hotels
Chemicals	
Basic metal products	
Machinery, equipment	

Countries

Australia	France	Sweden
Belgium	Italy	UK
Canada	Japan	USA
Denmark	The Netherlands	West Germany
Finland	Norway	

conducive to catching up among the presently advanced countries with large technological gaps and the USA as an undisputed leader. In order to test whether the catching-up factor is still of importance in explaining differences in productivity growth between leading industrial countries we analyse the rate of growth of production in fourteen OECD countries during the period 1970–85. The most substantial difference, as compared with other studies, is that we use disaggregated data; we study fourteen industries, where nine of the industries belong to the tradables sector and five to the nontradables sector. The countries and industries are described in Table 12.4. Our analysis also differs from previous studies in another important respect: the technology level is measured by total factor productivity and not by labour productivity as is customary.

Our model starts out from a production function:

$$Y_{ikt} = A_{ikt} g\left(K_{ikt}, L_{ikt}\right). \tag{12.6}$$

Output Y_{ikt} in a given industry i and country k at time t is a function of capital K_{ikt} and labour L_{ikt}. A_{ikt} measures the level of total factor productivity.

Differentiation with respect to time and some rewriting gives us an expression of the relative growth of output in industry i:

$$\left[\frac{\dot{Y}}{Y}\right]_{ik} = \left[\frac{\dot{A}}{A}\right]_{ik} + A_{ik}g_K\left[\frac{\dot{K}}{K}\frac{K}{Y}\right]_{ik} + A_{ik}g_L\left[\frac{\dot{L}}{L}\frac{L}{Y}\right]_{ik}. \quad (12.7)$$

$\left[\dfrac{\dot{A}}{A}\right]_{ik}, \left[\dfrac{\dot{K}}{K}\right]_{ik}$ and $\left[\dfrac{\dot{L}}{L}\right]_{ik}$ denote, respectively, the relative growth in TFP, capital and labour. K/Y and L/Y are the inverses of the average productivity of capital and labour. $A_{ik}g_K$ and $A_{ik}g_L$ denote the marginal productivity of capital and labour, respectively.

We may assume the marginal productivity of capital and labour to be equal across industries and across countries. A justification for this specification is that free mobility of factors within a country will equalize the marginal products within a country. Even in the absence of international factor mobility, free trade will, under certain conditions, equalize the marginal products in the tradables sector across countries, and indirectly also in the nontradables sector. Moreover, we do not assume anything about the functional form of the production function.

However, as mentioned above, lower marginal productivities of labour and capital in nontradables than in tradables in combination with a faster growing nontradables sector has been proposed as a (partial) explanation of catching up.[16] Different marginal productivities could be caused by factor immobility between sectors. Another reason might be measurement problems: failure to capture improvements in the quality of services leads to an underestimation of true productivity. To examine whether there are sectoral differences between the tradables and nontradables sectors we estimate the following model:

---

[16] A similar argument adduced to explain why poor countries have the possibility of growing faster than rich countries is that poor countries can attain a higher productivity at the aggregate level by shifting production factors from agriculture to manufacturing. One condition is, however, that the marginal productivity of labour should be lower in agriculture than in manufacturing. The results in Dowrick (1989) and Dowrick and Gemmell (1991) indicate that this may possibly be the case.

$$\left[\frac{\dot{Y}}{Y}\right]_{ik} = \beta_0 + \beta_{11}Z\left[\frac{\dot{K}}{K}\frac{K}{Y}\right]_{ik} + \beta_{12}(1-Z)\left[\frac{\dot{K}}{K}\frac{K}{Y}\right]_{ik}$$

$$+ \beta_{21}Z\left[\frac{\dot{L}}{L}\frac{L}{Y}\right]_{ik} + \beta_{22}(1-Z)\left[\frac{\dot{L}}{L}\frac{L}{Y}\right]_{ik}. \tag{12.8}$$

Z is a dummy variable that equals 1 if industry i belongs to the tradables sector and 0 if it belongs to the nontradables sector.

One may reasonably hypothesize that there are sectoral differences in the rate of technological progress and diffusion of technology. In particular, international competition may promote technical change and growth in the tradables sector. For this reason, the potential for technological catching up in tradables and nontradables may not have been the same by 1970, which is the initial year for our investigation. Hence, we allow for different catching-up effects in these two sectors. In our study we test whether there are systematic differences in the rates of technological progress and technological diffusion between sectors. To model this we assume that the relative growth in TFP is determined by a sector-specific factor as well as by a catching-up factor. Catching-up potential is measured by the initial technological gap in terms of TFP levels between a country k and the leading country in that industry. The catching-up factor is allowed to vary between the tradables and non-tradables sectors. The relative rate of growth in TFP in industry i in country k is then given by:

$$\left[\frac{\dot{A}}{A}\right]_{ik} - \lambda_j + \kappa_j \log\left[\frac{\tau_{ik}}{\tau_{il}}\right] \qquad j=1,2. \tag{12.9}$$

λ_j is the sector-specific factor ($j = 1$ for tradables), and we hypothesize that $\lambda_1 > \lambda_2$. τ_{ik}/τ_{il} is the catching-up factor. τ_{il} is the TFP level in the country with the highest productivity in industry i in 1970 and τ_{ik} is the TFP level in industry i in country k.

The indices of TFP levels are implicitly based on a Cobb–Douglas function:

$$\log \tau_{ik} = \log Y_{ik} - \alpha_i \log L_{ik} - (1-\alpha_i)\log K_{ik}. \tag{12.10}$$

Y_{ik} is value added and K_{ik} is the capital stock in industry i in country k. L_{ik} is total employment in industry i in country k. To be able to compare TFP levels across countries, the local currencies have been converted to a common standard by using the OECD purchasing power parity estimates with 1980 as the base year (Ward, 1985).

Under the assumption that labour and capital elasticities are the same in each industry across countries, factor shares should be equal across countries. Thus, we can use the international average factor shares in different industries as measures of α_i. The share of labour in value added in sector i in country k is calculated as

$$\alpha_{ik} = \frac{W_{ik}\left(L_{ik}/E_{ik}\right)}{Y_{ik}^*},\tag{12.11}$$

where W_{ik} denotes the wage sum; Y_{ik}^*, value added in current prices; L_{ik}, total employment including self-employed; and E_{ik}, total number of employees. The self-employed are included in the weighting scheme by assuming that they receive the same average rate of compensation, and total compensation is rescaled in accordance.

By combining (12.8) and (12.9) we get our basic model:

$$\left[\frac{\dot{Y}}{Y}\right]_{ik} = \alpha_0 + \alpha_1 Z + \beta_{11} Z \left[\frac{\dot{K}}{K}\frac{K}{Y}\right]_{ik} + \beta_{12}\left(1-Z\right)\left[\frac{\dot{K}}{K}\frac{K}{Y}\right]_{ik}$$

$$+\beta_{21} Z\left[\frac{\dot{L}}{L}\frac{L}{Y}\right]_{ik} + \beta_{22}\left(1-Z\right)\left[\frac{\dot{L}}{L}\frac{L}{Y}\right]_{ik}$$

$$+\beta_{31} Z\log\left[\frac{\tau_{ik}}{\tau_{il}}\right] + \beta_{32}\left(1-Z\right)\log\left[\frac{\tau_{ik}}{\tau_{il}}\right] + \varepsilon_{ik},\tag{12.12}$$

where $\alpha_0 = (\beta_0 + \lambda_2)$, $\alpha_1 = (\lambda_1 - \lambda_2)$, $\beta_{31} = \kappa_1$ and $\beta_{32} = \kappa_2$. ε_{ik} is a zero mean, normally distributed error. The average annual relative growth rates of the variables Y, K and L during the period 1970–85 is given by equation (12.5).[17] All data comes from the International Sectoral Data Bank (ISDB) compiled by the OECD. In Table 12.5 we present the results of the estimations of our regression model in equation (12.12).

In specification (i) we find that the marginal productivity of capital is equal in the two sectors.[18] The marginal productivity of

---

[17] To economize on computation, K/Y and L/Y are calculated by taking the average of the initial and final years.

[18] $\beta_{12} - \beta_{11} = 0.00$ [0.00]; t-value in brackets.

TABLE 12.5. *The Effect on the Rate of Growth in Output of Growth in Factors of Production, Technical Progress and Catching Up*

Variable	Parameter	(i)	(ii)
$\left[\dfrac{\dot{K}}{K}\dfrac{K}{Y}\right]_{ik}$	β_1		0.045 [3.65]
$Z\left[\dfrac{\dot{K}}{K}\dfrac{K}{Y}\right]_{ik}$	β_{11}	0.044 [1.12]	
$(1-Z)\left[\dfrac{\dot{K}}{K}\dfrac{K}{Y}\right]_{ik}$	β_{12}	0.045 [4.04]	
$Z\left[\dfrac{\dot{L}}{L}\dfrac{L}{Y}\right]_{ik}$	β_{21}	6464 [3.35]	6462 [3.52]
$(1-Z)\left[\dfrac{\dot{L}}{L}\dfrac{L}{Y}\right]_{ik}$	β_{22}	14974 [4.27]	14988 [4.33]
$Z\log\left[\dfrac{\tau_{ik}}{\tau_{il}}\right]$	β_{31}	0.000 [0.05]	0.000 [0.06]
$(1-Z)\log\left[\dfrac{\tau_{ik}}{\tau_{il}}\right]$	β_{32}	−0.012 [−2.73]	−0.012 [−2.67]
Constant	α_0	−0.002 [−0.32]	−0.002 [−0.31]
Z	α_1	0.010 [2.49]	0.010 [2.84]
Country dummies			
$\bar{R}^2$		0.507	0.511
n		162	162

Note: Brackets [   ] give White's (1980) heteroscedasticity consistent *t*-statistics.

labour is larger in the nontradables sector.[19] Therefore, in specification (ii) we assume that the marginal productivity of capital is equal in the tradables and nontradables sector (β_1). The marginal productivity of labour is still significantly larger in the

[19] $\beta_{22} - \beta_{21} = 8509$ [2.16]; *t*-value in brackets.

nontradables sector, $\beta_{22} > \beta_{21}$.[20] Contrary to what is commonly believed, a faster growing nontradables sector cannot explain the productivity slowdown in the OECD in the 1970s and 1980s, since the marginal productivities of labour and capital are not lower in that sector.[21]

There is no catching-up effect in the tradables sector, in contrast to the nontradables sector where a statistically significant catching-up effect is found. Our interpretation of this result is that the diffusion of technology had narrowed some of the technology gaps in the tradables sector at the beginning of the studied period (1970), and with that the potential for catching up was also decreased. Increased international competition, caused by trade liberalization in the 1950s and 1960s, and increased co-operation internationally among researchers and engineers are factors pointing in that direction. Technological diffusion in the 1970s and 1980s has probably been more complex than a one-sided transfer from an undisputable leader to the followers, a pattern that may have been valid in the 1950s and 1960s.

On the other hand, a catching-up effect is found for industries in the nontradables sector, which is not very surprising. Since the industries in that sector are not exposed to foreign competition, they have not been forced to adopt superior technology from abroad in order to survive. Technology is today often carried across national boundaries while remaining within the same firm. Multinational companies, which probably have played a large role in the diffusion of production technologies in the tradables sector, are represented to a far smaller extent in the sheltered industries. Hence, technology has spread more slowly across boundaries in the nontradables sector, and by 1970 a potential for catching up still remained to be exploited.

The sector-specific rate of growth of TFP is larger in the tradables sector, $\alpha_1 > 0$, which indicates that international competition promotes technical progress and faster diffusion of technology. We know, for instance, that investment in R&D is

---

[20] $\beta_{22} - \beta_{21} = 8526$ [2.42]; *t*-values in brackets.

[21] Dowrick (1989) reached the same conclusion for the service sector. However, he found a significantly lower marginal productivity for labour in agriculture, which implies that a reallocation of labour from agriculture to the rest of the economy leads to an increase in productivity.

considerably larger in the tradables sector, which could be a result of greater competitive pressure.[22] There may also be other explanations. Besides openness to international competition, the tradables and nontradables sectors differ to a large extent in character.

In sum, our results point to the conclusion that technological catching up in the tradables sector, although it was probably significant in the 1950s and 1960s, in particular among the OECD countries, has no longer been important after 1970. However, catching up still operates in the nontradables sector. Yet the relative growth of TFP, the sum of the sector-specific factor and the catching-up factor—$(\dot{A}/A)_i$ in equation (12.9)—is faster in the tradables sector, which indicates that international competition promotes technical change and growth. On average the TFP-growth in the fourteen OECD countries is 2.07 per cent in tradables and 1.61 per cent in nontradables.[23]

12.3 The simple catching-up effect: some concluding observations

A closer inspection of the catching-up studies shows that catching up has not occurred universally. The selection of time periods and countries is of decisive importance for whether empirical support for catching up is received.

Moreover, catching up and convergence have not always coincided. This is evident from Table 12.2, where the gap in labour productivity between the USA and the followers has decreased during the period 1960–85, whereas the dispersion among countries in productivity has increased. According to Gordon (1992), among the industrialized countries the catching up to the USA and the convergence pattern have varied between different time periods during the last century.

In our empirical studies we received support for the simple catching-up effect at the aggregated level during the period 1960–85 when capital accumulation and labour growth was

---

[22] See Englander, Evenson and Hanazaki (1988).

[23] The calculations are based on estimates from specification (ii) in Table 12.4 and the average technological gap in tradables and nontradables in 1970 (the beginning of the studied period).

controlled for. At the disaggregated level, in the most developed OECD countries, we found that simple technological catching up has not been important after 1970 in the tradables sector, while it still operates in the nontradables sector. However, international knowledge spillovers do not take place automatically. The receiving countries' capability to adopt foreign technology and to adjust it for their own purposes is essential for the success of diffusion. Therefore, one would expect that the extent to which technology transfers from leaders to followers exist depends on the followers' social capability of catching up.

13

Modelling the Effect of Social Capability

As already noted in Chapter 10, social capability is a necessary condition for a country to be able to benefit from catching up. The model we use to examine the effect of social capability on the catching-up process starts out from the model already presented in section 12.1.

To facilitate reading we repeat equation (12.3) defining the expression for the relative growth of output per employed:[24]

$$\frac{\dot{y}}{y} = \frac{\dot{A}}{A} + AL^\mu f_K\left(\frac{\dot{K}}{Y}\right) + (\mu - 1)\frac{\dot{L}}{L}. \tag{13.1}$$

Many authors have stressed the difference between potential technological spillover (dependent on the technological difference between the leading country and a follower), and the actual spillover (determined by the interaction between the technological gap and the follower's social capability). This idea can be formalized in a model that draws on Nelson and Phelps (1966).[25] Let us assume that in every period the relative change in the technological level is proportional to the technological gap:

$$\frac{\dot{A}}{A} = \Phi(s)\left(\frac{T - A}{A}\right), \qquad 0 < \Phi \leq 1. \tag{13.2}$$

T denotes the technological level in the leading country, and s is the social capability. Φ measures the speed at which the technology in the leading country is absorbed by the less advanced country. Φ is assumed to be positively related to the social capability of the country, that is, $\Phi'(s) > 0$.

If we postulate that T grows exponentially at the rate λ in (13.2) and then solve the resultant differential equation, we can see that A evolves as

---

[24] Unless expositionally necessary, time and country indices are suppressed throughout.

[25] A similar model is used by Edwards (1992)

$$A_t = \left(A_0 - \frac{\Phi(s)}{\Phi(s) + \lambda} T_0 \right) e^{-\Phi t} + \frac{\Phi(s)}{\Phi(s) + \lambda} T_0 e^{\lambda t}. \qquad (13.3)$$

As usual the second term on the right-hand side denotes the evolution of A in the steady state (A^*), while the first term captures the part of the evolution that is attributable to the out-of-steady-state effect. It is easy to show that the technological gap in the steady state will be:

$$G = \frac{T - A^*}{A^*} = \frac{\lambda}{\Phi(s)}. \qquad (13.4)$$

From our assumptions it also follows that increased social capability in a country reduces the steady-state technological gap. Thus, a country with a greater social capability will have a higher equilibrium level of technology and a smaller technological gap than an otherwise identical economy. This result is depicted in Fig. 13.1, where the two ($\dot{A}/A$)-schedules represent different rates of growth of A corresponding to a high (s_H) and low (s_L) social capability, respectively.

There are two interesting cases that may be used to shed some further light on the diffusion mechanism. First, consider two countries with the same social capability s_L, but with initially differing technological gaps G_1 and G_2, that is, the two countries start out at points a and b, respectively. The country with the larger technological gap will grow faster than the country with the smaller gap, but both countries will eventually converge to point c, where $\dot{A}/A$ equals λ and the equilibrium gap is $\lambda/\Phi(s_L)$. Second, consider two countries with different social capabilities s_H and s_L, but with the same initial gap G_1. In this case the country with the higher s will have a faster $\dot{A}/A$. Eventually, $\dot{A}/A$ approaches λ in both countries, and the technological gaps converge to the steady state values corresponding to the respective levels of social capability. The country with the higher s moves from d to e, while the country with the lower s moves from a to c.

As we saw in Chapter 10, there are a number of factors that may be important in determining the social capability of a country. Assuming there are n such factors, we may write $s = s(s_1, \ldots, s_n)$, and therefore $\Phi = \Phi(s_1, \ldots, s_n)$. In order to arrive

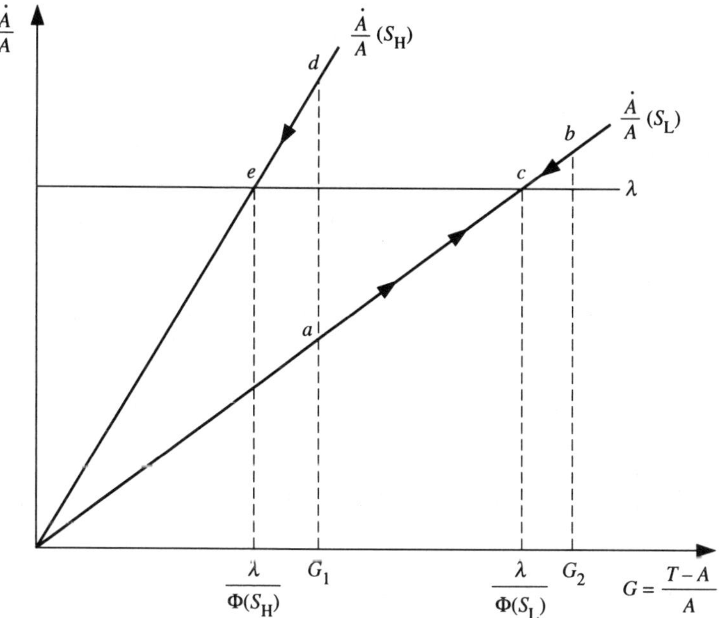

FIG. 13.1. *Technological Change as a Function of Technological Gap and Social Capability*

at an equation that can be estimated empirically, we simply assume that each factor interacts directly and in a linear fashion with the technological gap in determining the rate of technological change. Following the empirical practice already applied in Chapter 12, we measure the technological gap as $\log(\tau_k/\tau_l)$, where τ_k is the technological level in country k, and τ_l the technological level in the leading country. Given these simplifications, $\dot{A}/A$ in country k is assumed to be determined as:

$$\frac{\dot{A}}{A} = \alpha + \sum_{j=1}^{n} \beta_j \log(\tau_k/\tau_l) s_j + \varepsilon, \qquad (13.5)$$

where s_j denotes the jth variable determining the social capability of absorbing technology from abroad. In the next section we will try to identify the potential s_j variables.

Inserting (13.5) into (13.1) gives us our basic regression equation:

$$\frac{\dot{y}}{y} = \alpha + \gamma_1\left(\frac{\dot{K}}{Y}\right) + \gamma_2\left(\frac{\dot{L}}{L}\right) + \sum_{j=1}^{n} \beta_j \log\left(\tau_k/\tau_l\right)s_j + \varepsilon. \quad (13.6)$$

As already noted a number of determinants of a country's social capability have been suggested. In practice, lack of data restricts the choice of s_j. An obvious candidate is the stock of human capital in a country; a larger stock of human capital makes it easier for a country to absorb the new products or ideas that have been discovered elsewhere. A second potential factor determining the level of social capability is a country's degree of integration into the world economy. Unfortunately, due to lack of data these are the only determinants of social capability that are amenable to empirical testing. In our view, empirical proxies for other determinants are too crude to merit inclusion in the estimations.[26]

In the following two sections we will briefly review the evidence on the effect of the degree of integration into the world economy and the stock of human capital on economic growth, generally. In section 13.3 we will specifically test their effect on catching up.

13.1 Trade orientation and social capability

A potential factor determining the level of a country's social capability is its degree of integration into the world economy. Several arguments have been put forward to explain why greater participation in international trade promotes catching up and growth. First, it is commonly believed that international transfers of technology are related to trade flows. Imports of goods and services developed by trade partners bring about a more effective use of existing resources in the importing country and thereby raise the country's productivity level. Second, there is the obvious argument that the greater the part of the economy exposed to international competition, the greater the exposure to superior technology will be, and the greater the pressure will be to adopt such technology in order to remain competitive

---

[26] For example, Verspagen (1991) uses the per capita electricity generating capacity as a proxy for the quality of the infrastructure.

(Baumol, 1986; Alam, 1992). Third, Lewis (1955) argues that new ideas will be accepted more quickly in countries where people are accustomed to change, while in isolated countries a rapid absorption of new ideas is unlikely.

We use a straightforward measure to capture the effect of international integration on social capability: the trade intensity ratio, defined as the sum of exports and imports relative to GDP, *OP*. Obviously, this measure has its shortcomings as an indicator of a country's trade policy; factors other than the trade regime may influence a country's trade intensity. The trade intensity tends to be lower in large countries with a great deal of interregional rather than international trade. Countries may be unevenly endowed with some factors of production, and consequently have a higher trade intensity. For our purposes, these deficiencies are less severe. We consider trade a channel for international technology transfers and thus it probably matters little what the causes behind the variations in trade intensity are.

An alternative indicator of international integration is the World Bank (1987) classification of countries into groups with different trade regimes. The categorization is based on various measures of trade policy, tariffs, subsidies and quantitative restrictions. A drawback with the World Bank classification is that it is subjective. While a great deal of effort has clearly been made to derive a good classification, prior knowledge about growth performance may have affected the categorization. Another conceivable measure of international integration is the set of trade intervention indices constructed by Leamer (1988).[27] Those indices are continuous, comparable across countries and moreover, objective. Leamer obtains his indices from estimations based on a Heckscher–Ohlin model where differences between predicted and actual trade intensity ratios are used as indicators of trade barriers. One shortcoming of these indices is that they are based on a trade model which only partly, and sometimes poorly, explains the trade intensities. Both the World Bank classification and Leamer's measures would more directly capture the effect of a country's trade policy on its catching-up performance.

---

[27] Edwards (1992) finds a strong and robust relationship between those indices and economic performance; countries with more open and less distortive trade policies tended to have a higher growth rate.

                    Hansson and Henrekson

The familiar arguments of gains in productivity from international trade, dating back at least to Adam Smith, include specialization according to comparative advantage and realization of economies of scale. Trade permits a more efficient allocation of national resources, but it should be noted that these productivity gains are level effects and not rate effects. However, empirically it is difficult to disentangle static from permanent effects. Once-and-for-all improvements in productivity in most cases take place over a period of time. Furthermore, after World War II international trade has increased continuously in many countries due to lower trade barriers, resulting from tariff negotiations within GATT, and lower transportation and communication costs.

International trade may also raise a country's productivity by increasing the availability of intermediate inputs.[28] Assume that the aggregate production function in a country is

$$Y = AL^{\mu} \sum_{i=1}^{n} x_i^{\alpha}, \qquad 0 < \alpha, \mu < 1, \qquad (13.7)$$

where the x_i's are intermediate inputs, that is, various types of capital goods, and n is the number of inputs available. All available intermediates enter symmetrically into the production function, and if we for convenience assume that they have the same price, then the demand for each intermediate is $x_i = x$.

From these assumptions it follows that (13.7) can be simplified to

$$y = \frac{Y}{L} = AL^{\mu-1}K^{\alpha}n^{1-a}, \qquad (13.8)$$

where $nx \equiv K$ is the aggregate quantity of capital used. Differentiation with respect to time gives the following expression for the growth in labour productivity:

$$\frac{\dot{y}}{y} = \frac{\dot{A}}{A} + (\mu - 1)\frac{\dot{L}}{L} + \alpha\frac{\dot{K}}{K} + (1-\alpha)\frac{\dot{n}}{n}. \qquad (13.9)$$

International trade increases the availability of various capital goods; n is greater with trade. This means that increased inter-

---

[28] The idea originates from Ethier (1982) and it has been used in several endogenous growth models, e.g., Romer (1990).

national trade has a level effect on productivity. An increased trade intensity ratio, OP, could therefore be a measure of greater availability of capital goods and we will use the rate of growth in the trade intensity ratio, $\dot{OP}/OP$, as a proxy for $\dot{n}/n$. $\dot{OP}/OP$ may also capture the familiar productivity gains of increased international trade, further exploitation of comparative advantage and economies of scale.

In one strand of analysis, popular in particular in development economics, exports are expected to contribute to aggregate productivity and output growth. The reason is that the export sector is assumed to have positive external effects on the nonexport sector, notably through its favourable impact on management style and production techniques in the nonexport sector. Another argument is that the marginal productivities of capital and labour are higher in the export sector due to a more competitive environment.[29] Thus, a faster-growing export sector relative to the nonexport sector entails higher productivity growth. An expansion of exports also allows a country to increase its imports and this gives greater opportunities to relax bottlenecks, which affects output growth positively. Edwards (1993) contains a survey of such studies. It appears that most studies have found a positive and significant relationship between exports expansion and GDP growth. Yet, Edwards is not fully convinced by the empirical evidence. He states that the theoretical underpinning is inadequate, and that econometric problems such as endogeneity and measurement errors are not properly dealt with in many studies.

In an endogenous growth model, Rivera-Batiz and Romer (1991) advance a number of reasons why participation in a larger world economy may enhance a country's long-run growth rate. First, countries more integrated into the world economy are likely to have access to a larger knowledge base than more isolated countries. In their model the stock of knowledge affects the rate at which new knowledge is generated and this in its turn results in a higher long-run growth rate. Second, improved dissemination of technologies by increased exchange of goods and ideas forces firms to develop technologies that are innovative on a global scale and not only new to the domestic market. This will

---

[29] See the discussion in section 12.2 about different marginal productivities in the tradables and nontradables sector.

mitigate duplications of industrial research, that is, lead to fewer 'reinventions of the wheel'.[30]

To sum up, we have argued that international trade may promote a country's productivity growth directly and indirectly. The direct benefits of increased international trade come from further exploitation of comparative advantage and realizations of economies of scale, along with an increased availability of intermediate products. The indirect benefits are brought about by international trade as a factor determining a country's social capability of catching up; the hypothesis is that the more integrated a country is in the world economy, the more socially capable of catching up it is. In our empirical study in the next section, the direct effects will be captured by the rate of growth in the trade intensity ratio, $\dot{OP}/OP$, and the indirect effects by the average trade intensity during the studied period, OP.

13.2 Human capital and social capability

Human capital has been assigned several roles in the literature on economic growth. First, it is often seen as a separate factor of production—for example, by Mankiw, Romer and Weil (1992). Second, it is a source of innovative activity, and therefore an important input in the production of basic knowledge (Nelson and Phelps, 1966; Verspagen, 1991). Third, a larger stock of human capital makes it easier for a country to absorb the new products or ideas that have been discovered elsewhere, and hence the catching-up potential may be better exploited (Nelson and Phelps, 1966; Easterlin, 1981; Abramovitz, 1986). Fourth, there may be an external effect of human capital, that is, human capital embodied in a worker may raise the productivity of colleagues (Lucas, 1988).

In cross-country studies of economic growth, human capital has also proven to have significant explanatory power.[31] In these comparatively early studies, educational enrolment rates (a flow

---

[30] Most economists believe that a country's long-run growth rate is higher if it is trading internationally in comparison with in autarky. However, Grossman and Helpman (1991) have constructed a couple of examples where the reverse applies.

[31] See, for example, Baumol, Blackman and Wolff (1989), Barro (1991b) and Mankiw, Romer and Weil (1992).

variable) are used as a proxy for the stock of human capital. More recently, studies have begun to appear where stock variables are used. Wolff and Gittleman (1993) have used World Bank data to construct educational attainment rates in the population aged 25 or more for primary, secondary and tertiary education. They use enrolment and attainment rates as alternative regressors. Their main finding is that enrolment rates are almost uniformly more powerful as explanatory factors of per capita income growth than attainment rates, despite the fact that attainment rates are arguably a better indicator of education as a production input. A likely explanation for this result is bi-directional causation; high or rising enrolment rates might be an effect of growth rather than a determinant of growth. Another important result of the Wolff and Gittleman study is that educational attainment has a highly significant effect on investment in physical capital. Hence, human capital may have an important indirect effect on economic growth.

Barro (1992) reports preliminary regressions using a newly constructed educational attainment variable as a regressor. Educational attainment is measured as the average number of years of schooling in the population aged 25 and over. Annual growth rate of GDP per capita is used as the dependent variable, and the data set consists of seventy-three countries during five time periods (five 5-year averages). Barro also finds a strong independent effect of schooling on growth. An increase in the average number of years of schooling by 50 per cent increases the growth rate by 1 per cent per annum. However, when investment and fertility are added as independent regressors, the direct effect of schooling is approximately halved. Further regressions indicate that human capital to a large extent affects growth positively through its positive interaction with physical investment and its negative interaction with fertility. Thus, using stock measures of human capital, both studies emphasize the indirect link from human capital to economic growth.

Without exception, the cited studies indicate that the accumulation of human capital is of vital importance for economic growth, but it remains unresolved how important each of the hypothesized mechanisms presented at the beginning of this section are. From time to time, the point has been that although the positive association between educational attainment and growth seems robust, caution should be exercised in making a causal interpretation of this relationship; there is always the possibility that human capital investment has increased as a result of rapid economic growth. However, Katz (1992) shows that the microeconomic and macroeconomic research on the links between education and productivity are quite consistent with each other, which is strongly suggestive of a causal interpretation of the macroeconomic findings of positive effects of human capital investment on economic growth.

Although it is empirically intractable, a further factor worth mentioning is that investment in human capital is measured by the number of years of schooling, educational expenditure as a share of GDP, etc. But this is an educational input, not an educational output. How well educational input proxies educational output is likely to vary across countries.

As we know from human capital theory (Becker, 1964; Schultz, 1960), the decision to acquire human capital can be analysed as an individual investment decision. In other words, the individual decision to acquire and use human capital is governed by its rate of return on human capital. As is well known (see, for example, Psacharopoulos, 1993) the rate of return varies a great deal across countries and across educational levels. This fact makes it possible to have a case where the resources devoted to education are high but the measured growth effects are meagre. Hence, human capital investment may be endogenous, in the sense that the individuals adjust their actual investment in human capital (as opposed to the number of years of schooling) to the institutionally given rate of return.

Empirical research also shows that there is a positive correlation between formal education and informal human capital investment in the form of on-the-job training (OJT), etc. (Mincer, 1984). At the same time, strong incentives for OJT may be a partial substitute for weak incentives to formal education, and the wage structure may also encourage intensive and efficient use of the individual's human capital. As shown theoretically by Lazear (1979, 1981) a steep age/wage profile, a so-called deferred payment contract, may be productivity enhancing. Such a wage profile can be important in motivating employees to deliver maximum effort, to continue to invest in human capital and to accept technical change that increases the employer's chances of long-run survival. This is an additional aspect of human capital and economic growth which requires further research to be quantified. It is sufficient here to point out that institutional arrangements are important determinants of the effect of educational spending on economic growth.

In our own empirical work reported in section 13.3 below, we will focus on the effect of education on catching up. To construct the human capital variable we draw on data published in the *UNDP Human Development Report* (1990, 1991 and 1992). The stock of human capital, *HUM*, is defined as a weighted average of adult literacy rate in the population aged 15 or more during the period 1960–85 (*MLIT*) and mean years of schooling in the population aged 25 or more in 1980 relative to the USA (*RSCH80*). Mean years of schooling was highest in the USA. The weights are the same ones used by UNDP to calculate educational attainment in different countries:

$$MLIT - \tfrac{1}{3}\left(LIT60 + LIT70 + LIT85\right),$$

$$HUM = \tfrac{2}{3}MLIT + \tfrac{1}{3}RSCH80.$$

In our view, this is a better measure than either the literacy rate or the enrolment rate in secondary schooling, which are the measures used in almost all other studies.[32] Enrolment rates are flow rather than stock variables, and literacy is but one aspect of the level of human capital. Furthermore, among the developed countries the variation in literacy rates is extremely limited, despite the fact that there is substantial variation in educational levels even across countries at a higher level of development. At least to some degree, *HUM* avoids these limitations of other measures.

13.3 An empirical test of social capability

In this section we present some econometric evidence on the effect of social capability and catching up. Our basic regression equation was presented as equation (13.6) above. The data source for all variables except *HUM* (see section 13.2) is

---

[32] The only exceptions we know of are the above presented studies by Wolff and Gittleman (1993), Barro (1992) and Barro and Lee (1994).

Table 13.1. Descriptive Statistics

Variable	Period	Mean	Std Dev.	Min	Max	No. of Obs.
HUM		0.558	0.279	0.053	0.991	81
OP	1960–85	0.384	0.284	0.055	1.646	81
ȮP/OP	1960–85	0.006	0.022	−0.065	0.057	81

Summers and Heston (1991). As the dependent variable we use the rate of growth in GDP per worker, $\dot{y}/y$. Lack of data on capital stocks forces us to use y as a proxy for TFP. $\dot{K}/Y$ is proxied by investment as a share of GDP, I/Y.

The growth rates used in the regressions for country k are calculated as averages as in section 12.1. I/Y and OP are the respective arithmetic means during the studied period. τ_k/τ_l is proxied by initial y_k/y_l and the USA is taken to be the leading country in all regressions (subscript US). The same eighty-one countries as before are included in the regressions (Appendix II.1).

In Table 13.1 some descriptive statistics of the human capital and trade variables used are shown. It is noteworthy that there are large variations between countries in the variables.

Specification (i) in Table 13.2 is the empirical application of the theoretical model presented in Chapter 13 (equation 13.6). The results show a clear effect of human capital on the capability of assimilating technology from abroad; the parameter is highly significant. The parameter estimate of international economic integration has the expected sign, although it is not significant at the 5 per cent level. $\overline{R}^2$ increases in specification (i) compared to specification (ii) presented in Table 12.3, which points to the importance of social capability.

In Fig. 13.2 we plot the partial association between growth in total factor productivity $(\dot{A}/A)$ and the interaction between initial technology gap and social capability. $\dot{A}/A$ and initial gap·social capability are calculated from specification (i) as

$$\frac{\dot{A}}{A} = \frac{\dot{y}}{y} - 0.080\,\frac{I}{Y} + 0.142\,\frac{\dot{L}}{L} \quad \text{and}$$

$$\text{initial gap}\cdot\text{social capability} = \log\!\left(\frac{\tau_k}{\tau_{US}}\right)\!\left(0.013\,HUM + 0.007\,OP\right).$$

TABLE 13.2. *The Effect on the Rate of Growth in Labour Productivity of Catching Up, Social Capability and Growth in Factors of Production 1960–85*

Variable	Parameter	(i)	(ii)	(iii)
$\log\left(\dfrac{\tau_k}{\tau_{US}}\right)\cdot HUM$	β_1	−0.013 [−3.12]	−0.012 [−2.92]	−0.013 [−3.31]
$\log\left(\dfrac{\tau_k}{\tau_{US}}\right)\cdot OP$	β_2	−0.007 [−1.55]	−0.008 [−2.04]	−0.009 [−2.18]
$\dfrac{I}{Y}$	γ_1	0.080 [3.38]	0.095 [4.65]	0.066 [2.78]
$\dfrac{\dot{L}}{L}$	γ_2	−0.142 [−0.85]	−0.038 [−0.28]	−0.021 [−0.12]
$\dfrac{\dot{OP}}{OP}$				0.171 [1.76]
Constant	α	−0.005 [−0.70]	−0.009 [−1.62]	−0.007 [−1.01]
$\overline{R}^2$		0.320	0.405	0.346
n		81	80	81

Note: Brackets [ ] give White's (1980) heteroscedasticity consistent *t*-statistics.

The correlation in Fig. 13.2 between $\dot{A}/A$ and the interaction between the initial gap and social capability is −0.41, whereas the correlation between growth in total factor productivity and initial gap computed from specification (ii) in Table 12.3 is −0.37. This reaffirms that social capability plays an important role in catching up.

As we can see from the plot in Fig. 13.2 there are three outliers: Botswana, Egypt and Zambia. We carry out the diagnostic test DFFITS[33] to check whether these observations are influential and find that at least Zambia seems to have a significant effect on the regression line. In specification (ii) in Table 13.2 we therefore exclude Zambia. Unlike specification (i), the

---

[33] See Krasker, Kuh and Welsch (1983) for a description of the test.

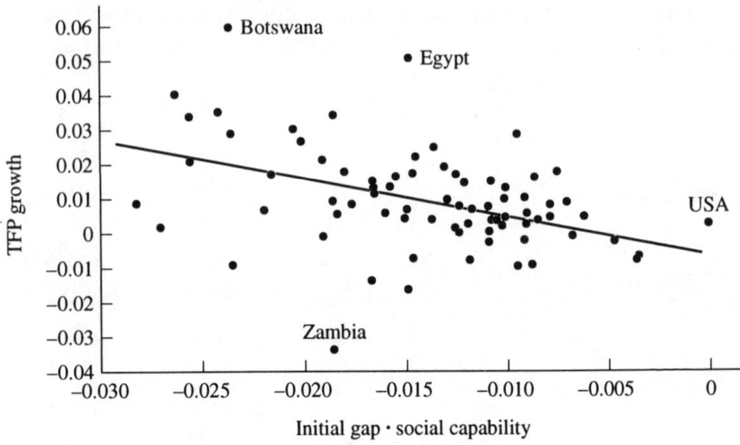

FIG. 13.2. *Partial Association Between Growth in Total Factor Productivity and Initial Technology Gap·Social Capability*

coefficient for $\log(\tau_k/\tau_{US})OP$ is significant. A closer inspection of the data for Zambia shows that the trade intensity ratio is higher than the average for the countries in the sample. But according to World Bank (1987) the trade regime in Zambia during the studied period has been strongly inward oriented.[34]

In specification (iii) in Table 13.2 we add the variable $\dot{OP}/OP$ to capture the direct effect of increased international trade stemming from further exploitation of comparative advantage and realization of economies of scale, along with increased availability of intermediate products. The parameter estimate for $\dot{OP}/OP$ has the expected sign and is significant at the 10 per cent level. It may also be noted that in specification (iii) the coefficient for $\log(\tau_k/\tau_{US})OP$ is clearly significant despite the fact that Zambia is included.

[34] OP for Zambia is 0.56 and the sample average is 0.38. The technology gap and HUM is similar to the value for other less developed countries. The reason for the high OP in Zambia is that Zambia is a leading exporter of copper. It is reasonable to expect that trade in mineral and agricultural products do not further technology diffusion to the same extent as trade in manufactures, especially trade in machinery and transport equipment (SITC 7). The case of Zambia shows that to capture the effect on a country's catching-up performance, a better measure may be the trade intensity in manufactures or the trade intensity for products classified into SITC 7.

Hence, summarizing our results using the Summers–Heston data base, we conclude that when capital accumulation and labour force growth are controlled for, there is significant catching up in labour productivity across countries. This effect is strengthened when the social capability interaction is accounted for, that is, both a higher level of human capital and deeper integration into the world economy facilitate productivity growth by technological diffusion from leader to followers. Furthermore, we obtain some empirical support for the hypothesis that increased international trade leads to productivity gains.

14

Government Expenditure and Economic Growth

Does government expenditure have a positive or negative effect on economic growth? A priori, we do not know. Arguments can be made in both directions.

To the extent that the well-known effects of the existence of collective goods, externalities and natural monopolies are important impediments to growth, the types of government expenditure that rectify these problems can be expected to have growth-enhancing effects. Following Barro (1990) we may label this 'productive' government spending.

Another problem is that the valuation of government output may lead to an overestimation of measured growth. In the different accounts, government goods and services are valued at their cost of production. This procedure gives rise to a number of difficulties which bias the researcher to find that increased government spending results in increased economic growth. This is due to the implicit assumption that government output is produced with a constant returns to scale technology, that all government production can be classified as final output rather than intermediate inputs lowering private sector production costs, and that the market value of government output is equal to the cost of production (Carr, 1989; Koskela and Virén, 1992).

Government expenditure is also part of GDP. Since both government consumption and investment are part of GDP when measured from the expenditure side, explaining GDP growth by changes in government spending involves explaining something partly by itself. In particular during periods when the government spending share has been increasing, this problem lends an upward bias to the estimated effect.

Kaldor (1966) claimed that a high rate of utilization has a beneficial effect on long-run productivity growth. In so far as an expansion of the public sector results in a higher utilization rate, there ought to be a positive effect on economic growth through the workings of Verdoorn's Law.

Furthermore, Myrdal (1960) stressed that a greater government involvement in the economy can foster growth because the greater involvement can be used partly to reduce social inequality, which is seen as detrimental to growth because it restricts the opportunities for low-income individuals to exploit their talent. Here we may also note Alesina and Perrotti's (this volume) finding that social conflict can be abated by increased government involvement.

As regards the growth-retarding effects of government expenditure, the most important of these effects deal with the distortionary effect on economic decisions that arise when spending has to be financed through taxation. Almost invariably, taxation inserts a wedge between the private and the social rate of return; taxation leads to an excess burden. In recent endogenous growth models such as Barro (1990) and King and Rebelo (1990), taxes create a wedge between the gross and net returns on saving, which leads to a lower rate of capital accumulation and hence a lower rate of economic growth. Lindbeck (1983), among others, has instead stressed the disincentive effects of large tax wedges on labour income in high-tax societies. Hansson (1984) assesses that the cost of increasing public revenue at the margin may be extremely high in a country like Sweden with a large public sector. It is also important to stress that there are many other important aspects of labour supply additional to the number of hours worked: degree of effort, worker morale, willingness to assume more responsibility in the work place, investment in human capital, transfer of labour to the informal economy etc. These empirically less tractable aspects may potentially be of great importance for the growth rate.

Other researchers have emphasized the fact that government activity may crowd out private production and private capital formation. Koskela and Virén (1992) have analysed how increased government demand for labour will put an upward pressure on real wages and hence crowd out private sector employment. In pooled time-series cross-section studies for OECD countries Landau (1983), Smith (1975) and Cameron (1982) have shown how government spending leads to crowding out of private sector investment and hence to lower economic growth.

A further argument pointing towards a negative effect of increased government spending on economic growth is that the risk for institutional sclerosis and rent-seeking increases. Olson (1982) has suggested that organized interest groups tend to evolve, and they strive to obtain advantages for their own group in the form of legislation or transfers that have the growth-retarding side-effect of worsening the functioning of the market economy. The scope for interest group action of this kind may be greater in countries with larger public sectors. Similarly, in the case of a large public sector the potential profits from rent-seeking activities are larger, which may lead to a greater diversion of resources into unproductive use (Buchanan, 1980).

This brief review of the arguments that have been proposed regarding the expected effect of government spending on growth leads us to conclude that there is no basis for having strong priors regarding the effect of government spending in general. We should also expect that different types of expenditure have divergent effects.

14.1　A survey of tests of the growth effects of government expenditure

The majority of empirical studies use a general regression approach (or a simple correlational approach). The studies are so diverse that it is difficult to make a complete survey and to draw generally valid conclusions. With this caveat in mind, we will briefly review the most important studies that we find relevant in the present context.[35] Barro (1991a) and Engen and Skinner (1992) have used the Summers–Heston data base to test for the effect of government expenditure on growth. Barro finds that the level of government consumption, excluding education and defence as a share of GDP, has a negative effect on the growth of GDP per capita. On the other hand, he finds no effect of government investment, whereas educational expenditure has a positive effect. Engen and Skinner use an explicit production

---

[35] For this reason, we do not deal with the Granger causality studies such as Holmes and Hutton (1990) and Conte and Darrat (1988).

function approach where they attempt to identify separate effects of expenditure and taxation. The main finding is that an increase in the tax ratio by 10 percentage points reduces GDP growth by as much as 3.2 per cent per annum.

Landau (1983, 1986) and Kormendi and Meguire (1985) are other studies that use a country sample including developing countries. Landau finds a highly significant negative effect of government consumption as a share of GDP on the growth rate of GDP per capita, although this negative effect disappears if the sample is restricted to the poorest half of the countries. In Landau (1986) the separate effect of transfers, educational expenditure and government investment is also assessed. All three are found to be insignificant. Kormendi and Meguire detect no effect from the change in the government consumption expenditure ratio on the average GDP growth rate in forty-seven countries during the period 1950–77.

In a number of studies the effect of the level of government as a share of national income on growth is assessed econometrically. In Table 14.1 a number of cross-section studies based on data sets dominated by rich countries are listed. It is generally found that a larger share of government spending has a significantly negative effect on GDP growth for OECD countries.[36] However, a recent study by Easterly and Rebelo (1993) does not find a negative relationship between the level of income taxes and growth of GDP per capita in OECD countries in 1960–88. One should also keep in mind the Levine and Renelt (1992) critique, that is, that the regression results may be sensitive to the choice of control variables.

In sum, the level of government consumption appears to have a fairly robust negative effect on economic growth, in particular in the richer countries.[37] For other types of expenditure the results are less consistent, although it is fair to say that expenditure for investment and educational purposes has at least no

---

[36] Yet another study that could have been used in the comparison is Korpi (1985), but he does not explicitly present the effect on the growth rate of GDP per capita of the relative size of the government sector in the case that is comparable to the other studies presented in Table 14.1. But from the text one can infer that for the eighteen OECD countries included in the study, the effect on the growth rate is negative for all measures of government expenditure used in the period 1960–73.

[37] See also Grier (this volume).

TABLE 14.1. *The Effect of Government Expenditure on Economic Growth in Developed Countries: A Summary of Earlier Studies*

Study	Period	No. of countries	Growth measure	Measure of Government	Effect
Barth and Bradley (1988)	1971–83	16	GDP	Cons.	−1.7
Landau (1983)	1961–76	48	GDP per capita	Cons.	−3.2
Smith (1975)	1961–72	19	GDP per	Total exp.	−1.0
		19	capita	Cons. + inv.	−2.5
Saunders (1985)	1960–73	21	GDP	Total exp.	−1.6
	1975–81	20	GDP	Total exp.	−0.6
Cameron (1982)	1960–79	19	GDP	Total exp.	−0.5
Katz *et al.* (1983)	1970–80	22	GDP	Tax receipts	0.0
Marlow (1986)	1960–80	16	GDP	Total exp.	−1.8
Grier and Tullock (1989)	1951–80	24	GDP	Cons.[b]	−0.32[a]

Note: Effect is defined as the estimated change in the annual rate of growth resulting from an increase in the relevant spending ratio by 10 percentage points. All government expenditure measures are related to GDP. Readers interested in further details are referred to the respective studies. All cited results are statistically significant.

[a] Refers to the growth in the share of government consumption. In this case, the interpretation of the effect is that an increase in the share of government consumption of 1% p.a. decreases the rate of growth of GDP by 0.32 percentage points.

[b] Refers to government consumption excluding defence and education.

negative effect on growth. The measured effects also seem to differ between developed and developing countries. There is a stronger tendency to find a negative effect of government expenditure on economic growth among the rich than among the poor countries.

Almost all studies that try to explain GDP growth by government spending shares suffer to differing degrees from a number of methodological problems. First, the change in GDP is definitionally related to the change in the part of government expenditure that is included in GDP (investment and consumption). In particular, this is likely to bias the researcher towards finding a positive effect of a change in the spending ratio on growth (Bairam, 1989; Gould, 1983). Second, there may exist a bias in the opposite direction as an artefact of a spurious correlation between output growth and changes in the government spending share. This would occur if an unusually high growth rate depresses the rate of change in the spending share (Engen and Skinner, 1992). Third, it is quite possible that countries that grow rapidly tend to increase government spending as a result of the increased income, that is, government spending may be endogenous (Rao, 1989; Conte and Darrat, 1988).

A further problem is a likely measurement error in government output. This valuation problem has already been treated above. Since it is likely to be greater for countries at a low level of development,[38] it is all the more questionable to include countries at very different levels of economic development in the same regression. In growth equations including both industrialized and developing countries it also appears to be essential to include human capital and probably a number of other control variables (Levine and Renelt, 1992), failing this, which is the case in most studies, the regression results may be biased.

Considering these pitfalls, we argue that it would be more appropriate to study the effect of government spending on productivity in the private sector, preferably at a disaggregated level. By doing so many of the problems of endogeneity, spurious correlation and the definitional effect can be circumvented. By concentrating on developed countries at similar levels of income the measurement problem and the problem of finding a comprehensive set of control variables can be alleviated to a large degree. The catching-up effect is still accounted for in the regressions, although those estimates are of less interest in this section. In the case of government expenditure the variation among OECD countries is much larger than for human capital (as it is measured) and trade orientation. See Table 14.2, where the nineteen OECD countries for which government expenditure data are regularly published are ranked according to the ratio of total government outlays to GDP in 1992.[39]

---

[38] First, the wage level in the public sector is more likely to be above the competitive level in developing countries (Lindauer and Sabot, 1983; Psacharopoulos and Tzannatos, 1992). Second, since the informal economy constitutes a greater portion of economic activity in developing countries (ILO, 1986), a larger part of private sector activity is not recorded in the national accounts.

[39] It should of course be noted that some of the observed differences are driven by differences in the tax treatment of transfers and the use of tax expenditures.

TABLE 14.2. *Total Government Outlays as a Percentage of GDP in nineteen OECD Countries, 1960 and 1992*

	1960	1992
Sweden	31.0	67.3
Denmark	24.8	59.5
Norway	29.9	57.5
Netherlands	33.7	54.7
Italy	30.1	53.2
France	34.6	52.0
Finland	26.6	51.7
Belgium	30.3	50.8
Austria	35.7	50.2
Canada	28.6	49.7
Germany	32.4	49.4
Greece	17.4	48.3
Portugal	17.0	46.1
Spain	—	45.1
UK	32.2	44.1
Ireland	28.0	43.9
Australia	21.2	38.3
USA	27.0	35.4
Japan	17.5	32.2
Weighted average	28.0	41.2
Unweighted average	27.7	48.9
Standard deviation	5.9	8.3

Note: For 1992 total outlays only include net capital outlays, while they are included gross in 1960. This reduces the expenditure share by roughly 1.5 percentage points for 1992.

Source: *OECD Economic Outlook* and *OECD Historical Statistics*.

14.2 Government expenditure and catching up: some empirical tests

In this section the same disaggregated model presented in equations (12.6) and (12.7) is used as the point of departure. In specifying how government spending affects the nongovernment sector we will assume that it exclusively affects the rate of growth of TFP. In modelling TFP we hypothesize that the relative rate of growth in TFP, $(\dot{A}/A)_{ik}$ in (12.7), is determined by a catching-up factor and by the relevant government spending measure, g_k.[40] Since the earlier distinction between tradables and nontradables is not the issue here, it has been suppressed. The relative rate of growth in TFP in industry i in country k is then given by:

$$\left[\frac{\dot{A}}{A}\right]_{ik} = \lambda + \kappa \log\left[\frac{\tau_{ik}}{\tau_{il}}\right] + \psi g_k. \tag{14.1}$$

τ_{ik}/τ_{il} is the catching-up factor. τ_{il} is the TFP level in the country with the highest productivity in industry i in 1970 and τ_{ik} is the TFP level in industry i in country k. ψ measures the effect of government spending on $(\dot{A}/A)_{ik}$. As before, catching up is defined in terms of TFP levels in different industries, which is measured as in equation (12.10).

By combining (12.7) and (14.1) we get our basic model:

$$\left[\frac{\dot{Y}}{Y}\right]_{ik} = \beta_0 + \beta_1 \left[\frac{\dot{K}}{K}\frac{K}{Y}\right]_{ik} + \beta_2 \left[\frac{\dot{L}}{L}\frac{L}{Y}\right]_{ik} + \beta_3 \log\left[\frac{\tau_{ik}}{\tau_{il}}\right]$$
$$+ \beta_4 g_k + \varepsilon_{ik}. \tag{14.2}$$

ε_{ik} is a zero-mean, normally distributed error term.

All data except for government spending comes from an updated version of the International Sectoral Data Bank (ISDB), which fully covers the period 1970–87. As in section 12.2, the data set covers fourteen countries and fourteen industries (see Table 12.4).

All government spending variables are from OECD sources, and they are related to GDP and the level is calculated as the average during the period under study.[41] Appendix II.2 contains descriptive statistics and exact sources of the data on the government spending categories used.

---

[40] Barro (1991a), Landau (1983) and several other studies also include a variable that controls for initial income or initial level of productivity. In most cases initial GDP per capita is used. With few exceptions, if any, this variable comes out with a negative sign in the regressions.

[41] As an alternative the level was calculated for 1965–82 in order to allow for the possibility that government spending might influence productivity with a lag. The results were virtually unchanged by this modification.

TABLE 14.3. *Government Consumption,
Investment and Total Outlays*

Variable	(i)	(ii)
$\left[\dfrac{\dot{K}}{K}\dfrac{K}{Y}\right]_{ik}$	0.027 [2.24]	0.026 [2.12]
$\left[\dfrac{\dot{L}}{L}\dfrac{L}{Y}\right]_{ik}$	7029 [8.67]	7530 [8.88]
$\log(\tau_{ik}/\tau_{il})$	−0.010 [−2.45]	−0.009 [−2.25]
GTOT 1970–87	−0.074 [−3.71]	
GC 1970–87		−0.136 [−3.48]
Constant	0.048 [5.34]	0.042 [5.49]
$\bar{R}^2$	0.495	0.502
n	153	153

Note: Brackets [ ] give White's (1980) heteroscedasticity consistent *t*-statistics.

The effect of government consumption and total outlays are
obvious choices for the empirical analysis. In addition, we have
chosen to look for a separate effect of educational expenditure,
which is a subset of *GC*, but should rather be considered as
investment in human capital (Barro, 1990).

In Table 14.3 we present results for the effect of catching up,
GTOT and *GC* on TFP-growth. First it should be noted that the
catching-up variable is significant. The point estimate for the
catching-up parameter indicates that TFP-growth is roughly 0.7
percentage points higher in an industry in a country at half the
productivity level of that industry in the leading country. Furthermore, consistent with the findings of most earlier studies,
both total government expenditure and consumption expenditure as a share of GDP have a highly significant negative effect
on TFP-growth. Specification (i) indicates that an increase in
GTOT by 10 percentage points would decrease the growth rate

of TFP by 0.74 percentage points per annum. According to the regression results in specification (ii), a commensurate increase of GC would lower the TFP growth rate by almost 1.4 percentage points per annum.[42]

As regards GC it is worth noting that it partly constitutes educational expenditures, GE, which is really a type of investment. In specification (i) in Table 14.4 we therefore distinguish between these two types of spending. Compared to the results for GC in Table 14.3, the negative effect of $GC - GE$ is larger, whereas GE has a positive, although not quite significant, effect on TFP-growth. The estimate of the catching-up parameter is virtually identical to what we found in the regressions reported in Table 14.3.

To further check the validity of the results when we have included one government expenditure variable at a time, we have also made regressions when all components of total spending are included and the different components sum to total outlays, see specification (ii) in Table 14.4. Here we see that GE is now significant at the 5 per cent level and the estimates of all other variables are almost identical to what was found above. Taken literally there are potentially very large beneficial effects from increasing educational expenditure—an increase of GE by one percentage point would increase the rate of TFP growth by 0.39 per cent per annum. This finding is consistent with other studies already cited, which emphasize the crucial role of human capital formation for economic growth. We cannot find any effect of increased government investment on TFP-growth—the estimates are not significantly different from zero. The absence of a positive effect may at first seem surprising; public investment is generally considered as an input to private production, and hence one would expect it to enhance private sector productivity. One conceivable explanation for this result is that inefficiencies in public-sector decision-making on average result in government investment with a low social rate of return.[43] Another possible explanation for this result is the suggestion

[42] Admittedly, these estimates are quite high, and we would like to warn the reader against jumping to policy conclusions. One cannot infer that an isolated and substantial decrease of the government spending share will all by itself boost long-run productivity growth. A major decrease of government spending would of course require a host of additional institutional and regulatory changes in the economy.

[43] See, e.g., Mueller (1989, ch. 14).

TABLE 14.4. *Education and All Government Expenditure Variables*

Variable	(i) 1970–87	(ii) 1970–87
$\left[\dfrac{\dot{K}}{K}\dfrac{K}{Y}\right]_{ik}$	0.026 [2.24]	0.024 [2.22]
$\left[\dfrac{\dot{L}}{L}\dfrac{L}{Y}\right]_{ik}$	7510 [9.12]	7080 [9.20]
$\log(\tau_{ik}/\tau_{il})$	−0.008 [−2.19]	−0.010 [−2.63]
$GC - GE$	−0.168 [−4.14]	−0.157 [−4.06]
GE	0.186 [1.26]	0.393 [2.34]
GI		0.034 [0.24]
GTR		−0.075 [−2.30]
Constant	0.031 [3.35]	0.033 [3.41]
$\bar{R}^2$	0.517	0.530
n	153	153

Note: Brackets [ ] give White's (1980) heteroscedasticity consistent *t*-statistics.

made by Barro (1990) that if governments are optimizing, then the reason different countries exhibit different investment spending ratios is that the relative productivity of public and private capital differs across countries. Therefore, in a cross-country regression one should not expect *GI* to be correlated with productivity growth.

In sum, we have argued that it is more appropriate to focus on the effect of government expenditure on the nongovernment sector, specifically on the rate of growth of TFP. To that effect, we use a production function approach, based on disaggregated data. Account is taken of a potential catching-up effect. The study covers fourteen industries in fourteen OECD countries during the period 1970–87. The results indicate that the levels of government consumption, transfers and total spending as a share of GDP have a strongly negative effect on the growth of TFP in the nongovernment sector. Educational spending has a positive effect and the level of government investment has no effect. An increase in the level of government consumption and in total outlays are estimated to lead to a decrease in the annual rate of growth of TFP in the nongovernment sector of 1.4 and 0.7 per cent per annum, respectively. Finally, the catching-up effect is significant, and is of an order of magnitude that makes it an important determinant of the growth rate of TFP among followers.

15

Limitations of Our Study:
A Brief Discussion

One limitation of our study is that it does not take into account the effect of domestic innovations on productivity growth. This problem is less severe for developing countries, where it is reasonable to expect that most of the new technology is transferred in one way or another from industrially more advanced countries. This means that much of the technological change in those countries is of a catching-up character, that is, it consists of assimilating and adopting technology originating from more developed countries. In the OECD countries, on the other hand, a significant share of technological progress and productivity growth is a result of the respective countries' own research efforts. Coe and Helpman (1995) have found that in the larger OECD countries (the G7), in particular, the domestic R&D stock is important for growth in TFP, whereas foreign R&D capital has a strong effect on TFP growth in the small open OECD countries.

In a study similar to ours, Verspagen (1991) made an attempt to capture the rate of productivity growth due to research activities in a follower country. The measure he uses is the sum of the per capita number of patents granted in the USA for inhabitants from the country in question. There are several drawbacks with this measure, which Verspagen also admits. Patent data have disadvantages as indicators of innovation, among other things, because they differ greatly in their technical and economic significance. Many patents reflect minor improvements of little economic value, while some patents can be extremely valuable. Moreover, many external (US) patents during a period may not indicate domestic innovation, rather they may simply reflect an increased internationalization of the economy. The empirical impact of the variable is quite weak; the coefficient is at most significant at the 10 per cent level (in a one-tail test).

A second limitation of our study, which is potentially of great relevance, relates to a point raised by Mancur Olson (1996). When we attempt to answer the question 'What makes a country socially capable of catching up?', it is of course true that we identify two factors that appear to be of vital importance, namely, trade orientation and the per capita level of human capital. On the other hand, we implicitly assume that these factors are exogenous, in the sense that we do not attempt to explain what ultimately lies behind the variation in these factors across countries. Olson argues (without explicitly using the concept of social capability) that the social capability of a country is instead a result of its social institutions and social policies. With this perspective in mind, our results could be interpreted as indicating that the only countries that tend to enjoy much catching up, even though catching up is open to all low-income countries, are those with tolerable institutions and policies, notably relatively free trade, and institutions and incentives that attract and facilitate the accumulation of needed human capital. According to Olson's interpretation this means that it is wrong to assume that most countries are on the frontiers of their aggregate production functions, and how far removed a society is from this frontier is then not a function of the constraints it faces, but rather a result of its own arrangements and choices.

Third, it should be mentioned that attempts have been made from a neoclassical perspective to take account of the effects of non-economic or institutional factors on economic growth. Barro (1991a,b) attempts to explain variations between countries in growth of real GDP per capita by including measures of political instability and the extent of imperfectly functioning markets among the regressors. He finds a negative relationship between growth in real GDP per capita and both political instability and the extent of market imperfections. Further efforts to take account of the effects of political instability on economic growth (and investment) have been made by Alesina and Perotti (this volume). Rather than using 'raw' figures on political instability, such as the number of political assassinations or the number of coups, which is the route taken by Barro (1991a,b) and Benhabib and Spiegel (1992), they apply an index based on a principal components analysis.[44] Alesina and Perotti find the

---

[44] The index is taken from Gupta (1990).

expected negative effect of political instability on investment and growth.

The importance of the institutional framework for economic growth has been emphasized by economic historians.[45] Security of property is a necessary condition for high rates of capital accumulation and growth. These writers have demonstrated how strong an effect more secure property rights have had on the economic development in the West. Recent studies on the growth performance among nations during the last decades seem to confirm that finding;[46] countries which subscribe to the rule of law, to private property and to market allocation of resources have grown faster than countries in which political, civil (legal) and economic liberties are circumvented. However, there are many problems involved in constructing comprehensive measures of the institutional framework among nations, and naturally, the above results hinge on how dependable these measures are.

Roubini and Sala-i-Martin (1992) have focused on the financial sector and its influence on economic growth. A large part of an economy's savings are intermediated towards productive investment by the financial sector. Hence, if the allocation of capital is worse in a financially repressed economy, then for any stock of inputs the aggregate output is less the more financially repressed an economy is. If the marginal product of capital is lower, then such a repressive policy will hurt economic growth. Financially repressed economies are characterized by credit rationing and artificially low real interest rates. In a cross-country study, Roubini and Sala-i-Martin obtain empirical support for a negative relationship between the degree of financial repression (measured by real interest rate distortions) and economic performance.

This brief review is sufficient to indicate that the political economy of economic growth is at present a lively area of research. Not least, a great deal of effort is expended on collecting and constructing internationally comparable data series on institutional, political and other pertinent factors that may help to explain cross-country differences in growth rates. This

---

[45] See, e.g., North and Thomas (1973) and Rosenberg and Birdzell (1986).

[46] e.g., Scully (1988), Scully and Slottje (1991) and Torstensson (1994).

development will also make it possible to refine the empirical testing of the catching-up hypothesis, since it may allow the concept of social capability to be more appropriately modelled than in this chapter.

16

Conclusions

In this study we have largely focused on a thorough assessment of the importance of catching up for the explanation of differences in growth performance across countries. We have also specifically treated the effect of government spending on productivity growth.

In general, there has been a strong belief in the catching-up hypothesis. This conviction was reinforced by Baumol's and Abramowitz's studies on Maddison's data for sixteen countries. A closer inspection of those studies shows, however, that catching up has not occurred universally. The selection of time period and countries is of decisive importance for whether empirical support for catching up is received.

Our study at the aggregate (national) level verifies that a simple catching-up effect has operated during the period 1960–85, when capital accumulation and labour growth are controlled for. The greater a country's technological gap relative to the leading country in the world (the USA) at the beginning of the period, the larger its rate of growth in labour productivity. Empirically, we have proxied a country's level of technology by its labour productivity.

To test for the existence of catching up at the most aggregate level may be too crude, and we have argued that a test procedure using disaggregated data is more appropriate. First, there may be systematic differences between sectors in technological catching up. Second, it is unlikely that one country can be identified as the undisputed technological leader in all industries. Rather it is more likely that technological leadership in different industries is domiciled in different countries. Our disaggregated study is only possible to carry out for fourteen OECD countries. On the other hand, it has the advantage that we can measure the level of technology in terms of total factor productivity, which is a more suitable measure than labour productivity.

During the period 1970–85 we do not find catching up in the tradables sector, whereas catching up has operated in the non-tradables sector. The results point to the conclusion that technological catching up in the tradables sector, although it was probably important in the 1950s and 1960s, has no longer been important after 1970. This indicates that in the part of the economy facing direct competition from foreign rivals, the potential for fast TFP growth based on catching up was depleted by the early 1970s. This is all the more likely considering that technology is today often carried across national boundaries while remaining within the same firm. On the other hand, multi-national companies have not been important in the nontradables sector.

Despite the fact that no technological catching up has occurred in the tradables sector, the relative rate of growth in TFP has been faster in tradables than in nontradables. Hence, international competition seems to promote technological change.

In our aggregated study we have operationalized the concept of social capability, that is, we have also taken account of the fact that a lower level of technology in a country is not a sufficient condition for attaining a higher rate of technological change than initially more advanced countries. We have presented a simple theoretical framework in which the effects of social capability on technological diffusion from leaders to followers is modelled. The main element in the model is the interaction between the technological gap and social capability. Two potential determinants of social capability arc highlightcd: thc stock of human capital and the degree of integration into the world economy.

Our results show that when capital accumulation and labour force growth are controlled for there is significant catching up in labour productivity across countries; an effect that is strengthened when the social capability interaction is accounted for. Both a higher level of human capital and deeper integration into the world economy facilitate technological diffusion from leaders to followers, which in turn promote the followers' productivity growth.

In an extension of our model, we try to capture gains in labour productivity from increased international trade that are likely to stem from other sources than catching up. These are specialization according to comparative advantage, realization of economies of scale, and, as emphasized by new growth theory, the greater availability of intermediate inputs resulting from increased international trade. The results from this extended model confirm the previous findings of the importance of social capability for catching up. They also show that there is an independent effect of the change in trade intensity and trade regime on productivity growth.

A final aspect covered in depth in this paper is the effect of government expenditure on productivity growth, and possibly how it affects the realization of the catching-up potential. Theoretical reasoning is not sufficient to determine whether government expenditure should be expected to have a positive or negative effect on growth and productivity. This issue has to be solved by empirical testing. A large number of studies with this purpose have been conducted. While the results are mixed, it is fair to say that the majority of them find a negative effect of government spending on economic growth. This is the case for government consumption in particular.

We have argued that for a number of reasons—notably measurement problems, the fact that government consumption and investment are part of GDP and a likely endogeneity of government spending—it is more appropriate to focus on the effect of various types of government spending on the rate of productivity growth in the nongovernment sector, preferably using disaggregated data. For this purpose we use a production function approach where a potential catching-up effect is allowed for. The developed model is applied to disaggregated data for fourteen OECD countries and fourteen industries during the period 1970–87.

Our results are quite distinct and consistent. The level of total outlays, consumption and transfers invariably have a negative impact on the rate of growth of total factor productivity. Government investment is not found to have any effect on TFP growth. On the other hand, educational expenditure exerts a positive influence on TFP growth. In a regression combining transfers, consumption excluding education, educational expenditure and investment, all previous findings for the different spending categories taken separately reappear. In that regression, which we consider to be the most convincing, the positive effect of educational expenditure is reinforced.

Finally, we would like to emphasize that the catching-up factor means that there is a potential for poor countries, by borrowing technology, to grow faster than rich countries. Whether or not the poor countries utilize this possibility depends partly on the way they shape their policies. New technology will probably be transferred to a larger extent to countries that are integrated with the world economy than to countries with inward-oriented policies. A country that has long invested in developing its educational system—and thereby may be expected to have a well-trained labour force—has a greater capacity to adopt new technology than a country that has neglected its educational system. It is also likely that a large share of government expenditure impedes economic growth. We would thus warn against taking a too mechanical view of catching up and income convergence, namely, that poor countries must necessarily grow faster than rich countries. Rather, as De Long (1988, p. 1148) states: 'the capability to assimilate industrial technology appears to be surprisingly hard to acquire, and it may be distressingly easy to lose.'

APPENDIX II.1

List of Countries in the Extended Sample

Algeria; Benin; Botswana; Burundi; Central African Rep.; Congo; Egypt; Gabon; Ghana; Ivory Coast; Kenya; Liberia; Madagascar; Malawi; Mauritius; Morocco; Niger; Nigeria; Rwanda; Senegal; Somalia; Sudan; Togo; Uganda; Zaire; Zambia; Costa Rica; Dominican Rep.; El Salvador; Guatemala; Haiti; Honduras; Jamaica; Mexico; Nicaragua; Panama; France; West Germany; Greece; Iceland; Ireland; Italy; Luxembourg; Malta; Netherlands; Norway; Portugal; Spain; Sweden; Switzerland; Turkey; UK; Australia; New Zealand; USA; Trinidad & Tobago; Argentina; Bolivia; Brazil; Chile; Colombia; Ecuador; Paraguay; Peru; Uruguay; Venezuela; Bangladesh; Hong Kong; India; Israel; Japan; South Korea; Malaysia; Pakistan; Philippines; Sri Lanka; Thailand; Austria; Belgium; Denmark; Finland.

APPENDIX II.2

GDP-Share of Various Government Spending Categories, Average 1970–87 for the 14 Countries

Category	Mean	Std dev.	Min	Max
Consumption, *GC*	18.28	3.99	9.43	26.16
Education, *GE*	4.98	0.92	3.53	6.45
Investment, *GI*	4.11	1.14	1.51	6.52
Transfers, *GTR*	21.43	6.09	13.02	33.67
Total outlays, *GTOT*	43.82	8.22	28.97	56.41

Source: Consumption and GDP in current prices are from *OECD Economic Outlook*, December 1992; Data on defence and educational spending are from *OECD National Accounts*, Vol. 2, 1992, except for Canada where they are drawn from Liesner (1989); data for all other spending variables are from *OECD Historical Statistics 1960–89*.

17

Comment

NICK CRAFTS

It is a pleasure to be asked to discuss such an interesting paper on economic growth. The authors offer us a rich diet of empirical results and find some new angles in what is becoming a very crowded field. My comments are mainly in the vein of asking for still more investigation with which to fill out what I broadly find a plausible story.

Hansson and Henrekson set themselves two main tasks: (a) to make a thorough empirical appraisal of the catching-up hypothesis and (b) to operationalize and test the importance of social capability for the achievement of catching-up. Their research is squarely in the tradition of Abramovitz (1986), Denison (1967) and Maddison (1987) rather than the Augmented-Solow model proposed by Mankiw, Romer and Weil (1992) or Barro and Sala-i-Martin (1992). Their models seek to endogenize TFP growth and highlight influences on the diffusion of technology but do not embrace the central claims of endogenous growth theory.

Before turning to the authors' results, it is useful to be reminded of basic background information on catching-up and convergence. Table 17.1 reflects the strong tendencies to convergence within Europe—by 1990 nine countries on the chart are within ±3.5% of the median. Table 17.2 demonstrates a catch-up of North America by Europe and Japan in manufacturing productivity. Here, however, it is important to note that the American lead over Europe is still very substantial in 1989, although lower than in 1973, while Japan, having overtaken Europe, continues rapidly to catch up the US.

The empirical findings of the paper are based on two data sets—the first is the more-or-less standard international cross-section on growth since 1960 derived from Summers and Heston (1991) while the second, from which the more novel results are obtained, is based on OECD sectoral data. Both data sets are

TABLE 17.1. *GDP per capita: Ranking of Sixteen European Countries (1950, 1970, 1990) in 1990 US Dollars*

1950		1970		1990	
1 Switzerland	8,782	1 Switzerland	16,379	1 Switzerland	20,997
2 United Kingdom	6,537	2 Sweden	12,199	2 W Germany	18,291
3 Sweden	6,464	3 W Germany	11,869	3 France	17,341
4 Denmark	6,221	4 Denmark	11,393	4 Sweden	16,867
5 The Netherlands	5,676	5 The Netherlands	11,322	5 Denmark	16,756
6 Belgium	5,209	6 France	11,313	6 Austria	16,620
7 France	5,110	7 United Kingdom	10,404	7 Finland	16,453
8 Norway	4,687	8 Belgium	10,142	8 Belgium	16,405
9 W Germany	4,267	9 Austria	9,667	9 Italy	16,021
10 Finland	4,087	10 Italy	9,652	10 Norway	15,921
11 Austria	3,675	11 Finland	9,203	11 The Netherlands	15,766
12 Italy	3,630	12 Norway	8,607	12 United Kingdom	15,720
13 Ireland	3,153	13 Spain	7,333	13 Spain	11,792
14 Spain	2,778	14 Ireland	5,672	14 Ireland	10,695
15 Portugal	1,753	15 Portugal	4,792	15 Portugal	8,398
16 Greece	1,422	16 Greece	4,613	16 Greece	7,394
Ratios 1st/16th	6.2		3.6		2.8
Ratio 4th/12th	1.7		1.3		1.07

Source: Prados (1993).

TABLE 17.2. *Comparative Levels of Labour Productivity in Manufacturing (UK Output per Employee = 100)*

	1870	1913	1929	1938	1950	1973	1989
UK	100	100	100	100	100	100	100
USA	204	213	250	192	263	215	177
Canada	132	230	256	218	227	229	185
Australia		138	102	101	96	86	81
Germany	100	119	105	107	96	119	105
Netherlands			102	117	88	133	128
Norway		90	109	95	103	104	85
Sweden		102	94	100	118	128	121
Denmark			115	98	88	89	93
France		79	82	76	84	114	115
Italy		59	59	49	68	96	111
Japan		24	32	42	20	95	143

Source: Broadberry (1993).

used to address each of the main concerns of the paper, although somewhat surprisingly, some aspects of social capability are included in tests on one but not the other.

The results obtained from the Heston–Summers data set are broadly consistent with a good deal of recent research. Catching up is found to be an important determinant of growth, along with investment, human capital and openness to trade. None of this would greatly surprise anyone familiar with Levine and Renelt (1992) who made a comprehensive overview of research in this area. They found that secondary school enrolment, the investment share in GDP and the initial income level had a robust effect on growth but nothing else did despite experiments to include a vast number of other variables.

I have four comments on the specific findings in Hansson and Henrekson

First, the reported results are somewhat less persuasive than those in Levine and Renelt because rather less appears to have been done to investigate their robustness and because the specification is perhaps too restrictive. Why not include government spending as a variable influencing TFP growth? How well

TABLE 17.3. *Actual and Forecast Convergence, 1950–86/7*
GDP/Hour (US = 100)

	Actual	Forecast		Actual	Forecast
Australia	78	81	Argentina	28	50
Austria	74	43	Brazil	25	29
Belgium	86	60	Chile	33	53
Canada	92	86	Colombia	28	38
Denmark	68	61	India	4	8
Finland	67	48	Korea	21	18
France	94	58	Mexico	27	35
Germany	80	47	Peru	20	34
Italy	79	48	Philippines	11	20
Japan	61	27	Taiwan	20	15
Netherlands	92	64			
Norway	90	61			
Sweden	82	67			
Switzerland	68	72			
UK	80	73			

Source: Crafts (1992) based on applying the Barro and Sala-i-Martin (1991) model to data from Maddison (1989, 1991).

would the results on openness be sustained as other variables are considered?

Second, the specification in Table 13.2 assumes a Maddison style catching-up model as against an Augmented-Solow framework in which human capital would enter directly as an argument in the production function, as for example in Levine and Renelt. This seems likely to lead the authors to lean rather too far towards a technology catch-up view of things with too little weight given to convergence towards the steady state in a world of both physical and human capital.

Third, Hansson and Henrekson correctly stress the inadequacy of present attempts to measure social capability and the importance of trying to do better. Table 17.3 underlines the point that models which regard catching up as automatic have a wide margin of error. At the same time, measurement of the key differences among OECD countries, if not between the first and third worlds, is very difficult and standardly used variables do not capture the subtleties of institutional impacts (Crafts and Toniolo, 1993). The authors have made a start but much more remains to be done.

Fourth, the results obtained from the 1960–85 data set may well not carry over to earlier periods. In any event, it would be interesting to know whether the apparent implication of their results, that is, that lack of human capital and/or protectionism thwarted catching-up before, say, 1950 or whether the results obtained for 1960–85 are contingent on a quite new possibility of technology transfer, as argued by Nelson and Wright (1992).

The results from the second data set, reported in Tables 12.5 and 14.4 are quite striking and might well stimulate further research as they raise a number of difficult questions. Perhaps the most interesting claim in the whole paper is the suggestion that there is no catching-up effect in the tradables sector after 1970. This needs to be thought about against the background of Table 17.2 which, after all, deals with the tradables sector. If these results stand up to further tests, they seem to call for clarification of the technology diffusion model which underpins the experience, especially since Japan, at least, does appear to have continued to catch up in this period.

Before accepting fully the apparent implication of the results of Table 12.5, I would want to see some further work. First, and most obvious, it would be nice to see results for subsamples, to explore the absence or presence of catching-up at finer levels of disaggregation and in the context of suggestions that some countries have more successful innovation systems than others (Pavitt and Patel, 1988).

Second, human capital needs to be brought into the picture. Failure to allow for its role in production potentially biases both the calculation of TFP levels and the relationship of changes in TFP to productivity gaps. Table 17.4 suggests this is potentially quite a serious issue. When human capital is explicitly measured—in this case using labour force skills—the UK appears to have a TFP lead over Germany in 1987, which would not show up if only physical capital were taken into account.

Let us, however, for the moment suppose that the main message of Table 12.5 is robust and that the differences in labour productivity shown in Table 17.2 largely reflect differences in

TABLE 17.4. *Productivity of Labour in Manufacturing, 1987*

Sources of German lead over UK	
Human capital	13.4
Physical capital	10.1
R&D	5.8
Efficiency	−7.5
Total	22.2

Source: O'Mahony (1992).

TFP, as Helliwell (1992) and Van Ark (1993) suggest. What might explain this result? There seem basically to be two quite different possibilities, one of which accords with Hansson and Henrekson's basic model and one which does not.

The first says that catching-up in Europe, but not Japan, ceased because of 'Eurosclerosis'. This seems rather doubtful given the continued catching-up reported in nontradables. The second says that North America and Europe are members of different 'convergence clubs' in the sense of Durlauf and Johnson (1992), as envisaged by new growth theory models with multiple equilibria. As Broadberry (1993) suggests, historically the latter seems strongly plausible and would be based on different home-market size and natural resources. In any event, the main point here is that Hansson and Henrekson's intriguing result underlines the need to explore further the nature of the international technological diffusion process.

Finally, let us consider the issues raised by the results in Table 14.4 which throw further light on the role of social capability in catching-up. The argument here is that a 10 percentage point increase in government consumption will reduce the TFP growth rate by 1.4% per year in the non-government sector. I am instinctively sympathetic to this suggestion but several points should be noted before we accept it without qualification.

First, if this argument is right, it suggests that the equations in Table 13.2 which omit government spending as a variable may be mis-specified.

Second, on the other hand, Levine and Renelt (1992) argue

TABLE 17.5. *Central Government Outlays*
(% of GDP)

	1938	1955
Austria	14.3	27.0
Belgium	11.0	20.9
Denmark	7.0	13.8
Finland	14.1	21.9
France	19.9	22.8
Ireland	11.6	35.0
Netherlands	19.4	27.3
Norway	8.1	19.0
Sweden	11.7	21.1
Switzerland	6.8	7.2
UK	20.2	28.0

Source: derived from Mitchell (1992); in some cases output is represented in both years by NNP.

that the effect of government consumption on growth is not robust and that might suggest that the equations in Table 14.4 are mis-specified. Certainly, some experiments to investigate their robustness would be welcome.

Third, Table 17.5 notes that the Golden Age of European catch-up growth was accompanied, in most countries, by a sharp rise in government budgets as a proportion of national output compared with the pre-war period. Obviously, this need not be inconsistent with the arguments of the paper (trade was liberalized, technology transfer became easier etc.) but it should give some pause for thought. The literal interpretation of Table 14.4 suggests that Europe would have caught up much more quickly in the Golden Age but for the expansion of the state which presumably (we are not told) encouraged rent-seeking, a haemorrhage of talent from the private sector and/or tax disincentives to factor accumulation.

Fourth, alternatively, as Eichengreen (1993) suggests, perhaps the expansion of the welfare state in post-war Europe was part of the achievement of a social contract conducive to wage moderation and high investment which ushered in the Golden Age. In such a context, a larger government sector may even have played a role in sustaining rates of return not dissimilar to that of low direct taxes in a conventional new growth model (Rebelo, 1991).

Perhaps the right overall reaction to the authors' results in Table 14.4 is to regard them as provisional and not necessarily applying more widely.

I hope these comments will not be misinterpreted. I enjoyed the paper and found it very stimulating. As with all good research, it not only gives some answers but it also opens up a fascinating agenda for further research.

18

Comment

KJELL ERIK LOMMERUD

In this interesting paper, Hansson and Henrekson pursue a twofold aim. First, it summarizes empirical research on the 'catching up' effect in economic growth, second, it presents the authors' own work in the field. Their own research on the topic, in turn, draws on three separate studies. I will use most of the allotted space to comment upon these studies one by one.

'Catching up' has to do with the diffusion of technology, but what is the precise content of the hypothesis? Catching up seems to refer to a situation where less developed countries grow faster than more developed ones, implying that there is a convergence in productivity and income levels. To have 'catching up' it is therefore not only necessary that a technological 'follower' is able to digest technology developed in the technologically leading country: for true catching up to occur, *either* the leader must suddenly start to grow slower for some reason *or* there must be an *increase* in the follower's capability to digest technological improvements. Further, Hansson and Henrekson delineate between 'catching up' on the one hand and 'convergence' on the other. As they use the concepts, catching up refers to a diminished gap between a technological leader and the followers, whereas convergence refers to a reduction in the variance of productivity among a group of countries.

In this forest of similar concepts, what are we really interested in? Personally, I think the most intriguing question is what shapes a country's capability to digest technology developed elsewhere. This question should be delineated from the question of whether or not successful digestion of technological improvements in the end leads to faster or slower growth than in some other country. In their empirical work Hansson and Henrekson

While preparing this comment I have benefited from discussions with Hildegunn Nordås.

lie close to this view, since what they try to explain is the growth for instance in total factor productivity or in labour productivity with the initial gap in productivity levels between that country and a leader as one of the explanatory variables. But when the authors, in the catching-up tradition, focus on the technological gaps between a 'leader' and the 'followers', one wonders if a convergence measure would not have been equally suited. For instance, in a developing countries context, it can be equally interesting to study how a poor country is able to adopt technology used in countries a little richer, rather than the extent to which they can profit from technological advances in the world's 'leading' nation. Be this as it may, the authors are at least quite clear about what they do and do not.

If the catching-up hypothesis is investigated at a very aggregate level, the issue more or less collapses into a study of the rise and fall of US technological leadership. This might be an interesting question in itself, but somewhat removed from the question of following countries' capability to adopt foreign innovations. A very natural idea then becomes to disaggregate the level of analysis to the industry level. Who the technological leader is can then vary between the industries. This is precisely the idea behind the first of the three studies that are reported in their chapters. In this study, the focus is on catching up in the developed world. The data set contains information from fourteen industries in fourteen OECD countries for the time period 1970–85. In this study, the technology level is measured by total factor productivity, and not by the customary measure of labour productivity. This is a clear improvement.

Hansson and Henrekson group their industries in two categories. Nine industries are categorized as the tradables sector, whereas five industries are grouped together as the nontradables sector. The way technology is diffused may very well depend on whether or not the final output is internationally traded. However, once industry data are available I do not see the rationale for working at a higher than necessary level of aggregation. To the extent that aggregate data yield results that cannot be detected in the underlying less aggregate data, suspicion is of course aroused. Given that the tradables/nontradables dichotomy is going to be used, the assignment of industries to one of the two categories can be criticized. Since rich OECD countries are the object of study, electricity and gas probably are tradables, at least between neighbouring countries. Insurance is a service, but perhaps an example of a service that can be traded internationally, especially when it comes to business insurance.

Why should it matter for the diffusion of technology whether or not the final output of an industry is internationally traded? One reason is that international contacts and 'outwardness' give better information about foreign inventions. One then suspects that the correct measure for openness would be the extent to which the technology and production equipment used in an industry are traded internationally, not necessarily that the output is a tradable.[1] Another reason could be that international competition forces firms to be more competitive, and to adopt the latest improvements in technology. The distinction between tradables and nontradables can then be seen as a proxy for the degree of competitiveness in the industry. This makes sense, but perhaps more direct measures for the degree of competitiveness could have been used. Transport and real estate may very well be competitive industries even though competition only comes from the national market.

Hansson and Henrekson's main finding is that there is no catching up in tradables, but that there are such effects in non-tradables. Their contention is that the technology used in these industries has spread more slowly, so that by 1970 there was still an untapped potential for catching up. This is interesting, but some questions arise: if there was such an untapped potential by 1970, what happened in subsequent years that made the followers capable of catching up, given that they did not have this capability in the 1960s? And regarding the tradables sector, given that they had successfully digested all technology originally coming from the leader by 1970, how did they manage to grow at the same pace as the leading country in subsequent years? Did they manage to go from a situation of rapid digestion of foreign invented technology to one where they themselves pushed technology forward *en par* with the once technologically leading country?

---

[1] Hansson and Henrekson assume throughout that technical change is neutral, which of course is at odds with the idea that technology spreads through trade with machinery and other equipment.

The second study reported in this paper concerns what determines a country's 'social capability', social capability precisely referring to the ability to digest technology available in other countries. This time the authors work with data from eighty-one countries; most data are taken from the well-known Summers–Heston data base. Hansson and Henrekson focus on international openness and human capital formation as the two main determinants of 'social capability'.

Openness might matter for catching-up capability for several reasons. This we have already touched upon in discussing the tradables/nontradables distinction. If the possibility of importing technology through capital goods is important, one would want a measure for barriers to trade in intermediate and capital goods. This is exactly what is used in Knight, Loyaza and Villanueva (1993), an alternative effort to study the effect of trade orientation on growth. Their data on trade barriers in intermediate and capital goods are drawn from Lee (1993).

The openness measure used in these chapters is the sum of exports and imports as a fraction of GDP. One advantage of such a measure is that these are readily available figures. It should, though, be used with care. If one imports only to 'repackage' for export, or in some other way only increases the value of the goods marginally, this measure will be highly inflated. This is said to be relevant for instance for a country like Singapore. Singapore is not included in the current sample of countries, and I do not know if any country actually in the sample should be excluded for this reason. Another aspect of the chosen openness measure is that it will pick out resource exporting countries as very open, even though the main part of the economy can very well be totally isolated from the world economy. The sample includes several resource-rich countries, and Fig. 13.2 tells us, for example, how much of an outlier diamond-exporting Botswana is.

On the human capital side, the authors use a measure that weighs the adult literacy rate with mean years of schooling in the population aged 25 or more. Such a measure perhaps captures the level of basic skills in the population. If this measure captures the capability to digest technological innovations, I think it does so at low levels of development only. For OECD countries the number of scientists and engineers, outlays on

R&D, and the like, must be more natural candidates for a relevant human capital measure. One possibility then would be to rerun the regressions used here, but only using those countries in the sample that belong to the developing world.

The authors conclude that both 'a higher level of human capital and deeper integration into the world economy facilitate productivity growth by technological diffusion from leader to followers'. This is interesting. With this type of study, though, where one attempts to explain a country's behaviour by only a very few variables, one becomes worried about omitted explaining variables. For example, 'openness' may very well be a phenomenon that goes together with attitude to foreign investments, to multinationals, with tax rules, with education policy. The policy implications of the results therefore become unclear.

In the last study, the authors look at the role government expenditure plays in economic growth. Although arguments can be made both for government expenditure to increase and decrease growth, the authors study, in this part of the paper, nineteen OECD countries. One can perhaps argue that since these are all countries with high government spending, basic investments in infrastructure have already been made, while on the other hand taxes approach levels where they start really to have detrimental effects on growth. This suggests for this sample of countries that one would expect a negative relationship between government expenditure and growth. Catching-up here enters the analysis in that when explaining total factor productivity growth in the different countries, the catching-up factor is one of the explanatory variables other than government expenditure. The authors' result is that government spending, either as an absolute amount or as a share of GDP, has a highly significant negative effect on total factor productivity growth. Again, an interesting result. One possible avenue for future research would be to try to disaggregate the analysis. Do different kinds of government expenditure influence growth differently? Is there a difference between, for instance, government investment and consumption on one side and transfer payments on the other? If government expenditure influences growth only through the tax burden, perhaps tax variables rather than expenditure variables should be used? Do various tax forms influence growth differently? A particular point concerns unemployment benefits. In some countries rapidly growing unemployment has been a factor behind growth in public expenditure. Does this harm growth because of the required tax income to finance unemployment benefit—or is unemployment benefit only correlated with the fact that there has been a negative productivity shock?

In conclusion, the chapters deal with important questions and provide some interesting empirical results. The results seem to imply direct policy conclusions such as: emphasize education, emphasize international openness and competitive domestic markets, be careful with expansion in the public sector. In some ways the analysis improves on existing work by being more disaggregate. However, one could wish for more. The level of aggregation is still rather high, and the number of explanatory variables rather few. For practical and reliable policy conclusion one needs an even more detailed analysis. At least as a complement to this kind of macroanalysis, I believe we really need microanalytic studies of technology adaption and productivity growth on the firm and industry level. The role of macrostudies is perhaps to discover broad trends—that can eventually guide later microeconomic studies. A further advantage of macrostudies is of course that it is possible to include data from a very large number of countries; microstudies will probably have to focus on one country, or a few at the most.

References

Abramovitz, M. (1986), 'Catching Up, Forging Ahead, and Falling Behind', *Journal of Economic History* 66: 385–406.

Aghion, P. and Howitt, P. (1992), 'A Model of Growth through Creative Destruction', *Econometrica* 60(2): 323–51.

Alam, M. S. (1992), 'Convergence in Developed Countries: An Empirical Investigation', *Weltwirtschaftliches Archiv* 128(2): 189–201.

Bairam, E. (1989), 'Government Expenditure and Economic Growth: Reflections on Professor Ram's Approach, a New Framework and Some Evidence from New Zealand Time-Series Data', *Keio Economic Studies* 25(1): 59–66.

Barro, R. J. (1990), 'Government Spending in a Simple Model of Endogenous Growth', *Journal of Political Economy* 98(5): S103–25.

——(1991a), 'A Cross-Country Study of Growth, Saving, and Government', in B. D. Bernheim and J. B. Shoven (eds.), *National Saving and Economic Performance* (Chicago, IL: University of Chicago Press).

——(1991b), 'Economic Growth in a Cross Section of Countries', *Quarterly Journal of Economics* 106: 407–43.

——(1992), 'Human Capital and Economic Growth', in *Policies for Long-Run Growth*, proceedings from a symposium sponsored by The Federal Reserve Bank of Kansas City.

——and Lee, J. W. (1994), 'Sources of Economic Growth', *Carnegie Rochester Conference Series on Public Policy* 40: 1–46.

——and Sala-i-Martin, X. (1991), 'Convergence Across States and Regions', *Brookings Papers on Economic Activity*, 107–82.

————(1992), 'Convergence', *Journal of Political Economy* 100(2): 223–51.

Barth, J. R. and Bradley, M. (1988), *The Impact of Government Spending on Economic Activity* (National Chamber Foundation).

Baumol, W. J. (1986), 'Productivity Growth, Convergence, and Welfare', *American Economic Review* 76: 1072–85.

——Blackman, S. A. B. and Wolff, E. N. (1989), *Productivity and American Leadership* (Cambridge, MA: MIT Press).

Becker, G. S. (1964), *Human Capital* (New York: Columbia University Press).

Benhabib, J. and Spiegel, M. (1992), 'The Role of Human Capital and Political Instability in Economic Development', Economic Research

Report (New York: C. V. Starr Center for Applied Economics, New York University).

Broadberry, S. N. (1993), 'Convergence: What the Historical Record Shows', paper presented to CEPR Conference, Europe's Postwar Growth, Oxford.

Buchanan, J. M. (1980), 'Rent Seeking and Profit Seeking', in J. M. Buchanan, G. Tullock and R. Tollison (eds.), *Toward a Theory of a Rent Seeking Society* (Texas A. and M. University Press).

Cameron, D. (1982), 'On the Limits of the Public Economy', *Annals of the Academy of Political and Social Science* 459: 46–62.

Carr, J. L. (1989), 'Government Size and Economic Growth: A New Framework and Some Evidence from Cross-Section and Time-Series Data: Comment', *American Economic Review* 79(1): 267–80.

Cass, D. (1965), 'Optimum Growth in an Aggregative Model of Capital Accumulation', *Review of Economic Studies* 32: 233–40.

Coe, D. T. and Helpman, E. (1995), 'Economic Growth in a Cross-section of Countries', *European Economic Review* 39(5): 859–87.

Conte, A. and Darrat, A. F. (1988), 'Economic Growth and the Expanding Public Sector: A Reexamination', *Review of Economics and Statistics* 70(2): 322–30.

Crafts, N. F. R. (1992), 'Productivity Growth Reconsidered', *Economic Policy* 15: 388–426.

——and Toniolo, G. (1993), 'Postwar Growth: An Overview', paper presented to CEPR Conference, Europe's Postwar Growth, Oxford.

De Long, J. B. (1988), 'Productivity Growth, Convergence, and Welfare: Comment', *American Economic Review* 78: 1138–54.

Denison, E. F. (1967), *Why Growth Rates Differ* (Washington, D.C.: Brookings).

Dollar, D. and Wolff, E. N. (1988), 'Convergence of Industry Labor Productivity among Advanced Economies, 1963–1982', *Review of Economics and Statistics* 70: 549–58.

Dowrick, S. (1989), 'Sectoral Change, Catching Up and Slowing Down. OECD Post-War Economic Growth Revisited', *Economics Letters* 31: 331–5.

——(1992), 'Technological Catch Up and Diverging Incomes: Patterns of Economic Growth 1960–88', *Economic Journal* 102: 600–10.

——and Gemmel, N. (1991), 'Industrialisation, Catching Up and Economic Growth: A Comparative Study across the World's Capitalist Economies', *Economic Journal* 101: 263–75.

——and Nguyen, D.-T. (1987), 'Australia's Post-War Economic Growth: Measurement and International Comparison', working paper no. 160, Centre for Economic Policy Research, Australian National University, Canberra.

Dowrick, S. and Nguyen, D.-T. (1989), 'OECD Comparative Economic Growth 1950–85: Catching Up and Convergence', *American Economic Review* 79: 1010–30.

Durlauf, S. N. and Johnson, P. A. (1992), 'Local Versus Global Convergence Across National Economies', NBER working paper no. 3996.

Easterlin, R. A. (1981), 'Why Isn't the Whole World Developed?', *Journal of Economic History* 41(1): 1–19.

Easterly, W. and Rebelo, S. (1993), 'Fiscal Policy and Economic Growth', *Journal of Monetary Economics* 32(4): 417–58.

Edwards, S. (1992), 'Trade Orientation, Distortions and Growth in Developing Countries', *Journal of Development Economics* 39(1): 31–57.

——(1993), 'Openness, Trade Liberalization and Growth in Developing Countries', *Journal of Economic Literature* 31(3): 1358–93.

Eichengreen, B. (1993), 'Institutions and Economic Growth: Europe After World War II', paper presented to CEPR Conference, Europe's Postwar Growth, Oxford.

Engen, E. M. and Skinner, J. (1992), 'Fiscal Policy and Economic Growth', NBER working paper no. 4223.

Englander, A. S., Evenson, R. and Hanazaki, M. (1988), 'R&D, Innovation and the Total Factor Productivity Slowdown', *OECD Economic Studies* 11: 7–42.

Ethier, W. J. (1982), 'National and International Returns to Scale in Modern Theory of International Trade', *American Economic Review* 72(2): 389–405.

Gerschenkron, A. (1952), 'Economic Backwardness in Historical Perspective', in B. F. Hoselitz (ed.), *The Progress of Underdeveloped Areas* (Chicago, IL: University of Chicago Press).

Gordon, R. J. (1992), 'Comment on Crafts', *Economic Policy* 15: 387–426.

Gould, F. (1983), 'The Development of Public Expenditures in Western Industrialized Countries: A Comparative Analysis', *Public Finance* 38(1): 38–69.

Grier, K. B. and Tullock, G. (1989), 'An Empirical Analysis of Cross-National Economic Growth, 1951–80', *Journal of Monetary Economics* 24(2): 259–76.

Grossman, G. M. and Helpman, E. (1991), *Innovation and Growth in the Global Economy* (Cambridge, MA: MIT Press).

Gruen, F. H. (1986), 'How Bad Is Australia's Economic Performance and Why?', *Economic Record* 62: 180–93.

Gupta, D. K. (1990), *The Economics of Political Violence* (New York: Praeger).

Hansson, I. (1984), 'Marginal Cost of Public Funds for Different Tax

Instruments and Government Expenditures', *Scandinavian Journal of Economics* 86(2): 115–30.

Hansson, P. and Henrekson, M. (1994a), 'Catching Up in Industrialised Countries: A Disaggregated Study', *Journal of International Trade and Economic Development* 3(2): 129–46.

————(1994b), 'A New Framework for Testing the Effect of Government Spending on Growth and Productivity', *Public Choice* 81(3–4): 381–401.

————(1994c), 'What Makes a Country Socially Capable of Catching Up?', *Weltwirtschaftliches Archiv*, Band 130(4): 760–83.

Helliwell, J. F. (1992), 'Trade and Technical Progress', NBER working paper no. 4226.

Helpman, E. (1992), 'Endogenous Macroeconomic Growth Theory', *European Economic Review* 36(2): 237–67.

Holmes, J. M. and Hutton, P. A. (1990), 'On the Causal Relationship between Government Expenditures and National Income', *Review of Economics and Statistics* 72(1): 87–95.

ILO (1986), *The Challenge of Employment and Basic Needs in Africa* (Nairobi: Oxford University Press).

Kaldor, N. (1966), *Causes of the Slow Rate of Economic Growth of the United Kingdom: An Inaugural Lecture* (Cambridge: Cambridge University Press).

Katz, C. J., Mahler, V. A. and Franz, M. G. (1983), 'The Impact of Taxes on Growth and Distribution in Developed Capitalist Countries: A Cross-National Study', *American Political Science Review* 77(4): 871–86.

Katz, L. F. (1992), 'Commentary: Human Capital and Economic Growth', in *Policies for Long-run Growth*, proceedings from a symposium sponsored by The Federal Reserve Bank of Kansas City.

King, R. G. and Rebelo, S. (1990), 'Public Policy and Economic Growth: Developing Neoclassical Implications', *Journal of Political Economy* 98(5): S126–50.

Knight, M., Loyaza, N. and Vilanueva, D. (1993), 'Testing the Neoclassical Theory of Growth: A Panel Data Approach', *IMF Staff Papers* 40: 512–41.

Koopmans, T. C. (1965), 'On the Concept of Optimal Economic Growth', in *The Econometric Approach to Optimal Planning* (Amsterdam: North-Holland).

Kormendi, R. C. and Meguire, P. G. (1985), 'Macroeconomic Determinants of Growth: Cross-Country Evidence', *Journal of Monetary Economics* 16(2): 141–64.

Korpi, W. (1985), 'Economic Growth and the Welfare System: Leaky Bucket or Irrigation System?', *European Sociological Review* 1(2): 97–118.

Koskela, E. and Virén, M. (1992), 'Is There a Laffer Curve between Government Size and Private Output: Some Evidence from a Market Price Approach', research report no. 20, University of Turku.

Krasker, W. S., Kuh, E. and Welsch, R. E. (1983), 'Estimation for Dirty Data and Flawed Models', in Z. Griliches and M. D. Intriligator (eds.), *Handbook of Econometrics*, vol. 1 (Amsterdam: North-Holland).

Landau, D. (1983), 'Government Expenditure and Economic Growth: A Cross-Country Study', *Southern Economic Journal* 49(4): 783–92.

——(1986), 'Government and Economic Growth in the Less Developed Countries: An Empirical Study for 1960–1980', *Economic Development and Cultural Change* 35: 35–75.

Lazear, E. (1979), 'Why Is There Mandatory Retirement?', *Journal of Political Economy* 87: 1261–84.

——(1981), 'Agency, Earnings Profiles, Productivity and Hours Restrictions', *American Economic Review* 71: 606–20.

Lee, J.-W. (1993), 'International Trade, Distortions, and Long Run Economic Growth', *IMF Staff Papers* 40: 299–328.

Leamer, E. E. (1988), 'Measures of Openness', in R. E. Baldwin (ed.), *Trade Policy Issues and Empirical Analysis* (Chicago, IL: University of Chicago Press).

Levine, R. and Renelt, D. (1992), 'A Sensitivity Analysis of Cross-Country Growth Regressions', *American Economic Review* 82(4): 942–61.

Lewis, A. W. (1955), *The Theory of Economic Growth* (London: Allen & Unwin).

Liesner, T. (1989), *One Hundred Years of Economic Statistics* (London: *The Economist* Publications).

Lindauer, D. L. and Sabot, R. (1983), 'The Public/Private Wage Differential in a Poor Urban Economy', *Journal of Development Economics* 12(2): 137–52.

Lindbeck, A. (1983), 'Budget Expansion and Cost Inflation', *American Economic Review* 73(2): 285–96.

Lucas, R. E. (1988), 'On the Mechanics of Economic Development', *Journal of Monetary Economics* 22(1): 3–42.

Maddison, A. (1982), *Phases of Capitalist Development* (Oxford: Oxford University Press).

——(1987), 'Growth and Slowdown in Advanced Capitalist Economies', *Journal of Economic Literature* 25: 649–98.

——(1989), *The World Economy in the Twentieth Century* (Paris: OECD).

——(1991), *Dynamic Forces in Capitalist Development* (Oxford: Oxford University Press).

Mankiw, N. G., Romer, D. and Weil, D. N. (1992), 'A Contribution to the

Empirics of Economic Growth', *Quarterly Journal of Economics* 107(2): 407–37.

Marlow, M. L. (1986), 'Private Sector Shrinkage and the Growth of Industrialized Economies', *Public Choice* 49(2): 143–54.

Mincer, J. (1984), 'Human Capital and Economic Growth', *Economics of Education Review* 3(3): 195–205.

Mitchell, B. R. (1992), *European Historical Statistics, 1750–1988* (London: Macmillan).

Mueller, D. C. (1989), *Public Choice II* (Cambridge: Cambridge University Press).

Myrdal, G. (1960), *Beyond the Welfare State* (New Haven, CN: Yale University Press).

Nelson, R. R. and Phelps, E. S. (1966), 'Investment in Humans, Technological Diffusion, and Economic Growth', *American Economic Review* 56(1): 69–75.

——and Wright, G. (1992), 'The Rise and Fall of American Technological Leadership', *Journal of Economic Literature* 30: 1931–64.

North, D. C. and Thomas, R. P. (1973), *The Rise of the Western World: A New Economic History* (Cambridge: Cambridge University Press).

Olson, M. (1982), *The Rise and Decline of Nations* (New Haven, CN: Yale University Press).

——(1996), 'Distinguished Lecture on Economics in Government: Big Bills Left on the Sidewalk: Why Some Nations are Rich, and Others Poor', *Journal of Economic Perspectives* 10(2): 3–24.

O'Mahony, M. (1992), 'Productivity and Human Capital Formation in UK Manufacturing', discussion paper no. 28, National Institute of Economic and Social Research, London.

Pavitt, K. and Patel, P. (1988), 'The International Distribution and Determinants of Technological Activities', *Oxford Review of Economic Policy* 4(4): 35–55.

Prados de la Escocura, L. (1993), 'Growth and Convergence in Historical Perspective: Spain, 19th and 20th Centuries', working paper no. D-93004, Ministerio de Economia y Hacienda, Madrid.

Psacharopoulos, G. (1993), 'Returns to Investment in Education: A Global Update', World Bank, WPS 1067.

——and Tzannatos, Z. (1992), 'Latin American Women's Earnings and Participation in the Labor Force', World Bank, WPS 856.

Rao, V. V. B. (1989), 'Government Size and Economic Growth: A New Framework and Some Evidence from Cross-Section and Time-Series Data: Comment', *American Economic Review* 79(1): 272–80.

Rebelo, S. (1991), 'Long-Run Policy Analysis and Long-Run Economic Growth', *Journal of Political Economy* 99: 500–21.

Rivera-Batiz, L. A. and Romer, P. M. (1991), 'Economic Integration and Economic Growth', *Quarterly Journal of Economics* 106: 531–55.

Romer, P. M. (1986), 'Increasing Returns and Long-Run Growth', *Journal of Political Economy* 94(5): 1002–38.

——(1990), 'Endogenous Technological Change', *Journal of Political Economy* 98(5): S71–102.

——(1994), 'The Origins of Endogenous Growth', *Journal of Economic Perspectives* 8(1): 3–22.

Rosenberg, N. and Birdzell, L. E. (1986), *How the West Grew Rich: The Economic Transformation of the Industrial World* (New York: Basic Books).

Roubini, N. and Sala-i-Martin, X. (1992), 'Financial Repression and Economic Growth', *Journal of Development Economics* 39(1): 5–30.

Saunders, P. (1985), 'Public Expenditure and Economic Performance in OECD Countries', *Journal of Public Policy* 5(1): 1–21.

Schultz, T. W. (1960), 'Capital Formation in Education', *Journal of Political Economy* 68(4): 571–83.

Scully, G. W. (1988), 'The Institutional Framework and Economic Development', *Journal of Political Economy* 96(4): 652–62.

——and Slottje, D. J. (1988), 'Ranking Economic Liberty Across Countries', *Public Choice* 69(2): 121–52.

Smith, D. (1975), 'Public Consumption and Economic Performance', *National Westminster Bank Review* Nov.: 17–30.

Solow, R. M. (1956), 'A Contribution to the Theory of Economic Growth', *Quarterly Journal of Economics* 70(1): 65–94.

Stern, N. (1991), 'The Determinants of Growth', *Economic Journal* 101(404): 122–33.

Streissler, E. (1979), 'Growth Models as Diffusion Processes: II. Empirical Illustrations', *Kyklos* 32: 571–86.

Summers, R. and Heston, A. (1991), 'The Penn World Table (Mark 5): An Expanded Set of International Comparisons, 1950–1988', *Quarterly Journal of Economics* 106(2): 327–68.

Torstensson, J. (1994), 'Property Rights and Economic Growth: An Empirical Study', *Kyklos* 47(2): 231–47.

van Ark, B. (1993), 'International Comparisons of Output and Productivity', unpublished Ph.D. Thesis, University of Groningen.

Verspagen, B. (1991), 'A New Empirical Approach to Catching Up and Falling Behind', *Structural Change and Economic Dynamics* 2(2): 359–80.

——(1992), 'Endogenous Innovation in Neoclassical Growth Models: A Survey', *Journal of Macroeconomics* 14(4): 631–62.

Ward, M. (1985), *Purchasing Power Parities and Real Expenditure in the OECD* (Paris: OECD).

White, H. (1980), 'A Heteroscedasticity-Consistent Covariance Matrix Estimator and a Direct Test for Heteroscedasticity', *Econometrica* 48: 817–38.

Wolff, E. N. and Gittleman, M. (1993), 'The Role of Education in Productivity Convergence: Does High Education Matter?', in A. Szirmai, B. van Ark and D. Pilat (eds.), *Explaining Economic Growth* (Amsterdam: North-Holland).

World Bank (1987), *World Development Report 1987* (New York: Oxford University Press).

PART III

Governments, Unions and Economic Growth

KEVIN B. GRIER

19

Introduction

There is currently an explosion of interest in the role of institutional factors in secular economic growth. Standard neoclassical economic growth theory is devoid of institutions and predicts that, in long-run equilibrium, growth rates will be equal across countries, or at most will vary with differences in labour force participation. Recently though, Romer (1986) and Lucas (1987) have developed growth models that contain some form of increasing social returns. These endogenous growth models imply that institutional factors and government policies can systematically affect economic growth, and there is now a large empirical literature examining these phenomena. Despite recent progress, the empirical relevance of policies and institutions for long-run economic growth is still hotly debated. Levine and Renelt (1992) argue that 'the broad array of fiscal-expenditure variables, monetary-policy indicators, and political stability indexes considered by the profession are also not robustly correlated with growth'. I believe that Levine and Renelt are wrong. What they see as fragile results, I see as overly averaged data and inappropriately pooled countries in their regression analysis.

In this paper, I offer a brief general assessment and critique of the empirical literature on institutions and economic growth. I then present some new empirical evidence on how the relationship between government and labour affects macroeconomic performance. Specifically, I study the centralized bargaining hypothesis most closely associated with Calmfors and Driffill (1988) and the leftist–corporatist government–unionization growth linkage espoused by Cameron (1984), Crouch (1985), Lange and Garrett (1985, 1987), Garrett and Lange (1989) and Alvarez, Garrett and Lange (1991). I find almost no support for the Calmfors–Driffill notion that both extremely decentralized and extremely centralized countries perform better that those in the middle. I do find some limited evidence of a positive synergy between corporatist governments and higher unionization rates.

Beyond this, my results show that, contrary to the Levine and Renelt critique, government policy actions, specifically growth in government consumption and the variability of inflation, are quantitatively important determinants of economic growth in all the samples and models presented. I use this to argue that government's effect on growth is best measured looking at actual policies rather than at typologies.

The paper is organized as follows. Chapter 20 contains a brief summary of recent work on institutions and economic growth. Chapter 21 is a general assessment and critique of the empirical literature. Chapter 22 presents the basic model used in all my empirical work, while Chapter 23 considers new evidence on the centralization hypothesis and Chapter 24 contains my results on corporatism and unionization. Chapter 25 examines whether centralization or corporatism have indirect effects on growth. Chapter 26 looks at the most recent experiences of the countries where unionization data is available, and Chapter 27 is my conclusion.

20

Literature

20.1 The new growth theory

The neoclassical growth model (Solow 1956) implies that, in equilibrium, output growth will equal population growth and the exogenously given rate of technological progress. Government policies and institutions can only affect growth temporarily in the transition from one equilibrium to the other. The neoclassical model also implies that if capital is mobile, cross-country convergence should occur over time with richer countries growing slower and poorer ones 'catching up'.

By postulating socially non-diminishing returns to some productive factor, endogenous growth models open up the possibility of policies and institutions having a longer-term or even permanent influence on economic growth.[1] There is also the potential for persistent non-convergence due to cross-national policy differences. These models provide the intellectual foundation for the explosion of empirical work exploring the relationship between governance and growth.

20.2 General empirical studies

In this section I discuss the general, large-sample, studies found mainly in the US economics literature (e.g. Kormendi and Meguire, 1985; Grier and Tullock, 1989; Barro, 1991; Mankiw, Romer and Weil, 1992). These empirical papers concentrate mainly on the effects of policy variables on economic growth. The basic economic model in these papers usually includes investment, population growth, and initial wealth. Barro (1991) examines data from ninety-eight countries averaged into a single

---

[1] Papers by Paul Romer, Robert Solow and Howard Pack in the winter 1994 *Journal of Economic Perspectives* symposia on the new growth theory provide three interesting views on the development, strengths and shortcomings of these models.

cross-section. He finds that initial literacy raises growth rates and government consumption lowers growth. Barro also reports that measures of coups or political assassinations lower growth in his sample. Grier and Tullock (1989) use pooled cross-section time series data on 113 countries at five-year intervals. They find that the growth rate of government consumption and the variability of inflation significantly lower growth in their OECD country sub-sample. Grier and Tullock argue for exploiting the time-series information available for each country and show that coefficients of their model differ significantly across subsamples.

There are several authors who study more specific institutional hypotheses related to growth in industrialized countries. For example, Alesina and Roubini (1992) and Alesina, Cohen and Roubini (1992) examine the effect of elections on growth, and Alesina and Rodrick (1992) and Persson and Tabellini (1992) study how variations in the distribution of income influence economic growth.

There is also a large empirical literature on how central bank independence or type of government affect inflation and deficit outcomes (e.g. Roubini and Sachs, 1989; Grilli, Masciandaro and Tabellini, 1991; Cukierman, Webb and Neyapti, 1992). Alesina and Summers (1993) argue that variations in central bank independence are not correlated with cross-country variations in economic growth.

20.3 Centralized bargaining literature

Calmfors and Driffill (1988, referred to as CD from now on) relate centralized bargaining to macroeconomic performance via real wages. In decentralized systems, attempts by individual bargaining units to raise real wages will swiftly cause the firms involved to lose market share and the workers to lose jobs. Thus union effects on real wages will be mitigated. In highly centralized systems, wage bargainers are alleged to consider the social effects of their actions and restrain wage demands. The intermediate cases are where real wages will be affected most by labour. Given that higher real wages reduce economic performance, CD then claim the existence of the famous 'hump-shaped' non-linear relationship between centralization and economic performance. Countries at either extreme of the centralization spectrum are predicted to do better than those in the middle. The CD hypothesis has gained a great deal of acceptance with a minimum of empirical testing and support. Calmfors and Driffill themselves begin by simply reporting average outcomes for employment and unemployment across the three categories of countries. They then create a centralization variable that imposes a hump-shaped relationship and then examine gross rank correlations between it and various macro indicators on the seventeen countries they consider. Heitger (1987) is often cited in support of the hump hypothesis. He too creates a 'corporatism index' that forces a non-linear relationship and then uses it in regressions explaining GDP growth. He finds the variable to be in the 1970s subsample. Rowthorn (1992) presents regressions showing a hump-shaped relationship between the change in employment (and unemployment) from 1973 to 1985 and the CD centralization index. Rowthorn uses a monotonic index and its square to test for a non-linear relationship.

Finally, Dowrick (1993) extends the CD index over time and presents pooled cross-section time-series results supporting the CD hypotheses. Dowrick uses adjusted productivity as his dependent variable, and takes one observation per decade over the 1960–89 period for eighteen industrialized countries. Dowrick also considers whether ordinary least squares is the proper estimation technique for time-varying cross national datasets.

20.4 Left-corporatist governments and labour literature

Turning specifically to government–labour interactions and economic growth, Cameron (1984) and Crouch (1985) discuss the role of union strength and type of government on strike activity, inflation, unemployment, and economic growth in the OECD during the 1970s. The general argument is that an inclusive form of governance, labelled corporatism, brings labour into the policymaking process. Again, this makes labour more aware of the social consequences of their wage demands and generates restraint. The main differences between this view and Calmfors and Driffill are (1) labour strength is measured by a variety of indicators, rather than only centralized bargaining; and (2) the relationship between labour strength and economic performance is monotonic, but its sign is conditional on corporatist governance. In corporatist countries, stronger labour improves performance, in non-corporatist (liberal) countries the relationship is negative. Cameron and others devise rankings of labour strength and classifications of countries, but like Calmfors and Driffill, provide no formal statistical tests of the theory.

Lange and Garrett (LG 1985, 1987; Garrett and Lange, 1989) undertook a multiple regression analysis and concentrated on the hypothesis that union strength affects economic growth differently, depending on the national political context. In effect LG use a different tool to investigate a specific hypothesis with the same data used by Cameron. The data covered fifteen OECD countries averaged from 1974 to 1980 into a single data point for each country. The political variable and union strength variable were taken from indexes found in Cameron (1984). Lange and Garrett find support for the hypothesis of positive synergy between corporatist governments and strong labour movements, but their results are strongly challenged by Jackman (1987, 1989).[2] Hicks (1988) and Hicks and Patterson (1989) defend Lange and Garrett, creating a total of seven published papers studying the same fifteen-observation sample!

Most recently, Alvarez, Garrett and Lange (1991) extend the analysis to a pooled sample of annual data for sixteen countries between 1967 and 1984. They choose to classify governments by the 'annual percentage of cabinet portfolios held by parties of the left' and they use a union strength index derived from Cameron that does *not* vary over the sample period. Alvarez, Garrett and Lange find that strong unions and left party governments or weak unions and right party governments are the cases with the best economic performance.

The literature on centralized bargaining and government–labour interaction has not made any real impact on American

---

[2] Jackman claims that all democratic governments have the same or similar aims for the economy and that Lange and Garrett's empirical results are faulty, due to model mis-specification and an overly influential observation.

economics so far. The main reason why, beyond chauvinism, is theoretical. The necessary link between lower wages and improved macroeconomic performance that drives both models is difficult to support. Most US economists implicitly use a competitive model in their thinking and associate wages with marginal productivity. Most would be sceptical of the proposition that higher real wages, holding other factors constant, necessarily implies poorer economic performance.

Further, efficiency wage models due either to adverse selection or moral hazard in labour markets are not consistent with the Calmfors–Driffill hypothesis. In efficiency wage models, either talent or effort is a positive function of the wage. In Shapiro and Stiglitz (1984), for example, the efficiency wage is set to eliminate shirking, and equilibrium unemployment results as an unavoidable consequence of the assumed moral hazard. In any employment situation, it is difficult to see how the efficiency wage would be related to the size of the bargaining unit. In efficiency wage models, differences in the costs of shirking or the probability of job loss such as differences in unemployment benefits across countries can lead to systematic differences in wages for otherwise identical jobs.

21

Problems and Pitfalls

In this chapter, I address three specific problems or shortcomings in the existing empirical work. My goal is not to belittle previous work, but to show what direction future work might consider and to motivate the empirical approach I use in the rest of this paper. Indeed, Cameron and Calmfors and Driffill have done a tremendous amount to advance the study of the relation between governance and economic growth.

21.1 Omitted variables

Informal empirical studies (e.g. Cameron, 1984; Calmfors and Driffill, 1988) do not do a good job of imposing *ceteris paribus* conditions on their hypotheses. Even many of the econometric models ignore the basic implications of growth theory in specifying their statistical models. For example, Rowthorn (1992) explains the differences in the change in unemployment across seventeen countries with the level and square of the CD (monotonic) Centralization Index. He uses no productivity variables or measures of initial conditions. Alvarez, Garrett and Lange use a lot of esoteric variables in their growth regressions, but they have *no* measure of initial conditions to allow for convergence. Further, they fail to use any variables to measure investment or fluctuations in the labour force growth.

As is well known, if relevant variables are omitted from a model, coefficients on any included variables that are correlated with the omitted regressors will be biased and inconsistent.

21.2 Inappropriate variables

Frequently, variables defined by Cameron or Calmfors and Driffill that are qualitative in nature and innocuous in an informal setting are used without much consideration in subsequent statistical analyses. The CD centralization index is a good case in point. There are two separate issues here. The first is using a qualititative variable as a quantitative regressor. The second is creating variables that force a non-linear relationship rather than testing for any non-linearities. Calmfors and Driffill construct both a monotonic ranking and another that has a hump built in. In the latter case, the first and seventeenth countries are assigned 1.5, the second and sixteenth 3.5 and so on to the middle country (New Zealand), which is uniquely assigned the number 17. Austria and the USA have the same number, as do Switzerland and Sweden.

CD and Heitger use a 'pre-humped' centralization index as an explanatory variable, while Rowthorn and Dowrick use the level and square of a monotonic centralization index. While either type of variable is ill-suited for a regression analysis, it is always preferable to test for, rather than impose, a non-linear relationship.

There are similar problems in the Lange and Garrett line of research. For example, left government is defined as the average percentage of cabinet portfolios held by left parties in each country. A linear regression specification requires a constant partial derivative; an increase from 10 per cent to 20 per cent in left cabinet portfolios must have the same marginal effect as an increase from 45 per cent to 55 per cent. This cannot be correct. A country with over a 50 per cent average of left-party ministers would have an actual left party government or left parties coalition government for some of the sample. Further, the union variable used is the sum of the percentage of the labour force unionized and a 'centralization of labour organization' index where each component is measured in standard deviations from the sample mean. This is a doubly manufactured variable. The centralization index itself is meant to be qualitative and not indicative of a proportional linear relationship, and the method used to sum the two components is arbitrary.

Qualitative variables should be handled with dummy variables that do not pre-impose symmetry or some pre-conceived relationship between the categories. Any analysis where the researcher both creates idiosyncratic index variables and then performs hypothesis tests using them has to be regarded with serious concern.

21.3 Overaveraged data

Though Dowrick (1993) is a welcome exception, most empirical studies of political influences on economic growth have not exploited the time-series properties of their data. Rather, they simply average whatever data is available for each country and then estimate a single, one observation per country, cross-sectional regression. This procedure is unfortunate for two reasons. First, it throws away a tremendous amount of information. Union densities vary over time as well as across countries; why not exploit that fact and gain efficiency in estimation? Second, with only one observation per country, very dissimilar countries frequently are forced to share the same coefficients. Grier and Tullock (1989), in models using one observation every five years, show that the growth process differs significantly across continents. Specifically, OECD, Africa, Asia, and South America all have a unique set of model coefficients and cannot validly be pooled into a single sample.

It is for this reason that I am not persuaded by the Levine and Renelt claim that government policies are not robustly correlated with economic growth. They use one observation per country and between 80 and 100 countries in their regressions. They then show that by including some variables or excluding others, policy variables change from significant to insignificant. Yet, their sample is inappropriately grouped together to begin with. Why should we be disturbed about unstable estimated coefficients when the sample cannot be expected to have the same coefficient describe the behaviour of each country even using the theoretically true model?

In the statistical work that follows below, I try to take these problems into account. I use a standard economic growth model as the basis of my statistical model. I capture, as best I can, the insights of the literature with qualitative dummy variables rather than quantitative index variables. I use data on union densities that vary over time and exploit the time-series properties of the data.

22

Data and Basic Model

The economic data used here come from Summers and Heston and cover the 1950–88 period. In order not to throw away information by over-averaging, I take five-year averages of the data, giving eight observations on each country. Since the data stop in 1988, the last observation for each country is a three-year average. Dropping this last time period does not substantively change any of the results reported below. The dependent variable in this study is real total GDP growth in 1985 international prices.

22.1 Variables

The model I use here is based on what has become the basic empirical model in the economics literature which implies that convergence effects, labour force growth and investment are the baseline factors that influence GDP growth.[3] These forces are represented by the following three variables:

1. *Initial real per-capita GDP*. This variable is included to capture convergence effects. With a fixed technology exhibiting diminishing returns to scale, poorer countries with a smaller capital stock should grow faster, 'catching up' to richer countries. This coefficient should be negative; richer countries will have slower growth. This result does not always hold for all countries and time periods, but seems generally confirmed for the industrial countries in the post war period.

2. *Investment*. While initial wealth differences measure the scope for catch-up by capturing differences in the marginal product of capital across countries, the actual rate of investment at any given marginal productivity will also affect growth in the

---

[3] Barro (1991) emphasizes these three factors. Levine and Renelt (1992) are sceptical even of the empirical relevance of investment

medium term. I use investment as a fraction of GDP in the regressions below. The Heston and Summers data group government and private sector investment together in a single variable.[4]

3. *Population growth.* Neoclassical growth theory predicts that equilibrium growth rates will be equal across countries, barring differences in labour force growth, which should create equal proportional changes in GDP growth. Population growth is used as a proxy for labour force growth here, and a positive coefficient near 1.00 is expected.

I also include policy variables that are, in my opinion, under government control over periods as short as five years, and that have proven to be significant factors in previous research. These variables are:

4. *Growth of government.* The variable used here is the growth of government final consumption as a percentage of GDP. Since this variable excludes government investment expenditures on infrastructure, a negative coefficient is predicted. I use the growth in government, rather than the level, because I do not want to impose the restriction that an increase in government size permanently lowers growth.[5]

5 and 6. *Inflation.* New Keynesian models with nominal rigidities imply that trend inflation can influence output. Further, there is still a lot of evidence that people expect inflation to be non-neutral. I use the *first difference of inflation* as a monetary policy regressor. Further, Hayek (1944) and Friedman (1977) argue that uncertain inflation increases the dispersion of relative prices and can lower economic efficiency and growth.[6] I use the

[4] Hansson and Henrekson (1993), using OECD data on fourteen OECD countries, are able to separate private and government investment. They find government investment does not raise private productivity growth, but that educational expenditures do.

[5] Engen and Skinner (1992) treat government consumption as an endogenous regressor, but also find significant negative effects. Hansson and Henrekson (1993) show that government consumption reduces private productivity growth.

[6] Grier and Perry (1993) use bivariate GARCH-M models to test whether average inflation or inflation uncertainty has real effects in the USA. We find inflation uncertainty is the variable that matters. This result is confirmed in a very different experiment here, as the standard deviation of inflation is consistently significant and the change in inflation is not.

TABLE 22.1. *Economic Growth in the OECD, 1951–1988*

Variable	Eq. 1 (OLS)	Eq. 2 (GLS)
Intercept	3.49	3.97
	(6.91)	(9.46)
Initial real per capita GDP	−0.00026	−0.00029
	(6.12)	(7.32)
Investment (%GDP)	0.0787	0.0672
	(4.85)	(4.31)
Population growth	0.8854	0.8319
	(5.93)	(6.47)
Δ in inflation	0.0093	0.0066
	(0.23)	(0.21)
Inflation variability	−0.0533	−0.0661
	(2.77)	(3.53)
Growth of govt. consumption (%GDP)	−0.4434	−0.3827
	(7.00)	(8.42)
R^2 (OLS)/log-likelihood (GLS)	0.654	631.28

Note: There are 8 five-year (except the final one which is a three-year average (1986–88)) average observations per country (N = 24 × 8 = 192). Seven time-period dummies are estimated, but not reported, in each equation above. Numbers in parentheses are *t*-statistics. Method of estimation in equation 1 is OLS with White's (1980) heteroscedasticity-consistent covariance matrix. Method of estimation in equation 2 is GLS with country-specific error variances and serial correlation.

standard deviation of the inflation rate over each five-year period as a second variable representing monetary policy.[7]

I use a statistical model that employs feasible generalized least squares to account for serial correlation and heteroscedasticity in the data. The specific model is well explained by Kmenta (1986, pp 618–21) and Greene (1993, pp. 448–56). I include time-period dummies in each equation. Since a large part of the

---

[7] A better measure of monetary policy uncertainty would be the standard deviation of money shocks, but the Heston and Summers data does not contain money-supply variables.

empirical work attempts to group countries into homogeneous categories, I do not include individual country dummies in the equations. The model described above is not problem free. There clearly are potential problems with endogenous regressors, and the model has not been derived in a way to allow structural interpretations of the coefficients. At most we can identify any robust partial correlations in the datasets used below.

22.2 OECD results

Table 22.1 contains OLS and GLS estimations of the basic model for the full sample of OECD countries. The growth rate of population and the growth of the capital stock (that is, investment) are both positive and significant as the standard economic growth model predicts. In both models, the coefficient on population growth is not significantly different from 1.0. Initial wealth is negative and significant, indicating a convergence effect in the OECD countries. A 1.0 standard deviation increase in initial per capita GDP corresponds to a 0.5 standard deviation decline in real GDP growth.

With respect to government policy variables, the first difference of inflation is completely insignificant, but the standard deviation is negative and significant. More variable inflation is associated with slower economic growth. The coefficient (−0.0661 in equation 2) implies that a 1.0 standard deviation increase in inflation volatility is associated with about a 0.2 standard deviation decline in real GDP growth. Growth in government consumption's share in GDP also significantly lowers growth. Here a 1.0 standard deviation increase in government growth is associated with about a 0.40 standard deviation decline in real GDP growth.

The OLS and GLS coefficients are quite similar, though the OLS model fails heteroscedasticity and serial correlation tests. The OLS model explains about 65 per cent of the variation in economic growth across the twenty-four countries and 8 five-year intervals. With this basic model as a guide, I now turn to consider the effect of centralized bargaining on economic growth.

23

Centralized Bargaining and Economic Growth

In this section, I examine the Calmfors–Driffill (CD) hypothesis in the context of the statistical model introduced above. Rather than actually using some index variable that imputes falsely precise differences between countries in my regression analysis, I take a simpler, dummy variable approach. Given that CD argue that either extremely decentralized or extremely centralized countries will do better, I define a dummy variable that equals 1.0 for the four most centralized and the four least centralized countries according to CD. They are: Austria, Norway, Sweden and Denmark (most centralized), and Canada, USA, Switzerland and Japan (least centralized).[8] I also use separate dummy variables for high centralization and low centralization.

The results are reported in Table 23.1. Equation 1 uses only initial per-capita GDP and the eight-country dummy variable. The CD effect is notably absent here. The t-statistic on the dummy variable is virtually zero. Equation 2 shows why. Here I use one dummy variable for the decentralized countries and another for the centralized ones. On average, Canada, the USA, Switzerland and Japan grew about 1 percentage point faster than their initial wealth level alone would predict. This effect is significant at the 0.01 level. The variable for Austria, Norway, Sweden and Denmark is actually negative, but not significant.

Equation 3 puts the two dummy variables in the full growth model used in Table 22.1. The Table 22.1 variables have the same signs, magnitudes and significance levels. The decentralized country dummy variable is still positive and significant, while the centralized country dummy remains insignificant. Given the

---

[8] Soskice (1991) argues that Switzerland and Japan are more centralized than CD claim.

TABLE 23.1. *Centralization of Bargaining and Economic Growth in the OECD, 1951–1988*

Variable	Eq. 1	Eq. 2	Eq. 3
Intercept	6.11	6.34	4.13
	(23.3)	(24.4)	(10.2)
Initial real per capita GDP	−0.00024	−0.00033	−0.00037
	(5.25)	(6.66)	(8.12)
Investment (%GDP)	—	—	0.0677
			(4.06)
Population growth	—	—	0.8507
			(6.40)
Δ in inflation	—	—	0.0111
			(0.37)
Inflation variability	—	—	−0.0633
			(3.41)
Growth of govt. consumption (%GDP)	—	—	−0.3907
			(8.06)
Dummy for high and low centralization	−0.0027	—	—
	(0.10)		
Dummy for low centralization	—	1.180	0.7487
		(2.74)	(2.43)
Dummy for high centralization	—	−0.310	0.2715
		(1.54)	(1.46)
Log-likelihood	593.43	599.40	635.47

Note: Low Centralization: Canada, USA, Switzerland, Japan. High Centralization: Austria, Norway, Sweden, Denmark. There are eight observations per country. Seven time-period dummies are estimated, but not reported, in each equation above. Numbers in parentheses are *t*-statistics. Method of estimation is GLS with country specific error variances and serial correlation.

policy-augmented economic growth theory model, a time-varying sample and simpler centralization variables, there is little support for the Calmfors–Driffill hypothesis. The four least centralized countries do grow faster than otherwise would be predicted (about 0.75 percentage points faster), but there is no evidence of a 'hump' here. These results also do not confirm the ancillary CD hypothesis that high centralization is better than low centralization, which is still better than intermediate centralization.[9]

---

[9] CD's 'revised' hump-shaped indices embody this exact ancillary hypothesis.

24

Corporatism, Union Density, and Economic Growth

Consider now the effects of union density on economic growth. I have data on union density for sixteen OECD countries from 1970 through 1985, taken from D'Agostino (1992).[10] I use four time periods per country, 1971–5, 1976–80, 1981–5 and 1986–8. In each case I use the union density figure from the year before the beginning of the period (1970, 1975, 1980, 1985) to lessen the possibility of simultaneity bias.

Again, rather than using variables that are author-created indices or that are ill-suited to linear regression analysis (index of labour organization, number of left cabinet portfolios), I simply use a dummy variable that equals 1.0 for the eight countries in the D'Agostino sample that are labelled corporatist by Crouch (1985). These countries are: Austria, Denmark, Finland, Germany, the Netherlands, Norway, Sweden and Switzerland. The rest (non-corporatist part) of the sample countries are: Australia, Belgium, Canada, France, Italy, Japan, the UK and the USA. In Table 24.1, I first investigate whether there is any general effect of union density on growth, then turn to the Cameron–Crouch model.

Equations 1 and 2 in Table 24.1 test for the existence of a simple relationship between union density and economic growth. There are four observations on each of the sixteen countries for a total of sixty-four data points. The results show that there is no significant linear or non-linear effect of union density on real GDP growth in these countries. The other variables continue to have the same general magnitudes and significance levels as in the full 192-observation sample used in Tables 22.1 and 23.1.

Equation 3 in Table 24.1 is my test of the Cameron–Crouch hypothesis that corporatist governments and higher union

---

[10] The data come from Table 2.10 on page 48. D'Agostino reports two sets of figures for Sweden. I use the average of the two.

TABLE 24.1. *Corporatism, Union Density, and Economic Growth in 16 OECD countries, 1971–1988*

Variable	Eq. 1	Eq. 2	Eq. 3
Intercept	2.68	3.32	2.54
	(4.19)	(3.62)	(4.46)
Initial real per capita GDP	−0.00027	−0.00028	−0.00017
	(5.99)	(6.18)	(4.61)
Investment (%GDP)	0.0933	0.0915	0.1064
	(8.25)	(8.15)	(13.3)
Population growth	1.2312	1.2063	0.7818
	(10.6)	(10.3)	(8.90)
Δ in inflation	−0.0374	−0.0289	−0.0695
	(1.28)	(0.99)	(2.60)
Inflation variability	−0.0830	−0.0833	−0.0718
	(4.99)	(5.25)	(5.49)
Growth of govt. consumption (%GDP)	−0.2980	−0.2988	−0.2832
	(5.54)	(5.56)	(6.81)
Initial union density	−0.0017	−0.0205	−0.0147
	(0.61)	(0.95)	(2.62)
Initial union density squared	—	0.0002	—
		(0.87)	
Dummy for corporatist country	—	—	−1.3335
			(4.63)
Corporatist country × initial density	—	—	0.0210
			(3.15)
Log-likelihood	254.09	254.47	265.85

Note: Corporatist: Austria, Denmark, Finland, Germany, Netherlands, Norway, Sweden, Switzerland. Non-corporatist: Australia, Belgium, Canada, France, Italy, Japan, UK, USA. There are four observations per country. Three time-period dummies are estimated, but not reported, in each equation above. Numbers in parentheses are *t*-statistics. Method of estimation is GLS with country-specific error variances and serial correlation.

density together can promote economic growth. Here the coefficient on union density is now negative and significant (−0.0147, *t*-statistic = 2.6). The corporatist government dummy variable is also negative and significant (−1.333, *t*-statistic = 4.6). The interaction term (corporatist dummy × union density) is positive and significant (0.0210, *t*-statistic = 3.1). The net effect of union density in corporatist countries is given by the sum of the coefficient on union density and the coefficient on the interaction term, which is (0.0210 − 0.0147) equal to 0.0063.

The interpretation of this equation is somewhat complex, but greatly simpler than the Lange and Garrett models. Holding constant the effects of union density and the basic growth model variables, corporatist countries grow about 1.3 percentage points slower than their non-corporatist counterparts. Every 10 percentage point increase in union density *lowers* the non-corporatist country growth rate by about 0.15 percentage points, but *raises* corporatist country growth rates by about 0.06 percentage points. These results are illustrated in Fig. 24.1.

The intersection of the corporatist–union density curve with the non-corporatist–union density curve occurs at a density of 38 per cent. In a sense, this is the break-even point between these two classes of social arrangements. The curves in Fig. 24.1 have the sample countries labelled at their 1985 density levels. Note that there are both corporatist countries with union densities less than 38% in 1985 and non-corporatist countries with 1985

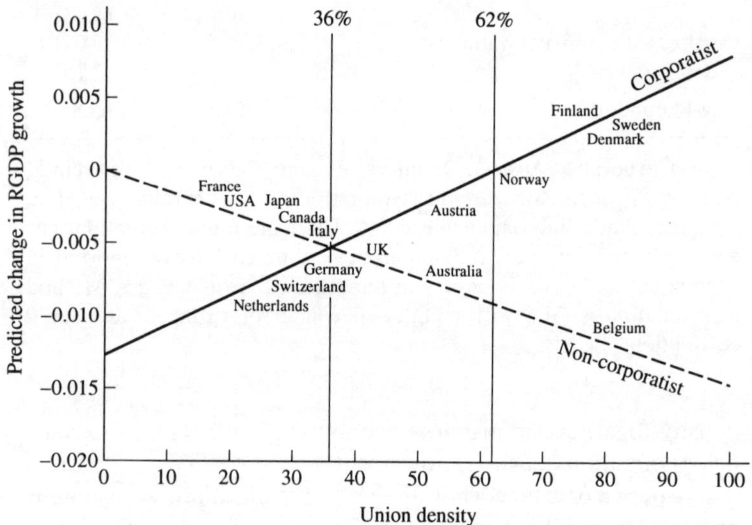

FIG. 24.1. *Corporatism, Unionization and Real GDP Growth in Sixteen OECD Countries, 1971–1988*

union densities greater than 38%. While the UK, Germany, and Switzerland are very close to the indifference point, the Netherlands, Australia and especially Belgium are significant outliers. A literal interpretation of my results is that, taking union density as given, these countries have the wrong form of government!

Taking corporatist status as given, the growth maximizing union density is 0.00 per cent in non-corporatist countries and 100 per cent in the corporatist group. The actual 1985 group averages are 38.2 per cent in the non-corporatist group (32.1 per cent if Belgium is excluded) and 56.8 per cent in the corporatist group. Among the non-corporatists, France, Italy, Japan, the UK and the USA all have unionization rates that decline over this 1970–85 sample which implies, *ceteris paribus*, improvement in economic growth. Australia's and Belgium's rates increase and Canada's is steady. In the corporatist sample, Sweden, Finland and Denmark have rising (growth enhancing) densities over the sample, while Switzerland, Germany and Norway have steady rates. Densities have declined in Austria and the Netherlands. The estimated model implies that the only chance for union density to actually have a net positive impact on growth is when density rates are above 62 per cent in a corporatist country. This point is represented by a vertical line in Fig. 24.1. As the figure shows, Finland, Sweden and Denmark are the only countries in the net positive portion of the graph as of 1985.

I am not totally comfortable with the corporatist classification scheme I use, and am frankly surprised by the strength of these results. Ignoring the corporatist labelling, the results can be interpreted as follows. After controlling for starting position, investment, population growth and government policies, France, Italy, Japan, Canada and the USA as a group have done significantly better than Australia, Belgium and the UK. The differences in growth performance between these countries is negatively correlated with differences in their union densities.

Similarly, holding constant the effects of initial wealth, investment, population growth and government policy, Sweden, Finland, Denmark and Norway have grown faster than Austria, Germany, the Netherlands, and Switzerland. The difference here is that better growth is positively correlated with union density.

I can also use this D'Agostino dataset to address some possible objections to my results in the previous section by giving my centralization variables another chance. In the results in Table 23.1, I use all the OECD countries, while Calmfors and Driffill only rank seventeen countries. I also use data from the 1950s, which CD do not consider. The data under consideration in Table 24.1 contain sixteen of the seventeen CD countries and start in 1971.[11] Re-estimating equation 3 from Table 23.1 with the dummy variables for the four most centralized and four least centralized countries on the Table 24.1 dataset produces the following result (t-statistics in parentheses):

$$\%\Delta RGDP = 3.08 - 0.0003(\text{Initial Wealth}) + 0.086(\text{Investment})$$
$$(5.6) \quad (7.1) \qquad\qquad (8.1)$$
$$+ 0.966(\%\Delta \text{Population}) - 0.04(\Delta \text{Inflation})$$
$$(8.5) \qquad\qquad (1.8)$$
$$- 0.09(\sigma \text{Inflation}) + 0.149(\text{Highly Centralized})$$
$$(5.5) \qquad\qquad (1.1)$$
$$+ 0.443(\text{Highly Decentralized})$$
$$(2.81)$$

Again, the 4 least centralized countries have a slightly (about 0.4 percentage points here compared to 0.75 in the full OECD sample) significantly higher growth rate holding the other regressors constant, but the hump is still missing. The most centralized countries are not significantly different from the rest of the sample. If the CD dummy variables are added to the corporatist–union density model of equation 3 in Table 24.1, the variables reported in the table retain their displayed signs and significance and the centralization variables are both completely insignificant.

Of course, as Calmfors and Driffill point out, the corporatist net is a wide one, and many scholars have difficulty seeing the similarities in the included countries (say, Sweden and Switzerland). As noted above, I share some of these reservations,

---

[11] The excluded country in the D'Agostino data is New Zealand. New Zealand is in the exact middle of the CD centralization ranking.

TABLE 24.2. *Union Density and Economic Growth in 10 OECD Countries, 1951–1988*

Variable	Eq. 1 1951–88	Eq. 2 1961–88
Intercept	2.27	1.49
	(3.60)	(2.59)
Initial real per capita GDP	–0.00033	–0.00029
	(5.42)	(5.46)
Investment (%GDP)	0.1238	0.1247
	(7.35)	(9.13)
Population growth	1.172	1.2330
	(3.36)	(5.28)
Δ in inflation	0.0003	–0.0451
	(0.04)	(0.82)
Inflation variability	–0.0551	–0.0729
	(2.47)	(2.78)
Growth of govt. consumption (%GDP)	–0.3639	–0.3561
	(6.01)	(5.68)
Initial union density	0.0097	0.0105
	(1.84)	(2.39)
Log-likelihood	287.24	238.94

Note: There are eight observations per country in eq. 1 (N = 10 × 8 = 80) and six observations per country in eq. 2 (N = 60). Time-period dummies are estimated, but not reported, in each equation above. Numbers in parentheses are *t*-statistics. Method of estimation is GLS with country-specific error variances and serial correlation. Countries in the sample are Austria, Denmark, France, Germany, Italy, Netherlands, Norway, Sweden, Switzerland, UK.

but my results do largely confirm the Lange and Garrett results using drastically different methods.[12]

There is, however, at least one other data set at my disposal. Visser (1989) contains union density data for ten OECD countries that I have compiled from 1950 through 1985. I use the

[12] There are two major differences between my work and that of Alvarez, Garrett and Lange. First, they stress left government strength and I stress corporatist status. Second their political variable moves over time and their union variable does not while my political variable does not move over time and my union variable does.

same five-year average datapoints and measure union density in the year before the first year included in each observation just as was done above. The countries in the Visser data are Austria, Denmark, France, Germany, Italy, the Netherlands, Norway, Sweden, Switzerland and the UK. Regression results for the 1951–88 period (eighty observations) and the 1961–88 period (sixty observations) are given in Table 24.2.

In these data, there is some evidence of a simple, modest but significantly positive, linear relationship between initial union density and subsequent GDP growth. In the full sample, the coefficient on density implies that every 10 percentage point increase in density raises GDP growth by about 0.1 percentage points. This effect is only significant at the 0.10 level. In the 1961–88 sub-sample, the effect of density is almost identical and is now significant at the 0.05 level. Three of these countries are *not* classified as corporatist (France, Italy and the UK) but yet the effect of union density in this sample is positive and (barely) significant. Using the corporatist dummy variable and density interaction term as in Table 24.1 above does not reveal any differences between the corporatist and non-corporatist countries in this sample. Union density matters, but not in the way predicted, and not in the way found above with a different sample.

25

Country Classifications and Government Policies

I have shown that inflation variability and government consumption growth are consistently negative and significant variables in OECD economic growth models. I have also argued that the direct evidence for the importance of bargaining arrangements or union density or corporatist governance is rather weak. Here I investigate whether centralized and decentralized

TABLE 25.1. *Does Centralization have Indirect Effects on Economic Growth?*

Country type	Investment		Growth of government consumption		Variability of inflation	
	Mean	Std. dev.	Mean	Std. dev.	Mean	Std. dev.
High (N = 32)	26.76	5.10	0.0030	0.0175	0.0482	0.0402
Medium (N = 72)	24.97	5.23	−0.0032	0.0155	0.0543	0.0413
Low (N = 32)	24.19	6.14	−0.0083	0.0188	0.0414	0.0463
Excluded (N = 56)	23.89	4.82	0.0057	0.0237	0.0773	0.0574

H_0: Investment in high and low centralization countries is the same. t-statistic = 1.82 (0.08)

H_0: Growth of govt. in high and low centralization countries is the same. t-statistic = 2.49 (0.02)

H_0: Inflation variability is the same in the excluded and included countries. t-statistic = 3.66 (0.01)

TABLE 25.2. *Does Corporatism have Indirect Effects on Economic Growth?*

Country type	Investment		Growth of government consumption		Variability of inflation	
	Mean	Std. dev.	Mean	Std. dev.	Mean	Std. dev.
Corporatist (N = 64)	27.53	5.05	0.0007	0.0175	0.0519	0.0415
Liberal (N = 64)	23.35	5.23	−0.0006	0.0164	0.0454	0.0430
Excluded (N = 64)	23.59	4.62	0.0047	0.0229	0.0762	0.0554

H_0: Investment in corporatist and liberal countries is the same.
t-statistic = 4.59 (0.01)

H_0: Growth of govt. in corporatist and liberal countries is the same.
t-statistic = 2.44 (0.02)

H_0: Inflation variability is the same in the excluded and included countries.
t-statistic = 3.82 (0.01)

H_0: Growth of govt. is the same in the excluded and included countries.
t-statistic = 2.60 (0.02)

countries, along with corporatist and liberal countries, systematically differ in their policy outcomes. That is, do these factors affect economic growth by influencing some or all of the significant explanatory variables in my statistical model?

I begin in Table 25.1 with the centralization classification of Calmfors and Driffill. The sample is divided into four groups. I distinguish between the four most highly centralized countries, the nine countries in the middle, the four least centralized countries and the seven OECD countries that Calmfors and Driffill do not consider. The most and least centralized countries differ in two significant respects. First, government consumption growth is much higher in the most centralized countries. Second, investment is higher in these most centralized countries. The first of these effects lowers growth; the second raises it.

It is also interesting to note how similar the excluded countries are, at least in terms of the variables considered here. The only significant difference between the seven excluded countries and the Calmfors and Driffill sample is that inflation is significantly more variable.

Table 25.2 repeats the experiment using the corporatist–liberal classification of the sixteen countries in the D'Agostino union density sample, along with the other eight OECD countries. The same general pattern emerges here. Investment is higher in the corporatist group, which tends to raise growth, but government growth is also higher, which is associated with lower GDP growth. There are now two factors that distinguish the eight excluded countries. They have significantly more variable inflation and faster government growth than the sixteen countries that have systematic data on union densities over time.

The significant differences in government policies between corporatist/centralized countries and non-corporatist/decentralized countries found here indicate that these institutional factors may have significant indirect effects on economic growth. This line of reasoning deserves much further study, but I will not pursue it here. In the next chapter, I consider the most recent (1984–8) growth performances of the sixteen countries in the D'Agostino sample.

26

Recent Growth Experience

Fig. 26.1 shows the annual average real GDP growth in the last five years of the Summers & Heston data (1984–8) for the sixteen countries for which I have union density data. The sample average growth rate is 3.14 per cent. There are eight countries with below average growth, Austria, Belgium, Denmark, France, Germany, the Netherlands, Sweden and Switzerland. The eight above average growth countries are Australia, Canada, Finland, Italy, Japan, Norway, the UK and the USA. Italy, Finland, Canada and Switzerland are very close to

TABLE 26.1. *Factors Explaining Growth Differences in 16 OECD Countries from 1984–1988*

Variable	Low growth group average	High growth group average	t-test for no inter-group difference
Real GDP growth	2.408%	3.876%	6.92
Investment (%GDP)	23.827	25.439	0.69
Growth of govt consumption	–0.011	–0.125	0.31
Std. deviation of inflation	0.160	0.106	2.72
Union density in 1985	50.72	44.26	0.51
Change in union density from 1975 to 1985	–0.041	–0.076	0.39
CD centralization index (Low number means more centralized)	6.875	11.125	1.74

Note: Low growth group is Austria, Belgium, Denmark, France, Germany, Netherlands, Sweden and Switzerland. High growth group is Australia, Canada, Finland, Japan, Italy, Norway, UK and USA.

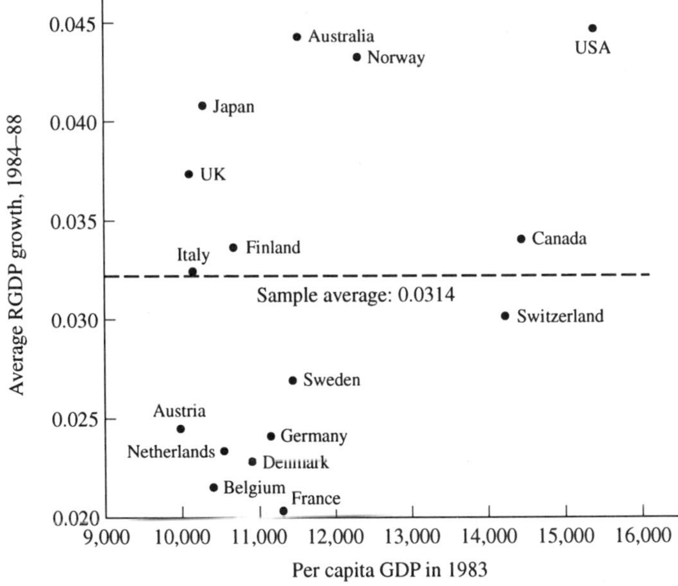

FIG. 26.1. *Economic Growth in Sixteen OECD Countries, 1984–1988*

the overall average. In this section, I group the above and below average countries into two groups and see whether any factors can be found that differ between these groups.

Before considering any statistical tests, note that of the six highest growth countries, five are non-corporatist, and of the six lowest growth countries, five are corporatist. High growth in Norway and low growth in France are the only factors that make this correlation less than perfect. I now perform some simple statistical tests for significant differences between these groups.

Table 26.1 reports my tests. First, the apparent difference in performance between the two groups is real. The top eight countries averaged 3.8%, the bottom eight only 2.4% and the difference is highly significant. The table shows that initial wealth, investment, government consumption growth, unionization and the change in unionization do not differ significantly between these groups. Inflation is significantly more variable in the lower growth group (at the 0.05 level), and the lower growth group has more centralized bargaining and a more fractionalized legislature, though these differences are only significant at the 0.10 level.

27

Conclusion

The empirical work reported here reveals three things. First, government policies affect economic growth in the OECD countries. The growth of government consumption and the variability of inflation are negative and significant factors in every regression reported in the paper. I believe that Levine and Renelt's rejection of this hypothesis is due mainly to their poor experimental design that forces drastically different countries to share a common set of coefficients.

Second, there is no Calmfors and Driffill (inverted) hump due to centralization of wage bargaining in GDP growth in the OECD. There is some evidence that the four least centralized countries grew faster than the other twenty, *ceteris paribus*, but highly centralized countries are not distinguishable from the rest of the OECD. There is also some evidence that government policies differ systematically between the most and least centralized countries.

Third, in the (non-random) subset of OECD countries where aggregate union density data is collected and reported, there is some type of relationship between unionization and economic growth. Whether this relationship generalizes to all countries and whether it really is dependent on corporatist governance remain open questions.

I hope that this paper helps convince researchers to exploit the time-series properties of their data judiciously and to use care in selecting appropriate regressors. I hope that future work will not ignore government policy actions by concentrating only on typologies.

I plan to extend this line of analysis in future work in two directions. First I want to model the sample selectivity inherent in the union density reporting countries. This is a frequently occurring problem in research on institutional factors and economic growth that has not received nearly enough attention. The sixteen countries with good union density data are not a randomly selected sample. If the factors determining data availability are correlated with the variables used in the regression model, the results are subject to selectivity bias. Second, more work is required to isolate the factors that create synergy between governments and unionization. I want to add time-varying measures of governments to the models used in this present work.

28

Comment

LARS CALMFORS

Kevin Grier's paper deals with an important subject, namely 'the role of institutional factors in secular economic growth'. It is a topic that for many years received surprisingly little interest in mainstream economics. Recent years have, however, seen an explosion of research in this area. It is true, as pointed out by Grier, that this new interest has been triggered off by the development of endogenous growth models—for example, Romer (1986) and Lucas (1987)—that may motivate why institutional factors have long-run growth effects. It is, however, surprising that no mention is made of the seminal work in the area by researchers such as Douglass North and Mancur Olson. Their contributions may not have the same formal elegance as those of the new growth theorists but they do expound all the more exciting visions of the essentials.

The main analysis in the paper is econometric. The baseline model examines the effects on growth of a number of 'standard' variables: initial wealth, population growth, investment, growth of government consumption and the change as well as the variability of inflation. To this is added an analysis of how the extent of centralization of wage bargaining and the degree of 'corporatism' affect growth. Both time-series and cross-country variations among the OECD countries are exploited.

As far as I can judge the econometric investigation is competently executed. My main objection concerns the lack of a well-specified theoretical model. This is a problem especially for the discussion of the impact of centralization of bargaining on growth. Here the main result is that there appears to be a monotonic negative relationship between the degree of centralization and economic growth, with more decentralized bargaining always leading to higher growth. This conclusion is contrasted with the Calmfors–Driffill (1988) hypothesis of a *hump shaped* relationship between centralization and macroeconomic performance, with intermediate degrees of centralization being associated with the worst macroeconomic outcomes.

Since I have a stake in the Calmfors–Driffill hypothesis I shall dwell on it. My main point is that it does not refer to economic growth at all; instead the argument was cast in a static framework. The simple idea is that real wages at a given point of time will be set lower under both centralized bargaining (because of internalization of the price effects of wage increases) and strongly decentralized bargaining (because of competition) than under intermediate centralization to the industry level (when both internalization and competition forces are likely to be weak). As a consequence bargaining at the intermediate level may produce the highest unemployment.

It is not at all clear to me why one should expect a hump-shaped relationship between centralization and real wages (unemployment) to carry over to centralization and growth. One possible reason might be that lower real wages (higher return to capital) stimulates investment, but that mechanism is ruled out in most of Grier's analysis since investment is included in the regressions as a *separate* variable. An alternative explanation has been suggested by Dowrick (1993), who claims that the degree of centralization may affect the willingness of labour to accept measures implying labour-augmenting technical progress: with bargaining at the level of the firm the perceived risk of employment losses is reduced because of the possibility of gaining market shares at the expense of others, with centralized bargaining the full social benefits of lower prices and higher output can be internalized.

However, one can also conceive of several other arguments leading to other conclusions. Moene *et al.* (1993) have emphasized how 'collective effort' on the part of the employees is likely to be higher when wage bargaining is decentralized to the individual firm and higher productivity there thus can be expected to raise wages. Ramaswamy and Rowthorn (1992) have analysed how the individual firms are free to set 'optimal efficiency wages' under decentralized bargaining at the firm level. One might hypothesize that both these mechanisms are conducive to a larger stock of human capital and thus to higher growth.

But there are also reasons why centralized bargaining may promote growth. Firms may be less willing to invest under decentralized bargaining because they know that this weakens their bargaining position (higher capital costs make them more vulnerable to industrial conflict, as stressed by Moene *et al.*, 1993). If centralized bargaining means less wage dispersion between old and new production units, the rate of structural change is likely to be speeded up (Moene and Wallerstein, 1992).

In sum, it seems difficult to motivate strong theoretical priors on the likely relationship between the extent of centralization of bargaining in the labour market and economic growth. This is even more true if one takes possible indirect effects into account. It is to be noted that Grier finds a positive association between centralization and investment (which in turn affects growth positively). It is also noteworthy that he finds a positive correlation between centralization and growth of government consumption (which in turn affects growth negatively). The latter relationship bears some relationship to the accommodation hypothesis of Söderström and Viotti (1978) and Calmfors and Horn (1985, 1986). They argued that a centralized trade union movement is likely to raise wages on the expectation that the associated tendency to higher unemployment will lead policy makers to expand the public sector.

How much could we then expect to get out of empirical studies of the association between institutions and growth? Levine and Renelt (1992) have pointed to the large sensitivity of the results in growth regressions to the specifications chosen: the inclusion of new explanatory variables often makes earlier ones insignificant. This is a general reason for regarding studies of this kind with a fair amount of scepticism. More precisely, we know nothing about how robust Grier's results on centralization and corporatism are with respect to the inclusion of other institutional variables.

An additional problem in the context of this study is that since bargaining systems in individual countries are so stable over time, studies of variations in the degree of centralization must by and large build only on cross-country differences. This means that the number of observations on centralization in Grier's analysis is restricted to the number of OECD countries (it is probably a reasonable judgment that it is not very meaningful to extend the investigation of the centralization/decentralization issue to non-OECD countries where political and labour market institutions are not at all comparable). The upshot is that the degrees of freedom if one were to study the impact of *several* institutional variables (including other characteristics of the labour market as well as political conditions) become very few. This problem is seriously exacerbated if one would try also to distinguish between different aspects of centralization (centralization in the firm–industry–nation dimension, centralization across regions and across professions, the number of bargaining levels, synchronization of pay deals etc.) and to take into account that a given level of 'formal' centralization will mean different degrees of 'effective' centralization depending upon the openness of the economy (Calmfors, 1993).

My conclusion is that because of these inherent problems empirical research on the macroeconomic impact of centralization of wage bargaining does not perhaps lead very far. It is always better to organize the knowledge there is in a systematic way, but in the end we may not have much more than individual country experiences that may be open to many interpretations. The best we can hope for is perhaps only to be able to reject those models that are squarely contradicted by the facts, but there are also likely to be many hypotheses that we cannot discriminate between empirically.

Let me end with two additional comments. First, Grier argues quite strongly that it is better to capture 'qualitative' variables like centralization and corporatism with dummy variables than with quantitative measures. I am not at all convinced. It is true that using rankings of countries in regressions may distort the picture under some conditions. But it is equally true that grouping countries only in broad categories may do the same under other circumstances. It is difficult to know which is the best strategy. The safest option would seem to be to try several methods.

Second and finally, the paper contains an interesting empirical analysis of the interaction between corporatist government and the degree of unionization. The conclusion is that corporatism and a high degree of unionization *as well as* non-corporatist government and a low degree of unionization are conducive to economic growth. This is not implausible. It is, however, a weakness of the analysis that it only considers the link between government and labour market organizations. Arguably, the extent of strong rent-seeking pressure groups in general (farmers, tenants, regional interests, various business cartels etc.) could be expected to hamper growth, as hypothesized by Olson (1982). Perhaps this is a more promising area for empirical research than the association between wage-bargaining institutions and growth because inter-country comparisons among a larger set of countries become more meaningful in this context. The Levine–Renelt critique of the sensitivity of the empirical results in growth regressions to specification changes is, however, likely to remain a serious problem.

29

Comment

JOHN D. STEPHENS

29.1 Grier's contribution

Kevin Grier's chapter advances our understanding of the determinants of economic growth in advanced capitalist countries by bringing together hypotheses from the literatures in economics and political science and subjecting them to rigorous empirical tests. As Grier correctly argues, past literature in economics has ignored the type of institutional variables of interest to political scientists such as collective bargaining systems, union strength, and party composition of government, while the political scientists fail to control for the basic economic variables such as investment, growth of the labour force, or initial level of economic development. Both economists and political scientists have been unimaginative, or unsophisticated in their statistical analyses. Almost all of the contributions to the literature are cross-sectional analyses. Such studies either include a very large number of heterogeneous countries at varying levels of economic development and with varying political regime form, or restrict the analysis to a small number of strictly comparable countries, typically the advanced capitalist democracies of Europe, North America, Australasia and Japan (the 'OECD democracies'). The large-N studies suffer from lack of data comparability and, more important, from the fact that the statistical relations within various subgroups of the sample are sufficiently different that generalizations drawn from the whole sample are of dubious value. Cross-sectional analyses of the OECD democracies typically are limited by the small number of cases: in attempting to test the full range of relevant hypotheses, authors quickly use up the degrees of freedom in the sample.

Grier has joined a handful of scholars in taking the obvious way out: pooling cross-sections and time series data for the narrower group of relatively comparable OECD countries. Pooling produces enough data points to test the hypotheses on the effects of a number of independent variables while simultaneously allowing for the full range of control variables to be entered in the analysis. Indeed, one of my main criticisms of the analysis is that he does not go far enough in this direction.

Grier makes several other improvements over previous analyses of this sort. First, in my opinion, he is correct in taking Calmfors and Driffill to task for an essentially arbitrary scale construction. His dummy variable analysis of high and low centralization as well as the alternative operationalization of corporatism by Crouch are both improvements on the Calmfors–Driffill scale. Second, contrary to many analyses of pooled data, especially by economists, Grier chose not to eliminate cross unit variation either through dummy variable least squares with dummies for the units or through generalized least squares with fixed unit effects. Such specifications treat cross-sectional variation as random noise that the analyst wants to eliminate. They are clearly inappropriate in a case like this in which the researcher is interested in the effect of relatively time invariant features of countries, such as bargaining systems.

The results of the analysis for two variables which are at least in part effects of government policy are unambiguous: the growth of government consumption and the variability of inflation both result in lower growth. The results for centralized bargaining, corporatism, and union strength are more ambiguous. In the regressions with dummy variables coded from the Calmfors–Driffill scale, only the countries with the most decentralized bargaining systems appear to have growth rates significantly different from zero, in this case in a positive direction. In all probability, this is due to the presence of Japan in this group as Japan has had growth over 50 per cent above the OECD average every decade since 1950. I will argue below that it is not the decentralization of bargaining *per se* that accounts for Japan's phenomenal success but rather its statist industrial policy. Thus, in my view, this statistical result is spurious. Grier finds his own result on the interactive relationship between unionization and corporatism puzzling and suggests that it requires further analysis. I concur with this and suggest a direction of inquiry below.

Before moving on to problems in the analysis and directions for further research, let me note two results that emerge from the group means displayed in Tables 25.2 and 26.1 as this will be of some importance for my subsequent discussion. Table 25.2 suggests that corporatism has a positive impact on investment which the earlier analysis showed to increase growth, and a positive impact on the growth of government consumption which the earlier analysis showed to decrease growth. This would lead one to hypothesize that corporatism has two different indirect effects on growth which cancel each other out. This makes sense from the social-class support base of most governments in corporatist countries as these countries are usually governed by social democratic parties or coalition governments including social democrats: union wage restraint boosts investment and social democratic governments compensate unions for restraint with increased public expenditure. Though the net effect on growth may be nil, the working class is better off because the welfare state effects a very significant redistribution of income to lower income earners, as recent studies employing the Luxembourg Income surveys have so clearly demonstrated (see, for example, Mitchell, 1990; Fritzell, 1993).

Second, Table 26.1 shows a clearly negative relationship between corporatism and growth in the 1984–8 period, though, without control variables, this is at best suggestive of a causal relationship. Note that this is in contrast to the analysis of the whole period which showed no such relationship. While this difference may be due to the exclusion of control variables in the later analyses (or might be a temporary artefact of this unusual period, a worldwide period of growth stimulated by Reagan's budget deficits), it also may be that the relationship has permanently changed. The Hicks, Garrett, and Lange cross-sectional studies cited by Grier which generally cover the period after the first OPEC oil shock to the early 1980s do indicate a positive not a negative relationship between 'social democratic corporatism' and growth.

29.2 Lacunae in Grier's analysis

Despite the advances Grier makes, there are lacunae in his analysis, above all, the omission of relevant independent variables included in previous studies, in particular Alvarez, Garrett, and Lange (1991), which is the most comprehensive analysis of growth in OECD countries carried out on pooled data. It may be that some of the variables in this article appear 'esoteric' (as Grier says) to economists, but surely openness to the international economy is a relevant control variable in the analysis of the causes of domestic economic growth. Moreover, one of these excluded variables, left government, is not only not esoteric, it is essential to testing the argument made by Garrett and Lange in a series of articles spanning almost a decade now. Central to Garrett and Lange's argument is the notion that a combination of strong and centralized unions and social democratic government is necessary for the 'social democratic model' to produce growth. The linkage is wage restraint. Strong unions are in a position to endanger the competitiveness of the national economy if they fully utilize their bargaining power. Centralization gives unions the capability to deliver wage restraint, as Grier following Calmfors and Driffill indicates. However, it does not necessarily make them willing to do it. Unions will be willing to restrain wages only if they are assured of a quid pro quo from the government, usually expansion of social benefits and social services or low unemployment or both. Unions are much more likely to trust social democratic governments to hold up their end of this deal and social democratic governments are much more likely to deliver the kind of policies unions want. Thus, it is essential to include an interaction term for presence of left government and strong and centralized unions to properly test the Garrett–Lange argument.

Incidentally, Grier's comment on why the centralized bargaining literature has made little impact on American economics seems to me to miss the point. This literature does not argue that low wages produce growth. In fact, countries with centralized bargaining have high wages compared with the OECD average. 'Wage restraint' in this literature has two meanings: 'underutilization of bargaining power' and 'holding wage increases at or below labour productivity increases'. In either case, the link to growth is straightforward: without wage restraint profits, a primary source of investment, would be squeezed.

Finally, Grier treats union centralization and corporatism as essentially the same phenomenon. They are very closely related as union centralization is a precondition for corporatism, but they are not the same thing. In Lehmbruch's (1984) influential formulation, corporatism is a system of interest intermediation, a bargaining process in which the constituent units are large interest organizations and the state. In practice, clearly the labour market partners are by far the most important 'interest groups'. He defines 'strong corporatism' as tripartite bargaining between the state and peak organizations of employers' associations and trade unions over broad economic policy—incomes policy, social expenditure, taxes, price levels and so on. In practice, only highly centralized employers associations and trade unions can enforce such a bargain.

Lehmbruch's corporatism scale would be an alternative, superior in my view, to the Crouch dichotomy which Grier uses. Most important for my purposes, Lehmbruch contends that two of the countries—Japan and France—cannot be classified on the ordinal scale and reserves a special category, 'concertation without labour', for them.[1] The label is descriptive enough and needs no further elaboration. This categorization dovetails nicely with Katzenstein's (1985) discussion of the interrelationship of types of industrial policy and modes of interest group organization. According to Katzenstein, the 'concertation without labour cases' and corporatist countries pursue different varieties of active industrial policy to encourage growth while the liberal countries with decentralized interest groups (including business and labour) intervene little in the economy. While wage restraint was an essential feature of corporatist industrial policy (it was not necessary in the 'concentration without labour' or statist cases because unions were so weak), it is only one piece in an overall state policy aimed at growth. Since the Vartiainen piece in this volume ably summarizes the experience of two

---

[1] Note that by this categorization, Vartiainen's (in this volume) East Asian cases, Taiwan and Korea, would be cases of 'concertation without labour' following 'statist' industrial policy. That labour was excluded from the policy making process in these two authoritarian regimes is obvious.

European corporatist cases, Austria and Finland, I need not go further here. The point for quantitative analyses such as Grier's is that one should follow Hicks (1988) and distinguish between the corporatist, statist, and liberal cases.

A final point along this line is that the degree of bargaining centralization (and industrial policy) changes through time. Thus, it is possible that Grier's result on the most recent period (assuming for a moment that it is correct) is not only due to the fact that the corporatist policies of the past do not work as well now but also to the fact that bargaining is not as centralized now as it was in the 'golden age of capitalism'. For instance, in Sweden, centralized bargaining broke down in the 1980s and arguably this made it more difficult to restrain wages. For quantitative analyses, this calls for the development of comparable measures of bargaining centralization and corporatism that vary through time within countries. These presently do not exist though the research project of Golden, Lange, and Wallerstein (1993) promises to rectify this lacuna.

29.3 Towards an understanding of the institutional and political bases of post-war growth patterns

Grier's results in Table 26.1 suggest that the institutional and political underpinnings of economic growth in the OECD democracies may have changed through time. While it is commonplace to observe that the rate of growth has declined in all OECD countries in the 1970s and 1980s due to a variety of domestic and international transformations, there is little agreement on why certain institutional and political arrangements which were once successful are no longer so. Let me take a few paragraphs to outline my view of this focusing on the corporatist cases and then suggest how the resulting hypotheses might be tested with the kind of data which Grier is using.

In the golden age of capitalism, from World War II to roughly 1971–3 (the break-up of the Bretton Woods system and the first oil shock), both statist and corporatist countries developed policy mixes that were relatively successful in promoting growth. Again I refer to the Vartiainen essay for a description of these policies I do want to emphasize one point that is often over-

TABLE 29.1. *Government Composition, Bargaining Centralization, and Budget Surpluses (percentage of years in which the budget was in surplus)*

Left % of total government seats[b]	Centralized bargaining[c]	Decentralized bargaining
(a) Before 1974[a]		
None	67	38
Under 25%	73	11
25–50%	58	52
Over 50%	92	46
Total	75	37
(b) After 1973		
None	28	6
Under 25%	13	4
25–50%	22	30
Over 50%	36	18
Total	30	10

[a] Depending on the country the first data points are between 1956 and 1960. The last year is 1988.

[b] Left (social democratic or communist) government share, scored 100% for each year when the left is in government alone, scored as a fraction of the left's seats in parliament of all governing parties' seats for coalition governments.

[c] Centralized bargaining: Austria, Belgium, Netherlands, Denmark, Norway, Sweden, and Finland. Decentralized bargaining: France, Italy, Germany, UK, Ireland, USA, Canada, Australia, New Zealand, and Japan.

looked. While all of the corporatist countries were Keynesian in the sense that they pursued counter-cyclical policies, they did not employ fiscal stimulus to promote growth and employment across business cycles.[2] As one can see from Table 29.1, governments in corporatist countries (those with economy wide

---

[2] Note that this does not deny the existence of an international Phillips curve in this period as shown by Hibbs (1977), with governments of the left favouring low unemployment at the expense of higher inflation. Rather it denies that deficit spending was responsible for the low levels of unemployment or high levels of inflation.

bargaining) ran budget surpluses three quarters of the time.[3] Moreover, the tendency to run a surplus increased with social democratic influence in the government such that those governments in which the social democrats formed 50 per cent or more of the parliamentary base of the government ran surpluses over 90 per cent of the time.

The budget surplus served two functions in this model. By dampening domestic demand, it facilitated wage restraint: Vartiainen points this out about Finland and it was also an important feature of the Rehn–Meidner model in Sweden. Second, it also facilitated cheap credit policies which were central to the industrial policy and the growth model. Essentially, these political economies were left-wing supply-side models. Not only were interest rates low but government control of credit markets was directed at producing industrial investment at the expense of consumer credit. For example, Mjøset (1986) characterizes Norwegian industrial policy as 'credit socialism', catching the centrality of cheap credit and state channelling of credit to critical industries in the Norwegian supply side policy. To be sure there were variations in policy instruments selected: with a relatively small state sector and concentrated, powerful, internationalized, and export-oriented business, Sweden was not able to follow the same sort of state directed investment policies pursued by Norway, Austria, and Finland, all of which had, or developed, large state sectors. Sweden relied on active labour market policy, low interest rates for business investment, very generous tax breaks for re-invested profits, and public savings in the supplementary pension funds, the last named of which were particularly important for investment in the housing sector.

With such austere fiscal policy, one would assume that the demand side would be a drag on growth. In these small, open economies, the demand side was taken care of by vigorous growth in the larger capitalist economies (and for Finland, markets in the Soviet Union) during the golden age. These countries never had a growth model that could be produced entirely by domestic policy.

---

[3] Switzerland, which runs a budget surplus every year for which I have data, is excluded from the table.

The experience of the first two years of the Mitterrand government has led many, even most scholars, to emphasize that economic internationalization has made traditional Keynesian demand stimulation policies (which were presumed to be 'social democratic' policies) to attack unemployment and stimulate growth unviable. However, as I have just emphasized, this was never the principal policy of the corporatist social democracies. Moreover, they were already very trade dependent and had very low tariff barriers during the golden age, so such a policy would not have been that effective, especially in periods of international recession. Following the logic of my argument, it is apparent that what was damaging to these models about the new conditions of the post-Bretton Woods/post-OPEC era was the combination of high international interest rates and the internationalization of financial markets which made both the cheap credit policies and the funnelling of cheap (essentially subsidized) credit to selected industries very difficult.

Earlier evaluations of the initial performance of the corporatist economies in the post-OPEC/post-Bretton Woods era emphasized their success especially in producing low unemployment but also in producing growth (see, for example, the contributions to Goldthorpe, 1984; Lindberg and Maier, 1985). Scharpf (1991) emphasizes that the successful fight against unemployment in Austria and Sweden was a product of a combination of fiscal and monetary stimulus with wage restraint. In the light of past policy as I have outlined it, this policy was a counter-cyclical 'bridging' strategy and could not be expected to result in long term growth as a substitute for a supply-side policy. Indeed, the domestic budget deficits (see Table 29.1(b)) necessary to carry out the stimulative fiscal policies contributed to the high domestic interest rates created by high international interest rates and the internationalization of financial markets. Thus, one might hypothesize that the growth downturn in the corporatist countries that Grier notes (again assuming this is a trend and not a blip) might be a product of their failure to find new supply-side policies which would restore growth across business cycles, that is, over the long run.

This is, of course, a very tentative sketch and I do not purport to have any definitive answers, but it does point to some hypotheses that might be tested with quantitative data. The most obvious one is the hypothesis that the effect of the corporatist (and statist and liberal) industrial policies vary through time. A first cut on this is either to create interaction terms or to divide the data set into two or three different time periods. The second, and much more difficult, step would be to attempt to measure the policy instruments themselves.

References

Alesina. A. and Rodrick, D. (1992), 'Distribution, Political Conflict and Economic Growth', in A. Cukierman *et al.* (eds.), *Political Economy, Growth and Business Cycles* (Cambridge, MA: MIT Press).

——and Roubini, N. (1992), 'Political Cycles in OECD Democracies', *Review of Economic Studies* 59: 663–88.

——Cohen, G. and Roubini, N. (1992), 'Macroeconomic Policy and Election in OECD Democracies', *Economics and Politics* 4: 1–30.

Alvarez, M., Garrett, G. and Lange, P. (1991), 'Government Partisanship, Labor Organization and Macroeconomic Performance', *American Political Science Review* 85: 539–56.

Calmfors, L. (1993), 'Centralisation of Wage Bargaining and Macroeconomic Performance: A Survey', *OECD Economic Studies* 21.

——and Driffill, J. (1988), 'Bargaining Structure, Corporatism and Macroeconomic Performance', *Economic Policy* 3: 13–61.

——and Horn, H. (1985), 'Classical Unemployment, Accommodation Policies and the Adjustment of Real Wages', *Scandinavian Journal of Economics* 2.

————(1986), 'Employment Policies and Centralized Wage Setting', *Economica* Aug.

Cameron, D. (1984), 'Social Democracy, Corporatism, and Labor Quiescence: The Representation of Economic Interest in Advanced Capitalist Society', in John Goldthorpe (ed.), *Order and Conflict in Contemporary Capitalism* (New York: Oxford University Press).

Crouch, C. (1985), 'Conditions for Trade Union Wage Restraint', in Lindberg and Maier (eds.), *The Politics of Inflation and Economic Stagnation* (Washington, D.C.: Brookings).

Cukierman, A., Webb, S. and Neyapti, B. (1992), 'Measuring the Independence of Central Banks and Its Effect on Policy Outcomes', *World Bank Economic Review* 6: 353–98.

D'Agostino, H. (1992), *Why do Workers Join Unions?* (Swedish Institute for Social Research, Stockholm University).

Dowrick, S. (1993), 'Wage Bargaining Systems and Productivity Growth in OECD Countries', mimeo, Australian National University.

Engen, E. and Skinner, J. (1992), 'Fiscal Policy and Economic Growth', NBER working paper no. 4223.

Fritzell, J. (1993), 'Income Inequality in the 1980s: A Five-Country Comparison', *Acta Sociologica* 36: 47–62.

Garrett, G. and Lang, P. (1989), 'Government Partisanship and Economic Performance When and How does "Who Governs" Matter?', *Journal of Politics* 51: 676–93.

Golden, M., Lange, P. and Wallerstein, M. (1993), 'The End of Corporatism?', in S. Jacoby (ed.), *Work and Society: Global Perspectives* (Los Angeles, CA: UCLA, Institute of Industrial Relations).

Goldthorpe, J. (ed.) (1984), *Order and Conflict in Contemporary Capitalism: Studies in the Political Economy of Western European Nations* (Oxford: Clarendon Press).

Greene, W. (1993), *Econometric Analysis* (New York: Macmillan).

Grier, K. and Perry, M. (1993), 'Inflation, Inflation Uncertainty and Relative Price Dispersion: Evidence from Bivariate GARCH-M Models', mimeo, George Mason University.

——and Tullock, G. (1989), 'An Empirical Analysis of Cross-National Economic Growth, 1951–80', *Journal of Monetary Economics* 24: 259–76.

Grilli, V., Masciandaro, D. and Tabellini, G. (1991), 'Political and Monetary Institutions and Public Financial Policies in the Industrial Countries', *Economic Policy* 13: 342–92.

Hansson, P. and Henrekson, M. (1993), 'A New Framework for Testing the Effect of Government Spending on Growth and Productivity', mimeo, Trade Union Institute for Economic Research, Stockholm.

Heitger, B. (1987), 'Corporatism, Technological Gaps and Growth in OECD Countries', *Weltwirtschaftliches Archiv* 123: 463–73.

Hicks, A. (1988), 'Social Democratic Corporatism and Economic Growth', *Journal of Politics* 50: 677–704.

——and Patterson, W. (1989), 'On the Robustness of the Left Corporatist Model of Economic Growth', *Journal of Politics* 51: 662–75.

Jackman, R. (1987), 'The Politics of Economic Growth in the Industrial Democracies, 1974–1980', *Journal of Politics* 49: 242–56.

——(1989), 'The Politics of Growth, Once Again', *Journal of Politics* 51: 646–61.

Katzenstein, P. (1985), *Small States in World Markets: Industrial Policy in Europe* (Ithaca, NY: Cornell University Press).

Kmenta, J. (1986), *Elements of Econometrics* (New York: Macmillan).

Kormendi, R. and Meguire, P. (1985), 'Macroeconomic Determinants of Growth: Cross-Country Evidence', *Journal of Monetary Economics* 16: 141–63.

Lange, P. and Garrett, G. (1985), 'The Politics of Growth: Strategic Interaction and Economic Performance in the Advanced Industrial Democracies, 1974–1980', *Journal of Politics* 47: 792–827.

————(1987), 'The Politics of Growth Reconsidered', *Journal of Politics* 49: 257–74.

Lehmbruch, G. (1984), 'Concertation and the Structure of Corporatist Networks', in J. H. Goldthorpe (ed.), *Order and Conflict in Contemporary Capitalism* (Oxford: Clarendon Press).

Levine, R. and Renelt, D. (1992), 'A Sensitivity Analysis of Cross-Country Growth Regressions', *American Economic Review* 82: 942–63.

Lindberg, L. and Maier, C. (eds.) (1985), *The Politics of Inflation and Economic Stagnation* (Washington, D.C.: Brookings).

Lucas, R. (1987), 'On the Mechanics of Economic Development', *Journal of Monetary Economics* 22: 43–70.

Moene, K. O. and Wallerstein, M. (1992), 'The Process of Creative Destruction and the Scope of Collective Bargaining', mimeo, Socialøkonomisk Institutt, Oslo University and Department of Political Science, University of California, Los Angeles.

——————and Hoel, M. (1993), 'Bargaining Structure and Economic Performance', in R. J. Flanagan, K. O. Moene and M. Wallerstein (eds.), *Trade Union Behaviour, Pay Bargaining and Economic Performance* (Oxford: Clarendon Press).

Mitchell, D. (1991), *Income Transfers in Ten Welfare States* (Brookfield: Avebury).

Mjøset, L. (ed.) (1986), *Norden Dagen Derpå* (Olso: Universitetsforlaget).

Olson, M. (1982), *The Rise and Decline of Nations* (New Haven, CN: Yale University Press).

Pack, H. (1994), 'Endogenous Growth Theory: Intellectual Appeal and Empirical Shortcomings', *Journal of Economic Perspectives* 8: 55–72.

Persson, T. and Tabellini, G. (1992), 'Growth, Distribution and Politics', in A. Cukierman *et al.* (eds.), *Political Economy, Growth and Business Cycles* (Cambridge, MA: MIT Press).

Ramaswamy, R. and Rowthorn, R. E. (1992), 'Centralised Bargaining, Efficiency Wages and Flexibility', IMF Working Paper WP/93/25, March.

Romer, P. (1986), 'Increasing Returns and Long Run Growth', *Journal of Political Economy* 94: 1002–37.

——(1994), 'The Origins of Endogenous Growth', *Journal of Economic Perspectives* 8: 3–22.

Rowthorn, R. E. (1992), 'Centralisation, Employment and Wage Dispersion', *Economic Journal* 102: 506–23.

Roubini, N. and Sachs, J. (1989), 'Political and Economic Determinants of Budget Deficits in the Industrial Democracies', *European Economic Review* 33: 903–33.

Scharpf, F. (1991), *Crisis and Choice in European Social Democracy* (Ithaca, NY: Cornell University Press).

Shapiro, C. and Stiglitz, J. (1984), 'Equilibrium Unemployment as a Worker Discipline Device', *American Economic Review* 74: 433–44.

Söderström, H. and Viotti, S. (1978), 'Money Wage Disturbances and the Endogeneity of the Public Sector in an Open Economy', in A. Lindbeck (ed.), *Inflation and Employment in Open Economies* (Amsterdam: North-Holland).

Solow, R. (1956), 'A Contribution to the Theory of Economic Growth', *Quarterly Journal of Economics* 70: 65–94.

——(1994), 'Perspectives on Growth Theory', *Journal of Economic Perspectives* 8: 45–54.

Soskice, D. (1991), 'Wage Determination: The Changing Role of Institutions in Advanced Industrialized Countries', *Oxford Review of Economic Policy* 6: 36–61.

Visser, J. (1989), *European Trade Unions in Figures* (Netherlands: Kluwer).

PART IV

Understanding State-Led Late Industrialization

JUHANA VARTIAINEN

30

Introduction

This paper attempts to interpret the experiences of some successful late industrializers in the light of economic ideas. Whether economic growth and successful structural transformation occur because of skilful public policies or on the basis of private activities coordinated only by a decentralized price system is of course a classic controversy within political economy. Many economists seem at least implicitly to read the empirical literature on growth in the light of this normative question.

We adopt the more modest aim of trying to suggest and understand some mechanisms of success in some countries. The paper is inspired by a study of the experiences of four small countries in particular: Taiwan, Korea, Finland and Austria. The growth performance of the first two is of course among the very best, but Finland and Austria, too, can boast a performance above the average of industrial countries. However, what the four cases all have in common is that they underwent a clear and rapid structural change and late industrialization in the 1950s and 1960s. In all of them, the state played a very active role in this transformation. We do not pretend that these recipes can generate superior growth in the long run. Yet development economics as well as modern theories of endogenous growth[1] suggest strongly that there are qualitative thresholds in economic development and that structural transformations whereby economies are industrialized do matter for the long run as well.[2] The classical if loose description of takeoffs and thresholds is of course the work of Rostow (1960), but similar ideas occur in the modern theory of endogenous growth or in treatises of the determinants of successful industrial clusters such as Porter (1990). An early Swedish contribution to the same tradition of ideas was Erik Dahmén's (1951) idea of a 'developmental bloc'.

---

[1] Many of these ideas were analysed already by Kaldor (1978).

[2] The positive growth effects of equipment investment in manufacturing industries is shown in De Long and Summers (1991).

All of the four countries are examples of successful state-led industrialization. Short of answering the grand question of markets versus state-led policies, these cases at least show that state-led industrialization has in some cases worked well and can therefore in principle be successful. Then a closer look at these experiences may be interesting. Whether these policies 'can' be replicated is a less well defined question. Ideally, everything can be replicated by rational agents who choose to do so, but this normative statement does not get us very far in understanding why some economies prosper and others do not. Interesting as it is to discuss what can be achieved by state policies, it may be even more illuminating to analyse the determinants of state action in the positive sense. Why have some states acted in ways that seem to have been conducive to success while some others have not?

This paper at least suggests some tentative answers to this question. But the results also emphasize the idiosyncracies of the case countries as well as the compositional fallacies involved in the idea of replication of policies. The most important limitation is the fact that this analysis is concerned with cases of *late* industrialization in *small* countries. Determinants of late industrialization are different from those of the mature industrial countries.[3] Inasmuch as the popular catching-up hypothesis is correct, it is important to see that not everybody can be a latecomer.[4] On the other hand, the discussion hopefully suggests at

---

[3] Patterns of late industrialization are different from the experiences of the mature industrialized countries, often because of their rapidity if for no other reason. This does, however, not by itself imply that one should see industrialization of the mature countries as a 'spontaneous' process. Even the traditional view according to which the industrialization of the old industrial countries was an essentially market-driven process has now been seriously questioned by economic historians. The attitudes of economic historians are surveyed by Supple (1980), whose theoretical positions have been influenced by Alexander Gerschenkron and Friedrich List. Supple emphasizes that the role of the state in industrialization has not been limited to the provision of a basic legal framework, public order and external security. Institutions favourable to industrialization have been actively encouraged, various public services organized and the state has even undertaken direct organizational activities in production. The Hungarian historians Berend and Ranki (1982) arrive at essentially similar conclusions in their study of several peripheral European economies.

[4] However, see Hansson and Henrekson (this volume) for a critical assessment of the catching-up hypothesis. The present paper can be seen as one attempt to come to grips with their 'social capability' variable, although our analysis is more concerned with 'political' capability.

least some recipes for well conceived development policies for such countries in which a similar potential for an industrial takeoff does exist.

The method of this paper consists of straightforward qualitative observation, description and interpretation of observations in the light of some economic and social ideas. Thus, there is no pretension to generality in the sense adopted by modern universalist economics nor in the sense of statistical analysis.

Comparisons of long-run growth rates in different countries, now based on the new large Penn World Table data set, are very interesting but fragile as Levine and Renelt (1992) have shown.[5] As argued by Elster (1993), entire societies are so complex that overall explanations of their performances are necessarily problematic. The commonplace statistical methodology employed in economics implicitly assumes that 'countries' are appropriate units of analysis, which seems to presuppose that they are in fact generated by a common mechanism and are sampled from a 'superpopulation' of 'potential' countries. Whereas firms and households and even industries[6] can perhaps be assumed to behave in ways that are universal enough so that similar economic models apply to all, this assumption is much more dubious for such incredibly complex entities as countries and societies.

The alternative, also advocated by Elster, is to look at *mechanisms*, particular and partial causal relationships that may be corroborated by all kinds of arguments, ranging from social theory and statistical inference to plain common sense and historical description.

---

[5] Levine and Renelt examine the robustness of the results generated by the new empirical growth literature. Their method is to use Leamer's extreme bound analysis to assess whether reported statistical regularities between growth rates and various explanatory variables are robust. Supposing one wants to examine the robustness of one particular explanatory variable, Leamer's method consists in varying the set of other explanatory variables and establishing lower and upper bounds for the coefficient of the variable of interest. The correlation between the variable and the regressand is said to be robust if the coefficient remains significant (and of the same sign) at the extreme bounds. Levine and Renelt find that there is generally no strong relationship between the policy indicators and growth.

[6] Cf. the paper by Henrekson and Hansson in this volume, where disaggregation of countries into industries permits more robust conclusions to be drawn.

The paper is organized as follows. Chapter 31 spells out, for the four countries in question, the stylized facts around which the discussion will be organized. Chapter 32 outlines some economic ideas and theoretical assumptions that help to make the country experiences intelligible. Chapter 33 summarizes these ideas with a simplified model of a corporatist economy with externalities. Chapters 34 and 35 then move on to discuss the empirical experiences of the four countries in the light of the model and some other economic ideas. Chapter 34 describes the content and the logic of the state's economic intervention in general terms, while Chapter 35 is more concerned with the political determinants of intervention. It tries to suggest some particular reasons why state intervention was successful and was implemented in ways conducive to success. Chapter 36 contains a specific historical description of each of the four countries in the light of the foregoing analysis, and Chapter 37 concludes with a discussion of the replicability and generality of these policy experiences.

31

Common Characteristics of the Four Late Industrializers

The experiences of the four case countries exhibit at least the following common characteristics that may have been associated with 'mechanisms' of success in state-led industrialization. The subsequent discussion will then present an attempt to make sense of these observations: (1) In all of the four countries, the state has been very powerful and interventionist, so that the practical organization of new investment has at times resembled that of the planned economies. (2) All have been extremely organized, corporatist economies where strategic decisions of economic and industrial policy have been taken in concert between the state and organized interest groups of business and labour. (3) In all of them, and in spite of the extensive étatist planning, the state and the political establishment have been ultimately committed to the liberal market order and respect of private property as a principle. (4) In all of them, for various historical reasons, the state has been politically strong and has also been endowed with a large and competent bureaucracy. (5) In international politics, all of them were situated in a contested borderzone between the two ideological blocks of capitalism and communism and all of them were confronted with a threat of loss of sovereignty. (6) In all of them, however, the outcome of World War II had shaken or disrupted the established organization of interests groups, so that a new corporatist network had to be built in the aftermath of the war.

Thus, in a nutshell, we ask whether these observations would lend support to a rudimentary 'theory' which predicts that state intervention and even planning can be very successful, in particular if it does not imply that the long-run incentives for private entrepreneurship are weakened; it is taken care of by a competent and highly meritocratic bureaucracy which sets its policy independently of organized interest groups and does not aim at maximizing the revenues of the individual bureaucrats; the state can deal with a coherent and balanced corporatist network of organized interests; the nation is confronted with a fragile position in international politics which means that the consequences of economic failure are fatal; and the political structure of the country has at the starting point been shaken so that established interest groups and rent-seeking routines have been discontinued.

32

The Economic Logic of State
Interventionism

The economic ideas that permit a positive interpretation of the successful late industrializers' experiences include the modern ideas of externalities and endogenous growth on the one hand and the theories of distributional conflicts in corporatist economies on the other. Supposing that one is willing to buy the set of assumptions of modern theories of endogenous growth, there are important implications for positive and normative theories of politics and political economy. Modern theories of growth are based on assumed externalities related to the returns of investment in education or to the spread of technical innovations. These assumptions contradict the usual neoclassical assumptions and lead to the conclusion that an economy's growth performance can be enhanced by, say, subsidized education or public support for investment in new technologies. They also lead to models of non-convex growth and increasing returns to scale.

There is of course no ultimate proof that this new 'view' of the economy is more correct than the one associated with the traditional neoclassical assumptions. Yet these theories, to some authors, seem to make better sense of the different countries' growth performances than the neoclassical growth model.[7] They also seem more in tune with many classical, empirically oriented discussions of economic development. As early as in 1960, W. W. Rostow presented his theory of the stages of economic growth where each 'stage' of growth was characterized by various self-enforcing mechanisms. Other, similar accounts of growth and development include Erik Dahmén's (1951) idea of a 'developmental bloc' and the notion of 'linkages' suggested by Albert Hirschman. Similarly, Michael Porter (1990) outlines the idea of industrial 'clusters' which generate an environment and a system

---

[7] For a contrasting view, see e.g. Crafts (1992).

of linkages favourable for industrial growth. These empirically inspired notions of blocs, clusters and linkages are plausible empirical candidates for counterparts of the theoretical notion of externality.

Thus, new ideas of growth contain powerful normative implications. If the related assumptions are true, there is an important potential role for the state in enhancing economic growth and development. But the assumptions of increasing returns also typically lead to outcomes that contradict assumptions of perfect competition. If the assumptions of non-convex endogenous growth are true, successful real economies will exhibit imperfect competition. If for example, industrial technology exhibits increasing returns to scale, successful economies will be dominated by a few large firms. This is indeed the case in many small economies. As shown in the various essays of Pekkarinen, Pohjola and Rowthorn (1992) and the related literature on corporatism, corporatist structures are typical for small economies (see also the discussion by Katzenstein, 1984 and 1985). One plausible explanation discussed in the literature hinges on economies of scale. If technologies exhibit increasing returns to scale at some intervals of the scale axis, some industry sizes are more advantageous than others and there may be a minimum size for a manufacturing sector, under which it cannot operate profitably in the international market. If this is the case, the structure of small economies will differ from that of the large economies. The small economies will be dominated by a few industries.

Furthermore, one expects that such an economic structure leads to a corporatist political structure. Big industries in small economies see that they can act strategically towards the state and towards other economic agents. This in turn makes it more worthwhile for other groups of agents to organize themselves.

Thus, the political economy of such small economies would and indeed often has been organized around two themes: the exploitation of economies of scale and the management of strategic conflict between organized interest groups. Both of these themes point to an extended role for the state. If the economies of scale are not exploited by the firms themselves—via, say, co-ordinated investment policies, joint research or simply mergers—it should be rational for the state to operate an active industrial policy. If, on the other hand, the economies of scale indeed lead to an oligopolistic economic structure and a corporatist political structure, the state must become an arbiter and manager of the inevitable strategic conflicts.

33

A Model of a Corporatist Economy with Increasing Returns

To summarize the ideas presented in the last chapter, consider a model economy with a few industrial sectors, the number of which we set to two for illustrative purposes. Call them sector 1 and sector 2. Each sector produces one good, so that the product market is made of two goods, good 1 and good 2. Assume that there are many entrepreneurs in both sectors; we can, however, normalize their number to unity in both sectors in order to make the exposition simple. At this level of generality we may think that each firm is owned by one individual, who is both the entrepreneur and the consumer of the model economy. Assume further that there are economies of scale associated with the accumulation of capital. If K and H are the capital stocks of the representative firms in both sectors,[8] let the firms' production technologies be characterized by the linear production functions

$$X = AK \tag{33.1}$$

and

$$Y = BH, \tag{33.2}$$

where X and Y are the outputs of the respective sectors and A and B are parameters that summarize the level of technological knowledge. These parameters, however, depend on the overall level of the entire industry's capital stock, so that

$$A = K^a \tag{33.3}$$

and

$$B = H^b, \tag{33.4}$$

where a and b are positive parameters on the range $(0,1)$. The industry-wide production functions exhibit increasing returns to

---

[8] One may think of K and H as a mixture of equipment and human capital, for example.

scale, so that, with the number of firms normalized to unity in both sectors, we have $X = K^{1+a}$ and $Y = H^{1+b}$. Assume further that the representative agent values both goods so that his preferences can be represented by a utility function

$$U = U(q_1, q_2) = q_1^c q_2^{1-c}, \tag{33.5}$$

so that a fraction $c \in (0,1)$ of money expenditure is allocated to good 1. Let good 1 be the numeraire (money) good. Furthermore, assume that new capital can be created in either sector by merging the two goods according to a Cobb–Douglas technology. More precisely, if an entrepreneur (in either sector) wants to increase his capital stock by an amount Z, he has to use an amount v_1 of good 1 and v_2 of good 2, where

$$Z = \text{constant} \times \left(v_1^c v_2^{1-c} \right), \tag{33.6}$$

where v_1 and v_2 are the amounts of goods 1 and 2, respectively. Note that the coefficient c in the production technology is the same as that of the utility function (33.5). This technical assumption is useful since the composition of nominal (that is, denominated in good 1) demand is now constant regardless of the level of investment: a share c of expenditure is allocated to good 1 regardless of whether it is used to investment or consumption.[9]

Let p denote the relative price of good 2 in terms of good 1. This relative price is determined by demand and supply. As explained above, the demand for good 1 is equal to $c(AK + pBH)$, where the term in parentheses is the total income of the economy, and this demand must equal the supply of good 1 which is AK, so that the relative price is given by

$$p = \left(\frac{1-c}{c} \right)\left(\frac{AK}{BH} \right). \tag{33.7}$$

Suppose now that the economy exists for two periods. Today's income is given by the initial capital stocks K and H and the production functions (33.1) and (33.2). Assume that there is no depreciation. Each entrepreneur has to decide how much of today's income is to be consumed and how much to be invested

---

[9] Utility maximization by consumers and efficient choice of inputs in the production of new capital implies that the share of either good in total nominal expenditure corresponds to the respective Cobb–Douglas parameter.

to create new capital by using the technology (33.6). In period 2, the entire output is consumed. Let subscript 2 refer to next period variables, so that K_2 and H_2 are next year's capital stocks and p_2 is next year's price level.

The model in equations (33.1)–(33.7) implies that this period's utilities of the respective entrepreneurs can be represented by functions $V_1(AK,p,K_2)$ and $V_2(BH,p,H_2)$. The utility of the sector 1 entrepreneur depends positively on today's income AK and negatively on the relative price p and investment K_2. The utility function of the entrepreneur in sector 2 is similar but increasing in the relative price p, of course. Finally, we can define functions $W_1(A_2K_2,p_2)$ and $W_2(B_2H_2,p_2)$ which represent the utilities of the typical entrepreneurs in the next period (A_2 and B_2 are the technology coefficients at time 2). Both functions increase in their first argument (output) whilst an increase in the price p_2 of good 2 in year 2 increases the welfare of sector 2 entrepreneur and decreases that of his sector 1 colleague.

A *decentralized organization* of the economy does not lead to a full exploitation of the economies of scale. The entrepreneurs solve Maximization Problem (i):

$$\text{maximize } V_1\!\left(AK,p,K_2\right) + \beta W_1\!\left(A_2K_2,p_2\right) \text{ with respect to } K_2,$$

and

$$\text{maximize } V_2\!\left(BH,p,K_2\right) + \beta W_2\!\left(B_2H_2,p_2\right) \text{ with respect to } H_2,$$

where β is the discount factor. The entrepreneurs take the future levels of technology A_2 and B_2 and next year's price level p_2 as given. For each expected price level p_2 and expected level of technology (A_2,B_2), there are optimal levels of investment (K_2,H_2) that come out of the maximization problem (i). The investment levels generate capital stocks that in turn determine the price-technology vector (p_2,A_2,B_2). The consistent perfect foresight equilibrium outcome is of course the fixed point of this composite mapping, i.e. an expected price-technology vector (p_2,A_2,B_2) such that it generates those amounts of investment (K_2,H_2) that in turn generate the expected vector (p_2,A_2,B_2).

The first best solution requires that the optimal investment programme takes into account the constraints (33.3) and (33.4). A benevolent planner can find a first best solution by solving Maximization Problem (ii):

$$\text{maximize } w\left[V_1\left(AK,p,K_2\right)+\beta W_1\left(A_2K_2,p_2\right)\right]$$

$$+\left(1-w\right)\left[V_2\left(BH,p,H_2\right)+\beta W_2\left(B_2H_2,p_2\right)\right]$$

with respect to K_2 and H_2, with constraints $A_2 = K_2^a$, $B_2 = H_2^b$ and

$$p = \left(\frac{1-c}{c}\right)\left(\frac{AK}{BH}\right) \text{ (as in equations 33.3, 33.4, and 33.7).}$$

In Problem (ii), the planner uses constant fractions $(w, 1 - w)$ to evaluate the welfare levels of the respective sectors. If the public authority is endowed with sufficient instruments, it can in principle impose this solution. For example, it can set a lump-sum tax on the entrepreneurs and then use it to subsidize invest-ment. Note, however, that this requires that the state authorities know the exact magnitudes of the parameters a and b. This is a stringent condition that is unlikely to be met in the real world. Moreover, the first best policy also requires that the state be able to operate a system of selective investment incentives, so that the level of the subsidy is set separately for each sector. This requirement may in turn run into political and legal difficulties.

Let us now call **corporatism** the variant of the model in which all the firms in each sector organize themselves into a corpora-tion which co-ordinates their investment policy. Suppose that the organized firms do know the magnitude of the parameters a and b. This assumption may be stringent, too, but it does make more sense than to assume that the state authorities have this information.[10]

Corporatism can now in principle improve the economy's per-formance. Corporation 1 will solve for K_2 by maximizing its expected welfare, taking into account constraint (33.3), while the corporation of sector 2 can similarly take into account constraint (33.4).

However, a new inefficient mechanism will now turn up. The corporations also perceive the price constraint (33.7) of the next period. This price constraint means that it is advantageous not to invest as much as would be implied by a first best solution: the more one sector invests, the lower will be the relative price of its own product in the next period. Thus, the corporatist solu-

---

[10] At least it makes sense to assume that the entrepreneurs know more about these parameters than the state authorities alone.

 Vartiainen

tion of the game without any state intervention is found by solving Maximization Problem (iii):

maximize $V_1\!\left(AK, p, K_2\right) + \beta W_1\!\left(A_2 K_2, p_2\right)$ with respect to K_2,

with constraints $A_2 = K_2^a$, $p = (1 - c)A_2 K_2/B_2 H_2$, and

maximize $V_2\!\left(BH, p, H_2\right) + \beta W_2\!\left(B_2 H_2, p_2\right)$ with respect to H_2,

with constraints $B_2 = H_2^b$ and $p = \left(\dfrac{1-c}{c}\right) A_2 K_2/B_2 H_2$.

Each corporation takes the investment programme of the other corporation as given. This corporatist setup defines a non-cooperative game, and the equilibrium of the economy is a Nash equilibrium of the game. In this equilibrium, the investment levels K_2 and H_2 fall short of the level implied by a first best solution, because each corporation wants to manipulate the relative price p.

However, the state can correct this inefficiency. All it needs do is to ration the relative price to a pre-specified level. If the price level of next year is set to p_2', the incentive for manipulating p by investing less is eliminated. The corporations now optimize their investment taking the price level p_2' as given, and the economic outcome is found by solving Maximization Problem (iv):

maximize $V_1\!\left(AK, p, K_2\right) + \beta W_1\!\left(A_2 K_2, p_2'\right)$ with respect to K_2,

with constraint $A_2 = K_2^a$, and

maximize $V_2\!\left(BH, p, H_2\right) + \beta W_2\!\left(B_2 H_2, p_2'\right)$ with respect to H_2,

with constraint $B_2 = H_2^b$.

The solution of this problem corresponds to one solution of the first best problem (ii).[11] The state can avoid a shortage or surplus of any of the two goods by setting the pre-specified price p_2' at the level which leads to market clearing. For each p_2', the corporations choose investment programmes that solve the maximization problem (iv). The corresponding capital stocks imply a price level through the price relation (33.7). If the state commits to the price level p_2' which leads to such capital stocks

---

[11] If one manipulates the first order conditions of Problem (ii) and Problem (iv), one sees that the first order conditions of the latter problem imply that the first order conditions of the former are identically true.

that they in turn generate that same price level p_2', the goods market will clear. Note that this requires that the state be really able to commit to a price policy. If the corporations believe that the authorities will re-optimize society's welfare in the next period, with the capital stocks given at that time, they will choose lower capital stocks. We will return to this point later.

The above model is suggested as a rudimentary theory of the state in a corporatist economy with increasing returns. If there are externalities related to investment, it is plausible to think that they may lead to a corporatist structure. The state may then have to step in to act as a mediator and limit the harmful consequences of unilateral strategic action. The model suggests a rationale for price rationing that is simply based on the need to limit the scope for strategic action.

A first best solution may in principle be attained without a corporatist structure (cf. optimization problem (ii)), but this seems to require that the state have an amount of information that is unlikely to occur in the real world. The real world of course contains many more variables than this model. Yet it is easy enough to imagine empirical counterparts to the mechanisms analysed in the context of the model. The model suggests that:

- the state might try to operate a selective industrial policy (cf. subsidies to investment in the model, if the state perceives the externalities (3) and (4));
- the state might want to operate a policy of low interest to affect investment (one interpretation for credit rationing in the context of the model is that the state tries to influence investment by lowering β, the discount factor);
- it may be advantageous for the state to encourage the build-up of corporatist structures (if the state authorities understand that their knowledge of the parameters a and b is less perfect than that of the industrialists themselves); however,
- the corporatist structure might lead to strategic conflicts which the state might have to mitigate by either selective industrial policies or administrative rationing of those prices which are seen as the strategic variables; therefore,
- the state must be strong enough to impose its own policies and must be able to commit to policies.

34

An Empirical Overview of State Intervention

Many of the suggested empirical counterparts can indeed be found in the country cases. There is no doubt about the degree of state involvement in the four countries. In all of them, the state has actively participated in the process of investment and capital accumulation. The menu of policy measures has been rich. The four countries have in varying degrees used:

- direct state ownership of key industries
- overall credit rationing and policy of low interest rates
- selective credit allocation to favoured industries
- selective administrative control over investment
- selective and general subsidies to investment
- administrative and political control of prices and wages
- publicly sponsored research on potential growth sectors and resource endowments.

So we see a rich menu of policy measures, which does make sense in terms of the simple economic model presented above.

The industrial policies of the case countries cannot easily be described or analysed in general terms. One important characteristic, however, which seems to be common for the industrial policy of the Asian miracles as well as Finland and Austria (and, more generally, for the Nordic countries) is the relatively little role of the neoclassical idea of competition and allocative efficiency in policy statements and policy formulation. The policymakers have instead been more interested in encouraging the growth of large firms capable to exploit assumed economies of scale (for the Nordic countries, see Hjalmarsson, 1991; for Korea and Taiwan, Chang, 1993 and Wade, 1989). This suggests that they have been motivated by assumptions of scale effects like (33.3) and (33.4) in the model. In other words, policymakers may have been more preoocupied with dynamic efficiency than with static competitive efficiency.[12]

Competition at home has even been actively suppressed. In Korea, for example, most industries have had restrictions on entry and capacity, and the Korean state has frequently used mergers and market-sharing arrangements to reorganize industries in which there have been 'too many' firms according to its judgement. The typical maker of industrial policy in our country cases has tended to see the objective of policy in terms of achieving industrial units large enough to survive in international competition.

In a small country, such policies have often meant that the company in question must acquire a monopoly position at home. This, however, has not been seen as a problem by domestic policymakers, since they have thought that the large domestic firm will anyway be confronted with competitive conditions on the international market.

The economic variable that has been most important to policymakers has been the allocation and amount of new investment, as the model would predict. The state has allocated direct subsidies to various industries. All the four countries have also used credit rationing and selective allocation of credit, so that some favoured projects and industries have had a privileged access to low-price credit. In Finland, for example, the central bank has even directly financed some investment activities.

Finally, as described in Chapter 36, the state authorities in all countries encouraged the build-up of corporatist structures, although the political balance of power has differed from country to country. But in all the four countries, the state has sought to establish a coherent corporatist structure with which it would be able to deal.

---

[12] The potential conflict between static efficiency and dynamic performance was pointed out early by Schumpeter (1942), who emphasized that free entry would discourage innovation because rents due to entrepreneurial innovation would be wiped out by competition.

35

Further Mechanisms of Success

The discussion has hopefully so far made some sense of the first two stylized facts of Chapter 31. The extensive state intervention obeys a sound economic logic—provided one is willing to buy the basic assumptions of externalities. However, what has been said hitherto should apply to almost any small economy. What has made the four countries successful? Why have the states been willing and capable to act in ways conducive to success? This section discusses stylized facts 3–6 and suggests at least some ways in which they may have contributed to good performance.

35.1 Stylized fact 3: extensive planning but abstention from a planned economy as a system choice

The third observation was that an extremely étatist and interventionist policy has coexisted with a commitment, of ultimate principle, to respect the right to private property and not to proceed towards a socialist planned economy. This is an issue that the economic discussion on planning versus markets has failed to appreciate fully. The question of whether 'planning can work' or not may depend crucially on whether it is attempted as a temporary way of organizing a transition towards a modern market economy or as a fundamental 'system' solution. In the former case, which is the one of all our case countries, the prospective entrepreneur can count on the system's commitment to keep the incentives of private entrepreneurship alive. In such a situation, even extensive and direct administrative interference might be tolerable in his eyes. In the latter case, the prospect of being able ever to recover the returns of today's investments is poor, and the environment for entrepreneurship is wrought with much more uncertainty.

Thus, basic political commitments may be as important as specific policies. Paradoxically, a regime that is fundamentally committed to respect private property and the private ownership of productive assets may successfully use wide-ranging planning and other radical ways of political intervention. These are then accepted by capitalists as temporary measures.

A left-wing regime, on the other hand, keen in its anti-market rhetoric, loses the confidence of domestic investors even if the practical policy package is not very radical and comprehensive. Thus, 'right-wing' interventionism may have a built-in advantage vis-à-vis 'left-wing' interventionism. As pointed out by Katzenstein (1984), there has at times been more planning in the Austrian economy than in some of its nominally socialist neighbours. Similarly, the accounts by Wade (1989) and Amsden (1989) show that Taiwan and Korea at best were not much behind the GDR in overall *dirigisme*. Yet Austria, Taiwan and Korea were also committed to and successful in becoming capitalist economies.

Another example which illustrates this comparison is that of Peru during the years of President Alan Garcia, 1985–8. Garcia's aim was to mobilize domestic investors in a national programme of industrial restructuring. Although his policies would probably not have been more interventionist than those of Taiwan and Korea, his basic political orientation and anti-IMF rhetorics aroused the suspicions of the national elites and his economic policy resulted in a failure.[13]

The experience of Austria is also instructive in this respect. In that country, a very extensive programme of nationalization was undertaken at the end of World War II and again in 1955 when the Soviet army withdrew from Austria and many enterprises that had been in its zone of occupation fell into Austrian hands. However, this was not seen as primarily an ideological decision, and it did not seem to hamper the willingness of entrepreneurs to co-operate with the state within the corporatist power structure.

---

[13] Of course, Garcia's explicit political project of reneging foreign debt was a clear breaking of the market-oriented rules of the game. Although stopping the interest payments on foreign debt increased the scope for short-term industrial policy, a rational domestic investor in Peru must have pondered whether a regime not committed to the fundamental property rights of capitalism would in the future guarantee a fair return on his own investment

35.2 Stylized fact 4: a large and competent bureaucracy in a strong state

The fourth stylized fact was the observation that the state has been 'strong' in all the four countries. This has meant that the state has been politically able to operate an interventionist policy, but it also has to do with the fact that there has been a large and competent bureaucracy which has enforced these policies. As emphasized by the Weberian tradition, rational management of the economy requires a meritocratic bureaucracy that is competent and autonomous enough to obey its own logic which is not one of individual utility maximization. The Weberian professional bureaucracy consists of career civil servants who are committed to their tasks and prestigious enough not to be easily corrupted by outside interests. Such a meritocratic civil service is also able to reproduce itself, since its prestige makes it possible to recruit from the best talents.

Thus, the quality of state institutions depends on history and traditions. In a political culture in which the public service is held in high esteem, it is easier to recruit amongst the best minds. This has been emphasized by Wade (1989) for Taiwan as well as Amsden (1989) for Korea. In Korea and Taiwan, the industrial pilot agencies were continuously able to retain their prestige and recruit able personnel. Corruption and mediocrity are self-enforcing phenomena as well: mediocre administrations can at best attract mediocre people, and corrupt regimes attract corrupt people and encourage the corruption even of those who originally tried to enhance the common interest.

Our success cases have all 'enjoyed' the services of a competent and prestigious administrative bureaucracy able to design and carry out successful industrial policies. We argued above that a successful state must be able to formulate credible and consistent policies that do not change overnight. This is precisely what bold and insensitive bureaucracies are good at.

By contrast, it is characteristic of weak states that they do not have genuine bureaucracies. Instead, the civil servants' behaviour follows the economic logic of individual maximization. In its most extreme forms, this is seen in the militarily strong but otherwise certainly weak African states where even administrative behaviour is aimed at individual revenue maximization. In an interesting book, Peter Evans (1995) describes at length the Zairian state, where 'everything is for sale', and 'personalism and plundering at the top destroys any possibility of rule-governed behaviour in the lower levels of the bureaucracy, giving individual maximization free rein underneath'. As Evans rightly points out, it is not bureaucracy but its absence that makes the state rapacious.

Another, less extreme case in point is related to the 'industrial organization of corruption', as analysed recently by Shleifer and Vishny (1993). The economy may tolerate a reasonable amount of corruption as long as this corruption is organized by a 'monopoly', so that an entrepreneur need not bribe a thousand officials to get a project completed. This is one more argument for a strong and centralized bureaucracy. A strong bureaucracy may harass the prospective entrepreneur with a lot of red tape, but if individual bureaucrats are well monitored within the system, the economic costs of corruption remain moderate. The monopolistic bureaucrat of the strong state expropriates a part of the economic surplus related to an investment project, but if the project is economically sound, it will be carried out anyway. The situation is very different with the uncontrolled bureaucracies of weak states: there the entrepreneur must bribe every official that can block the investment, and these competing bureaucrats together impose a much higher economic cost on the economy.[14]

The political and bureaucratic strength of the state has a nice interpretation in the economic model of Chapter 33. The efficient corporatist solution corresponding to the optimization problem (iv) requires that the state be able to *commit* to hold the price level at the chosen level when the latter period arrives, even if that choice would *ex post* seem to decrease the welfare of the economy. Now the ability to commit is precisely one plausible interpretation of 'strength' of the state power. Returning to the model, note what happens if the state cannot commit and make a credible announcement of next year's price level p_2'. Then the two corporations will understand that, whatever the state now says, it will reoptimize society's welfare in the next period by solving its optimization problem with the given capital

---

[14] For a formal analysis, see Shleifer and Vishny (1993).

stocks. Then they understand that they can *de facto* manipulate the price level, and the economy will again be in an inefficient equilibrium defined by optimization problem (iii). Both corporations will cut down their investment to increase the relative price of their product.[15]

35.3 Stylized fact 5: the external challenge

The fifth observation was that all the four cases have found themselves in a difficult situation in international politics. They have been situated in a contested borderzone of the world's two ideological blocks and faced with much more powerful countries. The very existence of Korea has been dependent on the constellations of international politics and on the willingness of the USA to maintain its military presence in the area. A similar story might apply to Taiwan, the existence of which has been continuously put into question. Taiwanese rulers were faced with the challenge of mainland China and an outright economic failure could have meant the very end of the Taiwanese State. In addition, the Taiwanese political elite represented an immigrant minority on the island, so that they could not even be sure of their support at home.

Finland and Austria have also shared a precarious international position. Both countries found themselves after World War II in the borderzone of two political power blocks, and both had a history of bitter internal conflicts and civil war. For Finland, a successful industrialization and an integration of the productive structure into the Western European economies was a powerful political objective as well as an economic motivation. The build-up of state-led corporatist structures from the 1960s onwards was a conscious political mobilization project encouraged by the state as well as many employers (see Jakobson 1992). The encompassing nature of Austrian corporatism probably also owes something to a political project of national integration and mobilization (see below).

---

[15] Rodrik (1992) presents a simple but very nice analysis of the importance of the ability to commit for development in general and trade policies in particular.

Thus, these countries could ill afford an economic failure. One plausible interpretation of this is that an external threat to the nation state changes the payoffs of the game in a fortunate way. In the context of the model of Chapter 33, imagine that the economy is corporatist but that the state authority is weak, so that it does not have the political power to ration prices and thereby impose an efficient investment programme on the economy. Then the Nash equilibrium of the game between the two corporations (cf. optimization problem (iii)) results in too little investment.

However, suppose now that there is an external threat to the nation, so that the economy is wiped out and everybody's payoff in period 2 is zero unless the output of period 2 corresponds to a threshold level. Specifically, let K_2' and H_2' be the levels of investment associated with the efficient problem (iv) when the price p is set at the implied market clearing level. Suppose that everybody's welfare is nil unless the outputs of both sectors reach the critical levels:

$$X \geq K_2'^{1+a}, \tag{35.1}$$

and

$$Y \geq H_2'^{1+b}. \tag{35.2}$$

In other words, the economy can survive only if it invests in a fully efficient way. This changes the payoffs of the game, so that efficient investment now becomes an equilibrium strategy for both players. In political terms, this means that the political authorities have an easy job in persuading the industrialists to undertake large investment programmes at the expense of short-term profitability. Thus, external threats can improve the state's bargaining muscle vis-à-vis the economy's organized agents.

35.4 Stylized fact 6: disruption of old elites

The last observation is that World War II and the related events had in all the four countries thoroughly shaken the power structure. We cannot really relate this observation to the analysis of the model economy, but it is a feature interesting enough to be mentioned in its own right. One may hypothesize that a weakening of ancient elites greatly enhances the freedom of action of an economically enlightened bureaucracy. Old power blocks generally resist change, almost by definition. The existence of an interest organization is a proof of some success in safeguarding a special interest (for otherwise it would not be profitable for the agents in question to keep up the interest organization). Inasmuch as structural change disrupts the established shares of incomes and resources, the successful interest organizations have on average more to lose.

This last stylized fact is also consistent with Mancur Olson's (1990) theory about the beneficial consequences of political disruptions: in the course of time, interest groups become more capable of seeking rents at the expense of others, so that a shake-out of a society's power groupings also diminishes the scope for harmful rent seeking. At first glance, this idea seems to conflict with the empirical finding according to which political upheavals tend to hamper economic growth.[16] These latter findings, however, are more concerned with long-term instability whereas it is not at all inconceivable that some particular political crisis may in its aftermath lead to a favourable growth surge. Note also that the political transformations of our four country cases all had to do with external circumstances so that by itself they were not a symptom of the state's political inability.

[16] See, for example, Alesina and Perotti (this volume).

36

An Overview of Country Experiences

This chapter briefly describes the individual experiences of each country case in the light of the foregoing discussion. We pay relatively more attention to Finland and Austria, since many excellent analyses (especially Wade, 1989; Amsden, 1989) have already been devoted to the two Asian miracles.

36.1 Korea

Korea illustrates most of the elements outlined above. The Korean state has been very strong not only towards labour but also towards business. The Korean state has offered large rewards for successful entrepreneurs, but it has also had the ability to discipline business: 'where Korea differs from most other late industrialising countries is in the discipline its state exercises over private firms' (Amsden, 1989, p. 14).

The historical roots of the strength of the Korean state have been analysed by Amsden (1989). The Japanese colonization of Korea left a vacuum of power after World War II, and the state was able to establish its power in the 1960s because of the weakness of social classes. The landlord aristocracy had been dispersed by land reform, the working class was too small and too weak to pose a serious challenge, and capitalists had become dependent on government subsidies. The military government nationalized the banks in 1961, which gave the state the power to determine the allocation and timing of industrial investment.

Thus there is no question of the strength of the Korean state. But it was also confronted with checks and balances that prevented a degeneration into pervasive corruption. Amsden emphasizes the role of the student movement as well as that of external pressures and the US administration. The student movement was important because it presented the state with a constant danger of rebellion which in turn 'disciplined' the government against the worst excesses of power. The students were in a pivotal position because the Korean strategy of industrialization relied on a rapid education of a class of salaried engineers and other white-collar workers.

The external challenge factor has also been present. The North Korean regime has provided a challenge which may have compelled the Korean rulers to pay more attention to overall performance and efficiency than would otherwise have been the case. Korea has not been a real democracy until recently and it is instructive to ask what did prevent a degeneration of its economy in the hands of an authoritarian state apparatus which was not really controlled by democratically elected bodies. The student movement may have played a role in controlling the actions of the state, but the external challenge of North Korea and the dependency on the US military commitment are another important explanation.

36.2 Taiwan

Taiwan's performance has been analysed by Wade (1989) and Amsden (1988), who both characterize Taiwan's industrialization from the 1930s to the 1980s as state-led. In the late 1940s, agriculture was still by far the most important sector in Taiwan, accounting for 90 per cent of exports. Four 4-year plans between years 1953 and 1968 brought a remarkably rapid industrialization. In accordance with the 'Scandinavian–Asian' model of industrial policy outlined above, Taiwanese industrial policies have emphasized the sectoral promotion of productivity at the expense of domestic competition.

Taiwan shares with Korea a past of Japanese colonialism. The strength of the Taiwanese state derives from the 'invasion' of the island by the two million military and civilian Nationalist mainlanders in 1949 after the defeat of the Nationalist army. The islanders had no army or powerful political structure to challenge the position of the Nationalist forces, and the Nationalist-mainlander government could enjoy unusually wide room for manoeuvre (Wade, p. 75). The monopolies originally owned by the Japanese colonialists passed to the incoming government. The government established multiyear development plans. They were not very detailed, but these government initiatives laid the basis for several branches of production (including plastics, fibres, cement and textiles). In the 1960s and 1970s, new export sectors such as steel, automobiles and shipbuilding were boosted, partly motivated by the idea of import substitution. Throughout this period, the government intervened heavily in favour of export industries. An impressive economic bureaucracy was set up to manage the governing of the economy.

In Taiwan's case, too, the Nationalist rulers were faced with a strict external challenge. Being the claimants of legal rule in mainland China, they could ill afford a failure in economic management. A challenge, external to the Nationalist party but internal to the Taiwanese society, was constituted by the native Taiwanese islanders, whom the Nationalists excluded from power positions (Wade, p. 237).

36.3 Finland

Finland provides an example of state-led corporatist industrialization where all the elements analysed in the above story have been present. Although Finland's severe crisis in the early 1990s has blurred the picture, it is clear that Finland's economic performance under the post-World War II period must be considered as very successful. The breakthrough of industrialization took place later than in the other Nordic countries. The economy was predominantly agrarian in the 1930s, and as late as around 1950 more than half of the population and 40 per cent of output was still in the primary sector. Per capita GDP was only half of that of Sweden (Andersson *et al.*, 1993). By the late 1970s, Finland had become a mature industrial economy.

Finland came out of World War II in a very vulnerable position between the power blocks of international politics. The victorious Soviet Union did not invade the country, but throughout the next forty years Finland was within the sphere of influence of Soviet foreign policy. Immediately after the war, the Soviet Union imposed a heavy war indemnity which required an extremely rapid build-up of industrial production. The way in which this challenge was tackled points the way to the organization of economic management that was to become prevalent for the entire period of state-led industrialization. The organization of industrial production was entrusted to a joint committee of civil servants, private industrialists and bankers.

This starting-point led to a conscious programme of state-sponsored industrialization and a build-up of a corporatist structure that was actively encouraged by the state. In the early 1950s, a strategic decision was made not to decrease taxes to the pre-war levels but to use instead the surplus created by the subtraction of war expenditure from the budget to increase investment by state-owned as well as private companies.[17] As a result of this and a tradition of fiscal orthodoxy, the Finnish state became an important net saver for the economy. The structural budget surplus did not vanish until the 1980s, and public saving accounted for as much as 30 per cent of aggregate saving during the 1950s and 1960s (see Kosonen, 1992). President Urho Kekkonen also thought that the trade unions would moderate their wage claims if a larger share of savings and investment were undertaken by the state.

The first phase of industrialization in the 1950s and early 1960s was characterized by active and direct state participation in the diversification of the economy (see Andersson *et al.*, p. 13). Several new state-owned companies were established and old ones were developed.[18] The 1950s in particular were a period in which wages as well as prices were regulated within a political bargain in which political parties as well as corporatist bodies took part (cf. the corporatist solution with price rationing in the model). Typically, the state would encourage long-term wage contracts with low wage increases and would then also regulate the prices of basic agricultural products such as milk. At the same time, it invested heavily in state-owned companies while the monetary authorities channelled cheap finance to manufacturing investment.

With the decision-making institutions, we see at work both an efficient bureaucratic tradition and a powerful corporatist network. The prestige and strength of the civil service have been

---

[17] A classical reference on this issue is the book by the later president Urho Kekkonen *Onko maallamme malttia vaurastua* (Has our country the patience to prosper), 1952, where he endorses a state-led investment strategy.

[18] The most important examples include Neste, which established a monopoly of oil refining and then continued into different lines of petro-chemicals and plastics.

repeatedly emphasized by Finnish historians. This tradition dates back to the autonomy period from 1809 to 1917 when Finland was under Russia's rule. Throughout this period, the civil service was in Finnish hands and its legalistic tradition provided a protective shield against the imperialistic aspirations of Russian politics. This is one important factor that explains the powerful and respected position of the Finnish civil service in comparison with the government and the parliamentary institutions. The civil service has played an important role in economic policy throughout the post-war years. In comparison with the East Asian countries, one may say that the Finnish state, if understood as the political power of a parliamentarian government, has been relatively weaker while business corporations and a relatively autonomous bureaucracy have been very strong.

The build-up of corporatist structures had already begun in the interwar years, but it was actively continued in the 1950s and the 1960s. In a way similar to Austria, key economic decisions have been taken within an informal network that has encompassed the leaders of powerful business corporations, the monetary authorities at the central bank and the top civil servants as well as government officials.

These are typical ways of corporatist concertation in which the state is but one actor among many others. But there is no doubt about the essential mechanisms: Finnish industrialization was 'managed' by a handful of corporatist leaders, top civil servants, bankers, central bankers and government officials. This half-official–half-corporátist decision-making structure dates back to the very birth of the independent state. The victorious White side of the civil war of 1918 was an improvised organization of the military, bankers, industrialists and right-wing politicians. Generally distrustful of republican democracy, they established a constitution which set clear checks and balances for a properly political intervention into the economy. The rights to private property in particular have enjoyed a strict constitutional protection. This can be seen as an important ingredient in the 'basic commitment' discussed above; a basic commitment that has probably been especially crucial for a country that has been situated at a contested zone between the world's ideological blocks.

The banks and the central bank have been an important headquarter of economic management. The credit markets were rationed until the 1980s and, similarly to Taiwan and Korea, credit was allocated to productive manufacturing investment while the households' demand for credit exceeded supply. From the 1930s onwards, the central bank became an authoritative agent of economic policy, well endowed with ties with the business community. The central bank also financed directly a number of selected economic activities.

Finnish corporatism had from the aftermath of the civil war of 1918 acquired a pro-business character. However, when the Finnish left and the trade union movement were strengthened after World War II, they were gradually encompassed into the established decision-making institutions without revolution in those institutions. The buildup of a coherent corporatist structure at the 'labour' side, that is, the comprehensive unionization of Finnish workers, was not resisted by the state. On the contrary, it was actively encouraged by the authorities in the 1960s, when the unionization rate increased from under 40 per cent to almost 80 per cent (see Pekkarinen and Vartiainen, 1993). This had its economic as well as political logic, both fitting well into the stylized story of managed industrialization of a small and vulnerable economy. From the point of view of the state authorities and the employers, the inclusion of workers in a corporatist structure was a protection against communist influence and a way to contain potentially dangerous political pressures. In economic terms, it was seen as a means of controlling wage inflation and distributive shares and limiting industrial conflicts. A concrete expression of this official acceptance of trade union organization was the introduction in 1967 of the tax deduction on the membership fee of a trade union.

Finally, we also see at work the phenomenon of old power networks being dissolved by the outcome of the war. Finland's defeat in the war against the Soviet Union discredited the bourgeois parties, and from then on the business community felt much more insecure and more in need of political support. This facilitated the practical management of the economy.

The étatist aspects of Finnish economic management were greatly enhanced by trade with the Soviet Union. This was organized politically, and close ties with the political elites became a source of lucrative business contracts as well.

36.4 Austria

The Austrian economy also underwent a process of late industrialization after World War II. In contrast to Czechoslovakia, Austria had never been part of the industrialized core area of Central Europe, and the outcome of the war left Austria with an economy that still relied to a great extent on agricultural output and primary production. Furthermore, the Potsdam agreement of 1945 gave the Soviets the right to seize German assets in their occupation zone and many Austrian factories were effectively dismantled and the machinery parts sent to the Soviet Union (Mjöset, 1992, p. 164). However, the period running from the late 1940s to the 1970s became one of heavy expansion for manufacturing industries. Iron and steel production as well as output of aluminium products expanded particularly rapidly.

Most of the mechanisms discussed above can be seen at work in Austria. The legal and formal institutions that have carried out the political intervention into the economy have been more similar to Finland's than those of the East Asian cases: the Austrian state has been relatively weak in comparison with the power of the various semi-official corporations. The Austrian state and the corporations of civil society have merged with each other in a remarkable way. In broad terms, the Austrian and the Finnish cases are reminiscent of each other.

Austria, too, had to struggle for survival from 1945 to 1952. After the liberation from Nazi rule, the economy was in chaos and the country did not enjoy full sovereignty. Austria was occupied by the Allied (including Soviet) forces until 1955. As in the other cases treated in this section, it is fair to say that an economic failure could have led to further losses of sovereignty.

This critical starting-point led to a remarkable mobilization of the nation's resources and the adoption of an industrialization strategy that depended on state action and corporatist concertation. This was a response to the external challenge as well as a reflection of the country's history. There had been a tragic civil war in 1934, when the Social Democrats, having been subjected to increasing provocation by the Nazis, took to arms. The victory of the conservative forces led to an authoritarian government, and the Austrian state's half-hearted attempt to counter Nazi-German infiltration was unsuccessful. The country was annexed to Germany in 1938. Thus, there were ample lessons of the dangers of internal strife and external threats. With reference to the discussion of Chapter 35, one can say that the outcome of the war certainly produced a situation where established internal power blocks were disrupted. 'Denazification' laws passed in 1946 and 1947 formally eliminated Nazi influence from the public life of Austria, and the labour movement had to reconstruct itself after years of repression.

The management of the Austrian economy has typically taken place in an informal borderzone of public decision making and private concertation. Yet there has been a strong centralization of power in economic policymaking, which, as far as the practical results are concerned, has been equivalent to a strong state. Whether all these decisions have been taken within the formal jurisdiction of state activities is then of secondary importance. As emphasized by Katzenstein (1984, p. 66), this concentration of power occurs 'in a political setting that does not recognise a distinction between public and private. Lines of formal authority are typically blurred. As bodies of public law, some of Austria's major interest groups exercise, in addition to their normal, autonomous operations, administrative powers delegated by the state'. A typical institution in this respect is the *Joint Commission*, which joins both state representatives and industrial organizations in deliberations about incomes policies and other economic policies.

The political management of the economy included, firstly, nationalization of a large part of the Austrian economy. At the end of World War II, the newly established Parliament decided to nationalize most of the assets seized by Germans after the Anschluss of 1938. Similarly, when the Soviet Union withdrew its forces from Austria in 1955, many of the enterprises formerly in the Soviet zone of influence fell into the hands of Austrian state. This vast nationalization reinforces the argument that stateled economic management can be perfectly acceptable from the point of view of private capitalists as long as it is not motivated by a Socialist ideology. It was clear in Austria that these nationalizations were not a reflection of ideological class struggle but instead an expression of the striving for national independence.[19]

There have been important elements of planning and political intervention within Austrian economic policy. There has been extensive regulation of prices and wages by political-corporatist bodies. The first wage/price agreements in 1947 were immediate responses to the inflationary chaos of the immediate postwar period. This coordination was institutionalized in 1951. The political-corporatist determination of prices has, remarkably, been by and large accepted even by the business community.

Finally, the public ownership of a large part of the banking sector and rationing of credit markets has 'socialized' a large part of investment decisions. This political determination of investment has introduced one further instrument which has made it easier to conclude corporatist agreements.

Many authors have emphasized the weakness of the Austrian state with respect to the corporations of civil society. We have argued above that this weakness is somewhat illusory, since the state and corporations have merged with each other and power has been centralized. Furthermore, Austria, too, has enjoyed a strong administrative tradition that dates back to the mercantilist unification of the most important German parts of the Habsburg empire in the eighteenth century (see Katzenstein, 1984, p. 63). The Austrian civil service has a reputation of great competence and is intimately involved in relations with business and trade unions. Measured by the number of officials per capita, Austria's welfare bureaucracy is larger than that of any other Western European country (Katzenstein, 1984, p. 63). So, we see, again, a competent bureaucracy richly endowed with formal and informal ties with organized economic agents. The East Asian one-party state is substituted in Austria with a network of corporatist arrangements and a state influenced by two remarkably stable political parties.

---

[19] In this respect it is important to note that the nationalization laws were passed unanimously by the Austrian parliament (Katzenstein, 1984, p. 49).

37

Conclusions

We have tried to understand the political and economic determinants of successful state intervention in industrialization. Can they be generalized to produce 'recipes' for success? It must be emphasized that these experiences relate to specific stages of economic development. Forces that generate long-run growth are different and still largely unknown. However, many theoretical and empirical arguments emphasize the importance of thresholds and qualitative leaps. The study of particular phases of industrialization and structural change is therefore an extremely important task for development economics. Whether state-led strategies like the ones analysed in this paper can generate growth in the long run is an altogether different question. The discussion by Katzenstein (1984) and many others has also pointed out weaknesses of state-led strategies in the long run. In the Austrian case, for example, Katzenstein (1984) argues that the economy's ability to produce innovations has not been very good.

There are also a number of compositional fallacies involved in the idea that the East Asian or Finnish experiences could be generalized. Firstly, these countries took advantage of a particularly favourable phase of the world economy. Secondly, Taiwan and Korea have protected and subsidized their growing industries in many ways. If all developing countries attempted to run similarly aggressive industrial policies, the international market would become much more difficult to penetrate for anybody.

The idiosyncratic nature of some of the proposed 'mechanisms of success' also renders the idea of replication meaningless. We have suggested that external threats posed by international politics may have consolidated the political institutions in a way that has produced good results. Yet it is clear that one would not wish to live in a world politically so unstable that the threat of conflict and destruction would be a major motive for economic development. We also suggested that former political upheavals might in these countries produce a situation where economically enlightened state bureaucrats had a large amount of room for manoeuvring. By the same token, development policies cannot be built on exceptional upheavals.

However, not all of the suggested mechanisms are self-defeating. The experience of the case countries suggests that a coherent and meritocratic bureaucracy dealing with a well-organized corporatist network can produce good results. The mainstream development policies advocated today by the developed countries perhaps pay too much attention to the creation of free exchange, at the expense of emphasizing the importance of social and political institutions that create stability, order and political acceptance of structural change (see Biersteker, 1990 and 1992). The incredibly complex system of implicit and explicit contracts and moral rules of which a mature market economy consists contains a lot of hidden order that has developed, whether spontaneously or not, during decades and centuries. In countries where such a system is not yet in place, a one-sided emphasis on 'freedom' of transactions may be ill-placed. As emphasized by Peter Evans (1995) the predatory states of Africa offer ample evidence of individual optimization going on at all levels of the state institutions. The economic cost of a competent bureaucracy, on the other hand, may be small when compared to the benefits it can bring about if it can impose a stable set of rules within which people can operate.

38

Comment

JONAS AGELL

This paper addresses an important question. What kind of social institutions, in a very broad sense, are likely to promote growth and development? Why have countries as diverse as Austria, Finland, Korea and Taiwan been success stories in the post-war period, while things have gone sour for countries like Peru and Uruguay?

The paper suggests a definite answer. The success stories have been characterized by a high degree of social corporatism. A powerful state, spearheaded by a competent bureaucracy, has actively intervened in the development process. The private sector has been dominated by a few large players, primarily organized labour and nation-wide business confederations. Strategic decisions on economic and industrial policy have been taken in concert between the state and the private players. The state has used a comprehensive package of sticks and carrots to mobilize and allocate investment in an environment characterized by increasing returns to scale and various growth externalities. An important additional role for the state has been to internalize various distributional conflicts, and to establish a reasonable measure of social harmony. Finally, the successful late industrializers have all been exposed to some stringent external threat, that has imposed an efficiency discipline on their ruling elites.

The paper draws much on the literature on social corporatism in already developed economies. In this literature, social corporatism is sometimes used as a more or less direct synonym for the economics of social democracy (this is particularly true in parts of the political science literature). As a prototype example, we may think of Sweden in the 1950s and 1960s. According to some writers this particular episode can be viewed as the realization of a highly successful social contract between the state, labour and capital. A strong government mitigated distributional tensions in society, and contributed actively to growth and structural change via the corporate tax system and extensive manpower programmes. An all-encompassing trade union movement shouldered its social responsibility, and accepted moderate wage claims, knowing that the similarly organized business sector would invest the residual in a way beneficial to productivity and future wages.

Is this too rosy a picture of recent Swedish economic history? I must confess that I have not the slightest idea. But maybe the question is not all that important. Whatever its shortcomings, the Swedish model still represents an interesting social experiment, that deserves careful scrutiny, both of its glorious past and of its more troublesome present.

Extending the grand vision of social corporatism to the context of development economics is certainly no easy task. A common theme in development economics is that latecomers in the industrialization process face quite different constraints than pioneer nations, like the UK or the USA. As a consequence, the lessons of pioneer countries may be of little value for latecomers. Also, in an area swamped with case studies, it is easy to get the impression that every latecomer is more or less unique, and that luck and coincidence play an important role. Due to differences in historical trade patterns, resource endowments and the extent of ethnic conflicts start-up conditions may not look the same everywhere. As a consequence, a policy that works in Korea may spell trouble in Ghana or Romania.

These peculiarities do not suggest that large-scale system thinking is a waste of time. Properly used, it helps us to frame interesting questions, and it reminds us of the skies above us. But we should not confuse map and reality. While the Arrow–Debreu model is an extremely useful pedagogical device that helps us to think 'big', we do not expect our students to view it as a literal description of any real world economy. While Marxian class analysis instructs us that social conflicts are important objects of study, most of us do not expect capitalism to end with a big bang. To me, much the same goes for the vision of social corporatism. While this vision underscores the fact that we need to know more about the role of the state and strong, organized private interests in the growth process, we should be wary of viewing it as a ready-made formula for economic success.

Having thus stated my own priors, I will organize my discussion under three main headings.

38.1 Internal consistency check or normative blueprint?

Juhana Vartiainen carefully outlines the kind of economic assumptions that are needed to make sense of social corporatism. Think of an economy characterized by increasing returns to scale and lots of sector-specific growth externalities. This is a rather deplorable situation, at least as long as every sector consists of a number of small competitive firms. What can we do to improve things? Well, a benevolent government might of course do something about it, using standard pigouvian taxes and subsidies. But, as Vartiainen points out, that may not be enough. If private sector agents have an informational advantage, which seems plausible, the government may intervene in the wrong way. So if we want to internalize the growth externalities we must look in another direction. This is where big business and organized labour enters the picture. By definition, such actors can remedy sector-specific externalities, and the assumption of increasing returns to scale means that there will be strong incentives for the build-up of corporatist and monopolistic structures.

By now our economy looks pretty centralized, but there is still no role for social corporatism and the state. But, as Vartiainen points out, a corporatist society is also a bargaining society, and we know that bargaining games may produce dynamically inefficient outcomes. In this setting we also know that an external co-ordinator may resolve the issues. Let's call her the state. The state must be able to do many things well. Mitigating distributional conflicts and providing a balanced package of sticks and carrots to steer investment is only one side of the coin. Some of the growth externalities may be due to infrastructure investments, education and large-scale research projects, which may only be handled by the state.

The state must also follow some rules of the game. It must be strong, in the sense of being able to resist pressure from special interests. The state bureaucracy must be competent, and devoted to national mobilization rather than maximization of its own well-being. To uphold the long-run incentives for private entrepreneurship the state must also respect private property—a requirement that draws a sharp demarcation line between the kind of social corporatism envisioned by Vartiainen and the planned economies of the former Eastern Bloc. However, as witnessed by the four countries singled out in the paper, the distinction between authoritarian rule and Western-style democracy does not seem to be an important one.

Now we are home and safe. We have a vision of a successful and highly corporatist development machinery, where every institution performs its well-thought-out task. There are two ways to interpret this grand story. The first one, which is the one that I prefer, is to view it as an internal consistency check. What kind of assumptions, economic and political, are needed to make sense of corporatism? Viewed in this light, I find Vartiainen's careful discussion very useful. Contrary to the gut reactions of many economists, he convincingly shows that there are a number of well-defined neoclassical market failures that may motivate corporatist structures. As a corollary he also demonstrates that unhindered *laissez faire* constitutes no quick and safe road to a development miracle.

The second interpretation is more troublesome. While Vartiainen is careful not to oversell his argument, there is throughout the paper a lingering tension between the theoretical assumptions and the discussion of the four empirical success stories. Sometimes it is easy to get the impression that Vartiainen also views the theoretical market failures as undisputed facts of life. The reader easily gets the impression that the comparative economic success of a handful of small open economies also demonstrates the empirical accuracy of the theoretical assumptions. Suddenly the vision turns descriptive—social corporatism *is* a superior development engine.

Apart from the simple point that there rarely is only one unique way of interpreting observed economic behaviour, Vartiainen's version of social corporatism relies crucially on the idea that externalities permeate every corner of the economy, and that the state (or the planning board) can identify them with some precision. No sensible person should reject the idea that social returns often differ from private ones. But every theorist (and perhaps growth theorists in particular) also knows that cleverly assigned externalities are a safe route to unconventional policy results. With a little imagination, it is indeed hard to think of any policy intervention that can not be rationalized by invoking the right kind of externalities. However, our empirical evidence on the importance of various growth externalities is very meagre, to say the least. While I am aware of some very interesting work on R&D spillovers (for example, Bresnahan, 1984; Griliches and Lichtenberg, 1984) and on the importance of growth externalities in manufacturing (for example, Bartelsman *et al.*, 1991), it seems yet short from the stage when we can start to think about policy, not to speak of grand system design.

38.2 Who disciplines the state?

Modern discussion of development dispensed with the notion of a benevolent social planner a long time ago. Understanding the development process requires an understanding of the interaction of political and economic constraints. As Vartiainen points out, there is no easy way to discipline the state. A democracy may certainly be hijacked by various special interests, just as authoritarian rule may promote the worst excesses of corruption and clientism.

To explain the apparent success of some corporatist economies Vartiainen proposes an interesting hypothesis. In countries like Austria, Finland, Korea and Taiwan, the state bureaucracy has been forced to be strong and to act competently because of a stringent challenge of international politics. As these countries were situated in a contested border zone between capitalism and communism, they could not afford economic mismanagement. The political authorities thus had a relatively easy job in persuading organized business and labour to undertake large investment programmes. By contrast, countries with a less delicate international position could survive with less efficient management of their economies.

I am no political scientist, so I do not feel very competent in evaluating this hypothesis. However, it seems a bit simplistic.

Should we, for example, view the current problems of the Finnish economy as the result of the collapse of the Soviet military threat? I also believe that one could just as well argue that there are many circumstances where external challenges may have a negative impact on the consistency of economic policy making. In any case, external threats are not a policy option. If social corporatism is to serve as a development strategy of more general interest, there must be some alternative mechanism to discipline the state.

38.3 How can we make social corporatism operational?

In his introduction, Vartiainen explicitly rejects the idea of using standard empirical and statistical methods to explore the link between corporatist structures and development. His explicit aim is to use 'straightforward qualitative observation, description and interpretation of observations in the light of some economic and social ideas'. By the end of his paper, Vartiainen briefly examines the experiences of Finland, Austria, Korea and Taiwan. He concludes that they indeed have a common denominator. All countries have been exposed to external threats, and they have all been characterized by highly corporatist structures, and active and competent state interference in the process of resource and investment allocation.

Today, when researchers run cross-sectional growth regressions backwards and forwards on their computers, this is clearly a rather unconventional methodological approach. However, in this difficult area, no sensible person should dismiss alternative approaches readily. From this perspective, quarrelling about sample-selection bias may seem a bit beside the point. I do believe, however, that the empirical parts of the paper would have benefited from a more extensive discussion about start up conditions. Spending one or two pages on each country, the reader learns a bit about politics and institutional structure, but very little about the kind of details that would interest a development economist. What does the resource structure look like? How have trade patterns shifted over time? What is the extent of direct foreign intervention and aid? How have terms of trade evolved? etc.

When it comes to development policy, Vartiainen adopts what one, for lack of a better word, may call a 'systems approach'. The emphasis is on broad corporatist structures on a high level of abstraction, and he pays much less attention to the fine prints of actual economic policy. These fine prints belong, however, to the bread and butter of most economists. In Chapter 35 the reader is simply told that the four selected countries have used a rich menu of policy measures, including direct state ownership of key industries, credit rationing and direct administrative control of investment in selective sectors of the economy, investment subsidies, and political control of prices and wages. I would have liked to see a much more extensive discussion of how these somewhat unorthodox development policies were designed and implemented.

At this lower, and much more concrete level of abstraction, I also believe that we can make some progress using standard quantitative methods. While it seems futile to ask for formal statistical tests of the economic efficiency of the grand vision of social corporatism, it makes perfect sense to try to assess the microeconomic costs and benefits of the adopted policy instrument. After all, evaluating microeconomic policy is what neo-classical economists are trained for!

38.4 Conclusion

While I disagree on a number of points, and some of my remarks have been rather critical, I enjoyed reading this paper. It raises a number of interesting issues, that can not easily be dismissed. However, to me a main lesson is that social corporatism is not a choice variable, that a country can switch on and off at its own will. In some countries, in some time periods, highly corporatist institutions may come hand-in-hand with development and a reasonable measure of social decency. However, we know very little about why these social compacts occur in the first place.

39

Comment

Villy Bergström

Microeconomic theory defines a narrow scope for government activity. It is confined to the supply of collective goods and interventions to correct, for example, externalities or monopolies due to increasing returns in production. A curious result of this micro theory is that this view of government often becomes a normative or ideological opinion among economists. Government *should* not do more than what can be motivated by the activities of 'the night watchman state', to use a Swedish phrase. In reality government activities cover a wide range. Governments supply private goods, they intervene in the distribution of incomes and in the function of markets without any existence of externalities.

Juhana Vartiainen's paper is an attempt at a realistic study of government involvement in economic life by studying four countries that were industrialized after World War II. Vartiainen finds that these four successfully industrialized countries have some traits in common: a strong state, an effective, uncorrupted bureaucracy, co-operation between state and capital, sometimes involving organized labour (corporatism) and a threatened international position between great powers.

By analysing a two-sector model of production and consumption, Vartiainen demonstrates several cases when decentralized market solutions are inferior to (benevolent) state planning or corporatist (co-operative) solutions with or without government intervention. These are principal results that are not extensively used when the four country cases are discussed. In fact, there is, in my opinion, too little specific information about how the successful industrialization got started and continued in the four countries analysed by Vartiainen.

In the case of South Korea, for instance, I have heard Korean economists describe in detail how the state involvement in industrialization was carried out. Export performance was encouraged. Every month president Park Chung Hee, who came into office in 1961, met with industrialists and capitalists of the country to discuss what they needed in terms of infrastructural investments by the state and in terms of national educational efforts. The demands were carried out. There was for instance an emphasis on education of engineers and technical workers. This procedure in South Korea is not in contradiction to the results given by Vartiainen's theoretical model.

This method of government may be possible only under political dictatorship, which may have been part of the stability conditions stressed by Vartiainen and the guarantee of property rights. But little is learned about 'the investment function' of the Korean business sector. For instance, was there emphasis on investment in machinery, regarded as decisive by De Long and Summers (1991)? Was the tax policy growth enhancing? How was wage policy led, in view of growth effects? These are questions that come to mind, but are not answered. There is much more discussion on rather general institutional factors, that constitute the environment in which the concrete actions took place.

Let me give an example of what kind of information is lacking in Vartiainen's paper, the case of Sweden. Sweden was not industrialized late. Takeoff happened in what historians call 'la belle époque', around the turn of the century. This period was marked by widespread industrialization in the whole of Europe. But growth in Sweden was also fast between the wars and after World War II, into the early 1970s.

The Swedish government was very active, mainly as a competent buyer of high technology. Ericsson, for instance, developed partly because the state telephone company worked together with Ericsson to build a telephone network in the country. The government hydro-electrical power agency worked together with ASEA for the electrification of the country and transmission of electricity over long distances. Orders were placed with competent specifications, which formed a basis for the diffusion of development costs in telecommunication and transmission of electrical energy.

In a small country this kind of home market co-operation may have been decisive for the later export performance of these two high-tech firms. The examples given here are not the only ones of this kind of government involvement in developing successful business operations.

In the post-war period other government policies added to successful growth, mainly a tax policy that encouraged capital formation, especially in machinery. There was a great discrepancy between statutory tax rates and effective tax rates, that could be achieved if profits were reinvested in capital formation. So there were tax breaks conditional upon capital formation. A profitable firm could typically avoid a statutory profit tax rate of more than 50 per cent and pay an effective tax of 25 per cent, sometimes much lower, by expanding.

Also, centralized wage policy was conductive to growth by putting pressure on profits in low productive firms and allowing profits for reinvestment in high productive firms. Wage policy thereby encouraged restructuring of less profitable firms and co operated with tax policy to stimulate capital formation in prosperous, high productive firms.

Vartiainen's descriptions of the four countries are very suggestive, as the different countries discussed in his paper had many institutional traits and conditions in common. I miss the specific information about actions of governments like those hinted at above but I do appreciate the realistic view of the government role in economic development and growth.

One of Vartiainen's suggestions is that state planning succeeded in the four countries included in his study because their governments respected private property and a liberal market order. Therefore, state planning was not seen as a danger or threat to private investors, and 'capital' co-operated with government.

This is an interesting point deserving careful discussion. In the Swedish judiciary tradition property rights have been regarded as a bundle of functions or rights. These rights can be decreased or expanded and they do not sum up to a well-defined amount called 'ownership'. They exist in different degrees in different countries, and they can vary widely over time (see Undén, 1928; Adler-Karlsson, 1967).

A country like China evidently can spur entrepreneurial spirit and capital investment by granting minor property rights such as profit sharing and some plant management control over production and investment. One example may be to turn state-owned firms into collectively owned co-operatives (see Weitzman and Xu, 1993).

Cultural differences between countries are reflected in differences in co-operative behaviour. In a country like the USA with wide property rights compared to China the introduction of only minor restrictions on property rights, such as environmental regulations or capital income taxation, may be very detrimental to entrepreneurship and capital investment.

Therefore I think the change of property rights compared to the cultural heritage in a country is a decisive factor for growth more than the existence of 'level' of property rights. In the four cases studied by Vartiainen the 'number of property rights' may have been increased during the periods of successful industrialization.

References

Adler-Karlsson, G. (1967), *Funktionssocialism* (Lund).

Amsden, A. H. (1988), 'Taiwan's Economic History: A Case of Étatisme and a Challenge to Dependency Theory', in R. H. Bates (ed.), *Toward a Political Economy of Development* (University of California Press).

——(1989), *Asia's Next Giant: South Korea and Late Industrialization* (Oxford: Oxford University Press).

Andersson, J. O., Kosonen, P. and Vartiainen, J. (1993), 'The Finnish Model of Economic and Social Policy: From Emulation to Crash', research report A: 401, Åbo Akademi University, Department of Economics.

Bartelsman, E. J., Caballero, R. J. and Lyons, R. K. (1990), 'Short and Long Run Externalities', NBER working paper no. 3810.

Berend, I. T. and Rànki, G. (1982), *The European Periphery and Industrialisation 1780–1914*.

Biersteker, T. J. (1990), 'Reducing the Role of the State in the Economy: A Conceptual Exploration of IMF and World Bank Prescriptions', *International Studies Quarterly* 34: 477–92.

——(1992), 'The "Triumph" of Neoclassical Economics in the Developing World: Policy Convergence and Bases of Governance in the International Economic Order', in J. A. Rosenau and E. O. Czempiel (eds.), *Governance Without Government* (Cambridge: Cambridge University Press).

Blomström, M. and Meller, P. (1991), Lessons from Scandinavian–Latin American Comparisons. In M. Blomström and P. Meller (eds.), *Diverging Paths: Comparing a Century of Scandinavian and Latin American Economic Development* (Washington, D.C.: Inter-American Development Bank, Johns Hopkins University Press).

Bresnahan, T. (1984), 'Measuring Spillovers from Technical Advance: Mainframe Computers in Financial Services', *American Economic Review* 76: 741–55.

Chang, H. J. (1993), 'The Political Economy of Industrial Policy in Korea', *Cambridge Journal of Economics* 17: 131–57.

Crafts, N. (1992), 'Productivity Growth Reconsidered', *Economic Policy* Oct.

Dahmen, E. (1951), *Entrepreneurial Activity and the Development of Swedish Industry 1919–1939* (Stockholm: Industriens utredningsinstitut)

Elster, J. (1993), *Political Psychology* (Cambridge: Cambridge University Press).

Evans, P. (1995), *Embedded Autonomy, States and Industrial Transformation* (Princeton, NJ: Princeton University Press).

de Geer, H. (1992), *The Rise and Fall of the Swedish Model* (Stockholm: Carden Publications and the FA Institute).

Griliches, Z. and Lichtenberg, F. (1984), 'Interindustry Technology Flows and Productivity Growth: A Reexamination', *Review of Economics and Statistics* 66: 324–9.

Hjalmarsson, L. (1991), 'The Scandinavian Model of Industrial Policy', in M. Blomström and P. Meller (eds.), *Diverging Paths: Comparing a Century of Scandinavian and Latin American Development* (Washington, D.C.: Inter-American Development Bank, Johns Hopkins University Press).

Jakobson, M. (1992), *Vallanvaihto* (Helsinki).

Kaldor, N. (1978), *Further Essays in Economic Theory* (Duckworth).

Katzenstein, P. (1984), *Corporatism and Change: Austria, Switzerland and the Politics of Industry* (Cornell University Press).

——(1985), *Small States in World Markets* (Cornell University Press).

Kosonen, K. (1992), 'Saving and Economic Growth from a Nordic Perspective', in Pekkarinen, Pohjola and Rowthorn (1992).

Levine, R. and Renelt, D. (1992), 'A Sensitivity Analysis of Cross-Country Growth Regressions', *American Economic Review* 82(4).

De Long, J. B. and Summers, H. L. (1991), 'Equipment Investment and Economic Growth', *Quarterly Journal of Economics* 106(2): 445–502.

Mjöset, L. (1992), 'The Irish Economy in a Comparative Institutional Perspective', Publication no. 93, National Economic and Social Council, Dublin.

Murphy, K. M., Shleifer, A. and Vishny, R. (1991), 'The Allocation of Talent: Implications for Growth', *Quarterly Journal of Economics* May.

Olson, M. (1990), *The Rise and Decline of Nations* (New Haven, CN: Yale University Press).

Pekkarinen, J. and Vartiainen, J. (1993), *Suomen talouspolitiikan pitkä linja* (WSOY).

——Pohjola, M. and Rowthorn, R. (1992), *Social Corporatism: A Superior Economic System?* (Oxford: Clarendon Press).

Porter, M. (1990), *The Competitive Advantage of Nations* (London: Macmillan).

Rodrik, D. (1992), 'Political Economy and Development Policy', *European Economic Review* 36: 329–36.

Rostow, W. W. (1960), *The Stages of Economic Growth* (Cambridge: Cambridge University Press).

Schumpeter, J. (1942), *Capitalism, Socialism and Democracy* (New York: Harper).

Shleifer, A. and Vishny, R. W. (1993), 'Corruption', *Quarterly Journal of Economics* 108(3): 599–618.

Södersten, B. (1991), 'One Hundred Years of Swedish Economic Development', in M. Blomström and P. Meller (eds.), *Diverging Paths: Comparing a Century of Scandinavian and Latin American Economic Development* (Washington, D.C.: Inter-American Development Bank, Johns Hopkins University Press).

Supple, B. (1980), 'The State and the Industrial Revolution 1700–1914', in C. M. Cipolla (ed.), *The Fontana Economic History of Europe 3: The Industrial Revolution* (Fontana).

Undén, Östen (1928), 'Några synpunkter på begreppsbildningen inom juridiken', in *Festskrift tillägnad A. Hägerström*.

Wade, R. (1989), *Governing the Market: Economic Theory and the Role of Government in East Asian Industrialisation* (Princeton, NJ: Princeton University Press).

Weitzman, M. L. and Xu, C. (1993), *Chinese Township Village Enterprises as Vaguely Defined Cooperatives* (Centre for Economic Performance, London School of Economics, ESRC).

Index